United States Congress

Hearings before the Committee on naval affairs

U.S. House of representatives, May 1894

United States Congress

Hearings before the Committee on naval affairs
U.S. House of representatives, May 1894

ISBN/EAN: 9783337221553

Printed in Europe, USA, Canada, Australia, Japan

Cover: Foto ©ninafisch / pixelio.de

More available books at **www.hansebooks.com**

FIFTY-THIRD CONGRESS.

HEARINGS

BEFORE THE

COMMITTEE ON NAVAL AFFAIRS,

U. S. HOUSE OF REPRESENTATIVES,

May 1, 4, 8, 18, 22, 25, 29, June 1, 5, 8, 12, 22, 1894,

ON THE

BILL H. R. 6338,

TO ABOLISH THE BUREAU IN THE TREASURY DEPARTMENT KNOWN AS
THE COAST AND GEODETIC SURVEY, AND TRANSFER THE WORK
OF SAID BUREAU TO THE HYDROGRAPHIC OFFICE IN THE
NAVY DEPARTMENT AND THE GEOLOGICAL SURVEY
IN THE DEPARTMENT OF THE INTERIOR.

AMOS J. CUMMINGS, *Chairman*, OF NEW YORK.
JACOB A. GEISSENHAINER, OF NEW JERSEY.
ADOLPH MEYER, OF LOUISIANA.
WILLIAM McALEER, OF PENNSYLVANIA.
JOHN M. CLANCY, OF NEW YORK.
HERNANDO D. MONEY, OF MISSISSIPPI.
J. FREDERICK C. TALBOTT, OF MARYLAND.
D. GARDINER TYLER, OF VIRGINIA.
LEVI T. GRIFFIN, OF MICHIGAN.
CHARLES A. BOUTELLE, OF MAINE.
JONATHAN P. DOLLIVER, OF IOWA.
JAMES W. WADSWORTH, OF NEW YORK.
CHARLES S. RANDALL, OF MASSACHUSETTS.
JOHN B. ROBINSON, OF PENNSYLVANIA.
GEORGE W. HULICK, OF OHIO.

JOSEPH BAUMER, Clerk.

WASHINGTON:
GOVERNMENT PRINTING OFFICE.
1894.

3

TRANSFER OF COAST AND GEODETIC SURVEY.

COMMITTEE ON NAVAL AFFAIRS,
Tuesday, May 1, 1894.

The Committee on Naval Affairs this day met, Hon. Amos J. Cummings in the chair.

The CHAIRMAN. We will give Prof. Woodward, of Columbia College, New York, a hearing on Mr. Enloe's bill providing for the transfer of the Coast and Geodetic Survey to the Navy Department, and the bill is as follows:

A BILL to abolish the Bureau in the Treasury Department known as the Coast and Geodetic Survey, and transfer the work of said Bureau to the Hydrographic Office in the Navy Department and the Geological Survey in the Department of the Interior.

Be it enacted by the Senate and House of Representatives of the United States of America in Congress assembled, That on and after the first day of July, eighteen hundred and ninety-four, the Bureau in the Treasury Department known as the Coast and Geodetic Survey be, and the same is hereby, abolished, and all the duties now performed by the Coast and Geodetic Survey, relating to the survey of the coasts of the United States and adjacent islands, including the survey of rivers to the head of tide water or ship navigation with such topography as may be necessary thereto, and the preparation of charts and nautical publications therefrom, and all soundings, examinations of temperature, and of the deep-sea and tidal-current observations, be, and the same are hereby, transferred to the Department of the Navy, and the Secretaries of the Treasury and of the Navy shall cause to be transferred to the Department of the Navy all the vessels, buildings now owned or controlled by the United States and occupied by said Coast and Geodetic Survey, and such of the records, materials, and employees of the Coast and Geodetic Survey, as may be necessary in order to carry out the purposes of this Act.

SEC. 2. That all of the duties now performed by the Coast and Geodetic Survey relating to the geodetic survey are hereby transferred to the Department of the Interior, and shall be performed by the United States Geological Survey attached to said Department, and such of the records and materials as belong to, or are used in, said work, together with such employees as may be necessary, shall be transferred to the Department of the Interior.

SEC. 3. That the chief of the Hydrographic Office shall be an officer not below the grade of commander, and he shall be entitled to the highest pay of his grade.

The CHAIRMAN. I want to say that this bill is recommended by the Secretary of the Navy and the Secretary of the Treasury. Prof. Woodward desires a hearing, and, with the permission of the gentlemen of the committee present, he will proceed.

STATEMENT OF PROF. R. S. WOODWARD, OF COLUMBIA COLLEGE NEW YORK.

Prof. Woodward then addressed the committee; he said:

Mr. Chairman and Gentlemen of the Committee: My colleagues and I, of Columbia College, New York, have drawn up a protest against this bill for the abolishment of the Coast and Geodetic Survey, and that protest has been submitted to the chairman. Your chairman has courteously offered to hear us further in protest with regard to this

5

proposed transfer, and my colleagues have asked me to come and present the case for them, not because I am especially well fitted to speak upon a question of this kind in an oratorical sense, but for quite a different reason. It has been my fortune, or misfortune, to be connected with three of the principal scientific services of this country. It has been my fortune, also, to have been connected with four different departments of the Government; first, with the U. S. Lake Survey during the last eleven years of its existence, a survey which was conducted for forty years, namely, from 1842 to 1882, by a corps of engineers of the U. S. Army, and in that business I, of course, had an opportunity to see how work of that kind is carried on under the War Department. Subsequent to that time I was connected with the Commission of the United States to observe the transit of Venus, a commission organized in 1872 under the U. S. Navy, and its duties continued until 1884. My connection with it lasted during the years 1882 to 1884. Immediately after that I became connected with the U. S. Geological Survey and stayed in that bureau until 1890, and during the following three years ending June last I was connected with the bureau in question, namely, the Coast and Geodetic Survey. Now, these four different bureaus, as I have said, have been conducted under different Departments, namely, the War Department, the Navy Department, the Interior Department, and the Treasury Department, and I have had perhaps exceptional opportunities to discover the modes of administration of business and the methods of conducting surveys or the scientific works of the kind carried on in those bureaus. It is for this reason rather than any other that I have been asked to represent my colleagues before the committee to-day.

Now, a considerable amount of correspondence has passed between your worthy chairman and myself concerning this business, and to some of that I wish to refer subsequently. But to begin with, it seems to me we should look very briefly—for I know your time is valuable—very briefly at the organization of the Coast and Geodetic Survey and the varying fortunes under which it has been suffered to exist since its organization in 1807. That organization, I may say, was due primarily to Thomas Jefferson. Through the influence of Jefferson and Gallatin that bureau was organized in 1807. It was assigned at that time to the Treasury Department; but owing to the fact that it was necessary in those days for the superintendent, at that time Mr. Hassler, to go to Europe to collect instruments and to provide equipment for the conduct of precise surveys, but little was done until about 1815.

You will recall that during this interval the war of 1812 occurred, necessitating attention to other business rather than the prosecution of such surveys. In 1818 this bureau was transferred to the Navy Department, and I wish right here to call attention to the fact that the discovery which has been made during the past few months that it might be better to have it transferred to the Navy Department is no new discovery. It continued with a sort of fitful existence under the Navy Department until 1832, when it was transferred to the Treasury Department. Then in 1834, it was transferred back again to the Navy Department, and in 1836 it went again to the Treasury Department. One might think, in reading this history, the United States had pursued a rather curious and vacillating policy in regard to a bureau of this kind. It has remained in the Treasury Department ever since.

In 1843 the Bureau underwent something like a reorganization and a definite plan was determined upon, and it is worth while to state in this connection that that plan was devised by a board consisting of

3 civilians and 6 Navy and Army officers (4 topographic engineers of the Army, and 2 officers of the Navy), and after mature deliberation they came to the conclusion that the proper place for this Bureau was in the Treasury Department and that the proper conduct of it should be under civilian administration. I would like to ask you to give some attention to that history and read for yourselves the reasons urged for that sort of administration, as I have not time to go into it to-day.

Now, from time to time since then, most prominently in 1848 and 1849, attempts have been made to get this Bureau, or some portion of it, back into the Navy, and although the subject has been repeatedly discussed in the halls of Congress the Bureau has been retained ever since in the Treasury Department. In 1884 the Government sought to examine into the workings of the various scientific bureaus of the Government, and amongst those that came under the consideration of the commission appointed from both Houses of Congress were the Weather Bureau, the U. S. Geological Survey, and the Coast and Geodetic Survey. That joint commission held sessions during two years and they took a vast amount of testimony, I can say, because I helped to prepare a portion of it. I was in the U. S. Geological Survey at the time. They collected a vast amount of information and heard a great amount of testimony——

The CHAIRMAN. In what year?

Prof. WOODWARD. During the years 1884 to 1886. I have here the report, to which I wish to refer in a few moments, of the joint commission. As I say, they collected a vast amount of testimony on this matter, and they finally made a report in the latter part of 1886. The report was not unanimous. There were 6 members of the commission and they stood 4 to 2 in favor of leaving the Coast and Geodetic Survey as it was in the Treasury Department and leaving the work to be carried on according to the plan adopted in 1843.

It is worth while, perhaps, to read very briefly, the conclusions of that committee, especially with respect to the transfer of any part of the work of this Bureau to the Navy Department. I see I have some quotations here which refer especially to the historical matter, but I feel obliged to pass over that and will simply refer you to it. There is some very interesting matter in this report of the committee. They made what you might call an exhaustive report on the subject, and here is the conclusion of the majority of the committee with regard to the maintenance of this work in the Treasury Department. They say:

> There is nothing in the testimony to indicate that the work now performed by the Survey can be more efficiently performed if the transfer is made, nor is it shown that the Navy can more economically execute the work; so there is no reason either on the score of efficiency or economy for making the change.

That is the net result of their conclusions. Now, as I said, there was a minority report. That report was written by the present honorable Secretary of the Navy. I have it with me and have within the past three or four days taken pains to read over not only the report of the majority of the commission but taken pains also to read very carefully the report of Mr. Herbert. This report, I may say, has interested me very much. It is an argument for which I have great respect. It is rich, it is ornate, and it is the work of a classical scholar. He has presented an argument in favor of the transfer in a most competent manner, and his report is worthy of careful attention.

I have read this report with great interest, and especially with reference to its literary merits, but let me say to you, gentlemen, that notwithstanding he has marshaled there all the arguments that can be marshaled, I think, in favor of this proposed transfer to the Navy, it is an argument rather of an advocate than of a judge. Singular as it may seem in the middle of this half—or rather near the close of this half century—the honorable Secretary of the Navy seems to be totally unaware there has any such thing as what we call modern science developed during the past two hundred years. A sort of strange opacity seems to have veiled his eyes to the advances of modern science, which have been just as marked along scores of lines as the progress in the direction of the steam engine and electricity. I need hardly tell you this, gentlemen, you are able to see for yourselves; but if the position that the Secretary of the Navy takes with regard to a question of this kind is proper, we would expect him to relegate every modern battleship to obscurity and go back to the dugout, and read by a tallow dip instead of by the electric light.

Such, then, is the history in brief of this Survey up to the present time. Now it is worth while to go into some few details with regard to it, and I shall begin with the consideration of the question of the economy expected to be secured by the proposed transfer. I will say, for the benefit of the members of the committee who have come in since I have began speaking, that I speak from experience in regard to this matter. I am not a doctrinaire who has been locked up in a closet in some college and has never seen the modes of administration of the Army or Navy, but I have been with the Army and Navy and know what these modes of administration are: I know what the modes of conduct are, so these things I am about to mention I state from actual experience, and not as a doctrinaire.

Suppose this transfer of the hydrographic work were made to the Navy Department; what would be the result? It is necessary in order to forecast what would be the result to consider what hydrographic work is. Most of you gentlemen, those of you who have not had time to look into the details of this work, see the net results of the hydrographic surveys embodied in the charts. That is the last product, but all that goes before that fails to come under your eye. It is a technical matter, gentlemen, and I can well understand that you may not have had time to look into it, but a great deal has to be done before the charts can be produced. There must be surveys made; we must know the latitudes and longitudes of points in that survey. These latitudes and longitudes require the making of astronomical observations, and there is a vast array of elaborate and difficult computations that have to be gone through in order to produce the proper results which are embodied on the sheet of paper with, perhaps, only a few black marks on it. Now, how has this work been done in the past history of geodesy and astronomy? It has been done by geodesists and astronomers, men who have devoted their lives to their business and not by dilettante officers, or *ex officio* scientific men who can go into the business for a few years and then leave it. A man to be proficient in that sort of work must understand it, just as a man to be proficient as a lawyer or a jurist must study law and jurisprudence.

Let us suppose this transfer was made, and see what would come of it. The first result would be this: Some naval officers would be put in charge of the administration of the work and then they would proceed to hire some competent scientific men to furnish brain and brawn to carry on the work. The result would not be economy. You would be feeding a lot of naval officers here and the real work would be done by civilians. Let me give an instance of conduct of that sort of work on the U. S. Lake Survey during the last eleven years of the administration of that work; and it is proper to state that the work was exceedingly well done, notwithstanding it was under the administration of an Army officer, but that fact serves only to emphasize the case. The exception in this instance proves the rule. You know it is the policy of our Army and Navy to set different officers at work at this or that piece of business and keep them only for a few years, but in the case of this efficient officer of the Corps of Engineers he was allowed to remain at that business during the whole of the last twelve years of the existence of the survey. He thus had time to develop a plan and perfect it.

Now, there were assigned to him from time to time younger officers of the Corps of Engineers. They were men mostly just from West Point and, like other college men who had recently come from college, they were inexperienced and had to gain experience. You know it would not do to put such men under the charge of a civilian who had acquired his knowledge; that would not do. It is the business of an Army or Navy officer, and very properly, to administer affairs and command something or somebody. Now, then, what did the gentleman who had charge of this survey do? He put these Army officers in charge of the steamers, which could transport parties back and forth, and left the more important work, the work which required knowledge and perseverance and brawn, to civil engineers who had graduated from colleges of the country. So it would be if you turn this work over to the Navy. They would hire civilians to do the real work, to furnish the brains and industry necessary to carry it on.

The CHAIRMAN. One word right there. You know the Navy is conducting coast surveys on the coast of Mexico?

Prof. WOODWARD. I shall speak about that later.

The CHAIRMAN. Do they hire civilians there, or do they do the work themselves?

Prof. WOODWARD. They do the hydrographic work—they have the Hydrographic Office; but they have not even done well enough to prevent the *Kearsarge* from running on Roncador Reef; I understand they sailed by a map fifty-nine years old.

The CHAIRMAN. If they are capable of making those surveys on the coast of Mexico, would not they be capable of making surveys on the coast elsewhere?

Prof. WOODWARD. So anybody of men are capable. The difficulty, however, is that the policy of the Army and Navy is inimical to that sort of work; they do not keep the men long enough in one sort of work to accomplish anything. Let me mention another case in the conduct of this kind of work. A few years ago one of my colleagues saw a base line measured by the geodetic survey of France working under the command of army officers. These army officers went out with their white gloves and set up umbrellas and they had some scientific experts to do the work. How many men do you suppose it took to measure that base? There were 57 men employed. Now, a year or two later the Coast and Geodetic Survey measured a base in southern Indiana. How many men do you suppose they had? They had 8 men. They did the work about twice as fast as the Frenchmen and it cost very much less. That is the way that sort of work is done.

Mr. TALBOTT. Were not these people in the employment of the Government, enlisted men?

Prof. WOODWARD. Some were employed as enlisted men, but experts were also employed; men who furnished the brains and everything but mere muscle, and in many instances they furnished the muscle also, as in the case of the Coast and Geodetic Survey. Those men are civilians. They are men who are trained to the work, men who make a profession and study of it and do not go into it for three years with the expectation that they are to be transferred to some other point.

Mr. TALBOTT. What is the difference in the education of a man who is a graduate from a college as a civil engineer and one who graduates from Annapolis or West Point; what is the difference in the course of study which makes one more proficient than the other?

Prof. WOODWARD. There is nothing, and that is not the question; let me explain to you what is the point. It is the policy of the U. S. Navy and the U. S. Army to shift men about from place to place. That is a very good thing and that is a very proper thing in the Army and Navy, because the practical business of an army and navy man is to fight. That is their business. It is to fight and command men, but when you go into the administration of scientific affairs it is not fighting; that is not it. You must get down to computation. It is a different sort of work, and it is for that reason that the Army and Navy officer very properly, I think, is not willing to take off his coat and go into the real work. He will hire some one else to do it. Let me give you an instance. While I was in the U. S. Lake Survey an Army officer was sent out to do triangulation work along with civilians. He stayed three days. The work lay in a sparsely settled part of the country and they were obliged to live on what they could get from the farmers, and as farmers did not have much fresh meat they had to eat salt pork and meats of that kind. The Army officer said that he would be damned if he would eat salt pork and climb hills for the United States, and he did not. It was very soon found that he could be transferred to some other place, and I do not blame him, because that was not his business; his profession is that of a fighter.

Mr. MONEY. But it is his business to do whatever he is ordered to do?

Mr. WOODWARD. Yes, it is; but they do not do it.

The CHAIRMAN. They have charge of improvements of rivers and harbors?

Prof. WOODWARD. Yes, sir; they have; and there are 500 or 600 civilian engineers who do the work. Look at the list and you will find that a great bulk of that work is done by civilian engineers. There is no doubt about it. I have been connected with the various workings of these bureaus, and I know exactly how they go on.

The CHAIRMAN. Why is it that the Coast and Geodetic Survey require the services of so many naval officers?

Prof. WOODWARD. They do not. They require specially-designed vessels for the prosecution of their work. They can not use the vessels of the Navy, and all the naval officer does is to command the ship. The men are enlisted under special rules and regulations, and not under the naval rules.

So, gentlemen, if you transfer this Bureau or this portion of the work of the Bureau to the Navy you will find in the end it will be bad economy for the United States; you will simply afford places for officers during these piping times of peace, and the real work will be done by civilians. But that is not the worst of it. The grade of work will be lowered. A man whose principal business is fighting, does not, as a general rule, take to scientific work where it is necessary to make a prolonged study of mathematical problems and astronomical calculations.

Look over the history of geodesy and astronomy. There is scarcely a name drawn from the Army or Navy. Everybody has heard of Sir Isaac Newton and La Place. Can you name anybody from the Army or Navy who is ——

Mr. MONEY. I can.

Prof. WOODWARD. Who?

Mr. MONEY. Commodore Maury.

Prof. WOODWARD. In the history of geodesy his name is scarcely known. Of course he wrote a very creditable book concerning winds, currents, and things of that sort, but his name will not go down in the annals of science along with that of La Place, Newton, La Grange, and men of that type. No, gentlemen; there is something very grotesque about this business, and I shall not be surprised if, in the course of a year or two, a bill is introduced in Congress to abolish the Supreme Court of the United States and relegate its duties to the advocate judges of the Army and Navy. It is not a bit more grotesque than the conditions contemplated in this bill. It is surprising, and the scientific men of this country are alive to it. They are in earnest. They are not mere dilettanti; they have looked into it. And right here it is worth while to pause and say a word about the *ex-officio* dilettante scientist. You see small boys astride broomsticks, imagining that they are riding horses. Now, a naval officer or an army officer sometimes gets on the scientific broomstick and imagines he is riding a scientific horse, but that is not so. A man to be a successful scientist, and to be worthy of mention in the annals of science, must do just as a lawyer does—as a jurist does; he must go through a period of prolonged study. It requires work to become efficient in that sort of business.

I want to say that I do not protest against the Navy. I am saying nothing against the Army or the Navy as such. I believe, from a large amount of observation, we have men in our Army and Navy who are just as capable, just as brave, and just as patriotic as the world has ever seen, but we must understand that when we come to scientific work it is not their business; their business is fighting, and we should never forget it. When the time of need comes, when it is necessary to fight, we shall find men who are worthy of their race, and worthy of our nation among our Army and Navy officers. I have sometimes seen strong reasons for protesting against the niggardly way in which Congress has treated these officers. They are worthy men and worthy of considerate care, but they are not scientific men. Science is not their business, and that is why we protest. It would be just as incongruous to put a lot of farmers or Coxey's army in charge of the Army of the United States as to put this geodetic work in the hands of Army and Navy officers; not that they could not do it, gentlemen, but the modes of administration of the Army and Navy are inimical to the prosecution of that kind of work. If you give the Army and Navy officer a chance to stay in his position, a chance to devote a life to the study of these subjects, he may become proficient and just as able as any other man.

Mr. MONEY. Let me ask you a question there, if it will not interrupt your argument.

Prof. WOODWARD. Certainly.

Mr. MONEY. You stated at the beginning of your remarks that this bureau has been shifted from the Navy to the Treasury and back again, etc.; what was the result of the work when it was under the care of the Navy before?

Prof. WOODWARD. That is a very good point, and I would like to read the history of it, but I have not time to go into it; but it would show that the work deteriorated under the Navy, and it was for this reason that it was retransferred and put in charge of a civilian bureau; and, as I stated, the plan of organization was drawn up by 4 topographical engineers of the Army, 2 officers of the Navy, and 3 civilians, and it was in accordance with their recommendation that the present organization was perfected and has been maintained.

Mr. MONEY. Another question, if you will permit. If this bill should be reported and acted on favorably, would these scientists who are now engaged in this Bureau be dismissed?

Prof. WOODWARD. Some of them; undoubtedly many of them would resign, because you know just as well as I do, and every member of this committee knows, a scientific man who has knowledge does not like to be lorded over by an Army or Navy officer.

Mr. MONEY. That is assuming an offensive sort of domineering spirit on the part of an Army or Navy officer which I do not suppose would be the fact, and I do not assume or admit that.

Prof. WOODWARD. You have never been under their domination?

Mr. MONEY. No; in regard to their character they are looked upon as gentlemen; you understand that?

Prof. WOODWARD. I do, but I have been under their dominion. Of course, they are considered gentlemen, but it is naturally the result of the Army and Navy discipline for them to be domineering. I have been under them and I know what it is. I served eleven years.

Mr. MONEY. *Crede experto?*

Prof. WOODWARD. Yes, sir. I have been called a "damned computer" and various other names of that sort. Let me tell you a little about the conduct of the Naval Observatory. The Observatory, by the way, has done some of the finest astronomical work which has been done. When the history of science comes to be written, gentlemen, if you and I should live to read it, we shall be proud of the work that has been done by the Naval Observatory. Who did it? The line officers? No; not line of officers of the Navy; but the professors of mathematics who have been permitted to stay there. They have been permitted to devote their time and attention and lives to it. There are some grand men who have gone out or will soon go out from that institution, men worthy of the highest standing in this country or any other country.

The CHAIRMAN. Then why is it that the college professors wanted this taken away from the Navy Department?

Prof. WOODWARD. Not all of them. I am opposed to that and was opposed to it when that measure was before your committee a year or two ago.

Mr. GEISSENHAINER. It seems that we will have it again this Congress, as they seem very persistent.

Mr. MEYER. Let me interrupt your train of argument for a moment——

Prof. WOODWARD. Certainly, providing it will not cut me short of time.

Mr. MEYER. You remarked that the business of a naval officer as well as an Army officer was fighting as I can see, but the mere business of fighting in the career of an Army or Navy officer occupies but very little of his time. Some of the Army and Navy officers in the service now who have been in that service for twenty-five years never have been in a battle. Do you mean to urge as an argument upon this committee that notwithstanding that fact a Navy or Army officer by reason of his being fitted for the business of fighting is not competent to acquire the necessary scientific knowledge referred to——

Mr. TALBOTT. No; he admits that, but he says that an Army or naval officer is not permitted to remain at this work long enough to become proficient in it.

Prof. WOODWARD. That is the way. There is no lack of ability on the part of these officers.

Mr. MEYER. You say they can not do scientific study with advantage. Take a naval officer who has been assigned to this geodetic survey for three or four years. Do you mean to say after he leaves that he will not have another opportunity and facility to continue that line of study?

Prof. WOODWARD. Yes, sir; he will be, as a rule, assigned to other duties and will have facility to acquire some other kind of business.

Mr. MEYER. Observe here, for instance, the steamer *Blake*. It does not state on the Naval Register what naval officers are on that.

Prof. WOODWARD. I can not say how many are at present.

The CHAIRMAN. I can state them to you (reading them over to Mr. Meyer).

Mr. MEYER. What civilians are on her?

Prof. WOODWARD. That steamer simply goes about from place to place supplying parties who do the work.

Mr. MEYER. What parties do the work?

Prof. WOODWARD. Shore-line parties, the hydrographic parties, the men who have to live in small boats and in tents on the shore carrying on the work of the Survey.

Let us now look at the other phase of this question, namely, that phase which proposes to transfer the geodetic work, the tidal, magnetic, and gravity work to the United States Geological Survey; that also is very grotesque. I have been connected, as I have stated, with the United States Geological Survey and I know its methods of administration very well. I know the distinguished director of the Survey very well. I have made a special study of him as well as some other things. He is a very distinguished geologist and anthropologist, but he makes no pretension to geodesy, magnetic, or gravity work, or any of the scientific work which is carried on by the Coast and Geodetic Survey, so that it would seem just as grotesque to transfer this peculiar work of scientific character to the Geological Survey as the other transfer I have mentioned. A man to carry on geodetic work, tidal work, magnetic work, must make a special study of them. Geology, it must be said, is relatively an imperfect science, not because men have not tried to make it perfect, but because from the very nature of things, from the very obscurity of the data available it has not yet become a reasonably perfect science. Geodesy, on the other hand, is a reasonably perfect science, and it seems very grotesque and very incongruous to transfer this work to the Geological Survey. Doubtless, it can be done if the Geological Survey takes hold of it and gets good men; in the course of ten or fifteen years' experience they will learn to do the work, but in the meantime the country would have to suffer the expense.

Mr. MONEY. That is if these gentlemen choose to resign who are now in, or if they are forced out by the change?

Prof. WOODWARD. Undoubtedly many of them would be forced out. I am going to speak shortly of what the results are when you shake up, by reorganization, a bureau every few years, or every few months. You can well understand what would happen if Congressmen were elected every six weeks. If you shake up these bureaus every year or two you will find what will happen. Not only would the grade of work deteriorate, but it would degenerate to mere dilettante science, which would be very expensive to the Government. I shall have occasion to refer to that by and by.

Now, there is a very important omission in the provisions of this bill. It may not be known to you gentlemen, but there is such a thing in the United States as the Bureau of Weights and Measures, a Bureau which has the administration of measures of weight, of length, of capacities, and things of that sort, and it is coming to be very important that that Bureau be administered with proper efficiency. That Bureau has been connected, for many years—ever since it started, I believe—with the Coast and Geodetic Survey, and the superintendent of the Coast and Geodetic Survey has had charge of the administration of it. What does this bill contemplate doing with that? Nothing; there is no mention of it. It is a very important kind of work; the work of levying duties, etc., depends upon having proper instruments for measuring and weighing, and for the testing of sugars, and other things. What are you going to do with it? It is proper that you should take charge of that. It was a Bureau which was also fostered by Thomas Jefferson. He had the foresight to see what was necessary with respect to the administration of that sort of work, and he provided for it, and you should also provide for it.

The CHAIRMAN. Do I understand you to say it is a bureau of the Coast and Geodetic Survey?

Prof. WOODWARD. It is a bureau by itself; it is appropriated for through the legislative bill.

The CHAIRMAN. No; through the sundry civil bill?

Prof. WOODWARD. No; it is not appropriated for under the sundry civil bill, but has been provided for in the legislative bill for many years.

Now, let me come to consider what I think to be the worst feature of this bill, and that is that it unsettles the affairs of this country. It unsettles scientific work and degrades it. When you come to shake up these bureaus you have to get a new set of men, and it has been well said, that "wherever workers are gathered together there also idlers abound, seeking to feed on the fruits of honest toil." There are plenty of them in Washington, as all you gentlemen know, and you know how hard the fight is between a man who is trying to attend to his business and the man who is seeking to get a place where he can simply be kept.

If you make this transfer, in all probability the next Congress will transfer it back again, and then in order to keep the bureau active as in the early years of the century, it will go back and forth. It will become a kind of political football, which is kicked from one side of the ground to the other. Do you think that will be creditable to us as a nation? That will inevitably result, gentlemen. I tell you, however, the scientific men of this country will never be satisfied to have the administration of this work in the incongruous condition that you propose to put it by this bill. To go back to my simile which I stated before, it would be no more incongruous to transfer the duties of the Supreme Court to the advocate-judges of the Army and Navy; not a bit more incongruous. On the other hand, if we are to go down in history worthy of the conduct of this sort of work, we must do it well.

Now, let me refer to the line of argument which is pursued by the honorable Secretary of the Navy. I admire that argument very much, and it is worth while for gentlemen in favor of the bill to read it carefully, as it will furnish a far better argument than I have seen advanced in the debate on this question. However, he seems to be totally unaware of the progress of modern science and he seems to have a curious notion that these bureaus, like the Geological Survey and the Coast and Geodetic Survey, are due not to the phenomena of nature, but to the machinations of scientific men. Certainly it would be a curious thing if they should be due to the machinations of scientific men. Jefferson never thought of that. But they are due to the phenomena of nature and they will last as long as we have commerce and navigation; as long as we have any respect for the phenomena of nature. So long as the tide washes the beach at Sandy Hook, just so long will you need carefully prepared tidal tables, and just so long will you need carefully prepared charts.

Millions of dollars sometimes depend upon the location of a buoy; 5 or 6 feet may swamp a vessel, one of those splendid vessels that now cross the Atlantic. Five or 6 feet only, gentlemen. I am not a mere doctrinaire from the closet who has come here to talk to you. I have seen how these things go. I recollect being out on Lake Huron when the lake was very smoky. You will recall the forest fires in Michigan in 1871, and it was frightfully dangerous to be out on the lake at a time when the fog added to the complication of smoke. We spent two days and nights there, and had to exercise scrupulous care. Why? Because there was a great danger of running into a vessel at any time. You know a steamship has to keep out of the way of sailing craft. Now, how did we find out our position. There had been a careful hydrographic survey made of the lake, made not by a Naval officer, but by civilians trained to the work, men who had made a study of it, men whose bread and butter depended on their competence to do the work, and we found our position and steered for a safe place by making soundings in the lake. It was possible from the carefully prepared chart of the lake to find out where we were in the dark, so to speak. Now, to attain that sort of perfection requires not a dilettante or an *ex officio* scientist, but it requires men of knowledge, men who have made a study of these subjects, and I do not want to see, and my colleagues of Columbia College and the scientific men of this country do not want to see, our science degenerate to mere dilettanteism, but they want it made better. They will meet you with approval in every case where you can devise reforms for its perfection. They are not disposed to defend in all respects the past history of this or any other government bureau. I, at any rate, am not prepared to do so, but when we judge of this or that bureau we must judge of it as we do of every other human institution. They are subject to human frailties; men may commit crimes in them as well as in other branches of Government service. No one, I will say, can approve every act of Congress. You will admit that as well as I.

Now then, it is worth while to consider the animus of the author of this bill. I hope he is present. Where is my friend, Mr. Enloe? I know him quite well, and I am sorry he is not here, as I wish to speak very briefly in regard to his animus. Does any member of this committee believe that the author of this bill is animated by a statesman-like desire to diminish the expenses of the country or to raise the type of scientific work done in this country?

The CHAIRMAN. I certainly believe that.

Prof. WOODWARD. Well, I have tried to believe it. I have taken that as my working hypothesis, and I have also examined into the question and studied the evidence. I have looked into his speeches on this subject before the House, and I have read all what he has had to say about it. I have had personal interviews with him, not this year, but two years ago. Let me give you a bit of personal experience. Two years ago Mr. Enloe was fighting this Survey, and it seems he was specially after my scalp. I was employed in that Survey and came here to it during the time of the Fifty-first Congress. I came, as Mr. Enloe says, as a "donation." Do I look like a donation, gentlemen; a scientific donation to the Coast and Geodetic Survey? Now, Mr. Enloe has lived here or been here in Congress for several years within a stone's throw of that Bureau. Why has he not gone down to that Bureau and found some trustworthy information concerning it?

The CHAIRMAN. He tells me he has visited the Bureau in search of information, but he has failed to find it.

Prof. WOODWARD. That is what he says, but I am credibly informed he has never taken any due pains to find out the workings of that Bureau, and I want to read a little extract here and show how much information he had on this subject. In the course of the debate on this matter by Mr. Enloe on the sundry civil bill two years ago, he offered several amendments cutting off the hydographic appropriation of the Survey, and amongst other things he said that he had been informed that I was engaged in a curious kind of work here; that I was engaged in seeking to discover a new method for the formation of "ice bars." Do you know what that means? Does any gentleman know what that means? If any man here does, let him speak up. I do not know, but let me explain that to you. First I will read from the Record in order not to do Mr. Enloe any injustice. He says, with respect to the appropriation:

As it stands now it is expended under the direction of the Superintendent of the Coast Survey. He has charge of the entire force and funds, and directs where the work shall be done; but as the sum is appropriated in a lump, and no particular direction given to it, he can take it and apply it anywhere in the country to any particular work he desires. He could spend every dollar of it in investigating the formation of ice bars.

Now, that is not so; specific appropriations are made and specific mention is made of localities where the work is to be done. But, do you know what that means in regard to ice bars? I was engaged at that time in the investigation and perfection of two new methods of measuring bases. Since that time the scientific world has had occasion to consider my work and has approved of it. I am willing to risk my reputation before the scientific public and before this committee, too, if they will make a competent examination of it, but when a man shows that he has no more information than the author of this bill shows in this debate, I am not willing to risk my reputation. At that time, gentlemen, I was trying to get out of the service of the Government, because I found it afforded no adequate opportunities to a man who had any ability or industry in him. During the time that this question was up for debate I came here and talked with Mr. Enloe about it, and sought to explain to him that I was neither a "donation" nor a loafer and desired to remain in the service only long enough to complete the investigation then nearly done. I had in my pocket at the time an offer of a professorship in a college to which, had it been necessary, I should have gone and furnished the money to complete that investigation in a creditable fashion to the Government and to myself.

The CHAIRMAN. What was that investigation?

Prof. WOODWARD. It was the perfection of two new methods of measuring bases which have been completed and tried, and have met with the approval of the scientific world.

The CHAIRMAN. What does the "ice bars" have to do with that?

Prof. WOODWARD. Let me explain. One of these kinds of apparatus is known as the "iced bar," and the peculiar feature of that was, as Mr. Enloe could have found out, that we packed the measuring bar in melting ice to control the temperature. To determine or control the temperature of a measuring bar has been a great subject of study for two hundred years, from the time of Sir Isaac Newton. We have an apparatus wherein we pack the measuring bar in melting ice and keep it at a fixed temperature. I will not go into that, because if any of you wish to examine that question you can do so. I am willing to stand by the decision of the scientific world but not by the decision of a Congressman who did not take the trouble to look the matter up.

Now I would like to refer in this connection to an argument used by the honorable Secretary of the Navy.

The CHAIRMAN. Before you read that let me ask a question. Is it your opinion Mr. Enloe has a personal motive in introducing this bill?

Prof. WOODWARD. Yes, sir; that is my private opinion.

The CHAIRMAN. Then let me ask you what motive had Senator Chandler in introducing the bill in the Senate?

Prof. WOODWARD. He has been under the influence of naval officers for many years. I have had a chance to see that, and I could relate an anecdote concerning that and will possibly do so, but that is going back to another matter.

The CHAIRMAN. How about the approval of the Secretary of the Treasury?

Prof. WOODWARD. I have not seen the argument of the Secretary of the Treasury; I would like to see it. I have not seen any public statement from the Secretary in regard to this matter.

The CHAIRMAN. I think you will find in Mr. Enloe's speech on the sundry civil bill that he read a letter from the Secretary of the Treasury.

Prof. WOODWARD. That is something I had not seen. Let me say that on an occasion two years ago Mr. Enloe offered several amendments, all of which were defeated I may say, curtailing the work of this Bureau, cutting down the scientific force, cutting down the salary of the Superintendent in particular, and Mr. Herbert could not stand the assault, and here are the words he used on that occasion.

Mr. Chairman, I desire to say only a few words. Something has been said in the course of this debate about gentlemen having appointees in this Bureau whom they desire to protect, and in view of what I am about to say I think it well to preface the statement by the assertion that I have never had an appointee there; never have applied for one; and I have made a good many harsh criticisms heretofore on the way the work was done, and that I am not disposed to retract them. I think much unnecessary work is done in the Bureau, principally in geodesy, magnetism, and electricity——

I will say there is scarcely any work done in electricity in that Bureau——

and those connected with its management have manifested an intention to prolong the existence of the Bureau and its work indefinitely.

The Coast Survey will be a perpetuity if its officials can effect it. But when it comes to the question of reducing the salary of the chief of the Bureau or any other salaries of its officers, it seems to me that the work they do, if it is worth doing at all it is worth doing well, and that when men do work well they ought to be paid for it. The committee on appropriations have examined the matter carefully and do not recommend a reduction of the salary, in that they indicate their opinion that the sum of $6,000 is not too much to secure the services of a man of the attainments of Prof. Mendenhall.

Now, gentlemen, I shall take but a little more of your time. Let me say to you that Dr. Mendenhall is a scientific man, a scholar and a gentleman, and a man who is known and respected abroad as well as at home; he is a man who is a credit to us, and scientific men look with fear upon any transfer of this Bureau which would contemplate putting it in the hands of men in whom the scientific public has no confidence.

Lastly let me refer to what seems to be the spirit of this bill. It is destructive and retrogressive instead of being constructive and progressive. As I have said before, the scientific public is not prepared to justify the past history in all respects of this Bureau; but we think it proper in judging to judge it as we do other human institutions, by the net results, and the Coast and Geodetic Survey, it must be admitted, has in many ways and places done a vast amount of very creditable work. There is one gentleman attached to the Survey who has been there forty years, a scholar whose industry rivals that of President Cleveland himself.

Mr. TALBOTT. What is his name?

Prof. WOODWARD. His name is Schott. He is a man of marvelous industry and has prepared many able papers and investigations and results which he has worked out, and it seems to be a pity to destroy that Bureau, and cast a slur upon the reputation of that man who has been an honorable servant of the Government for forty years.

The CHAIRMAN. This will cast no slur upon his reputation?

Prof. WOODWARD. It seems to me it would cast a very serious slur upon the reputation of such men, because the proposed destruction of the bureau is equivalent to charging that its present conduct is inefficient or corrupt. Let me say to you, gentlemen, that I have no personal affiliations with that service, and no interest in it except those proper to a private citizen; I am out of it. I am glad to say I am out of the government service. It is dog's life to a man who seeks to be industrious and to attend to his business. In many respects it is fine for the hangers-on, as the work is largely a matter of administrative routine which runs itself. It is a misfortune, however, that our scientific bureaus are not under a single scientific head. The ideal system, I believe, would be to put them all in one department where their work could be correlated under and represented by a cabinet officer. With the present system, you can see that a corps of civilians, like those of the Geodetic Survey, are placed at a great disadvantage when a controversy of this kind comes up and when naval officers who would like to get a slice of the scientific work are able to enlist the aid of the honorable Secretary of the Navy. Believing, then, that the spirit of this bill is destructive and retrogressive, we most earnestly protest against it.

I thank you, gentlemen, for your attention on behalf of myself and my colleagues, and I shall be glad now to answer any questions with regard to matters of detail, concerning which I may have acquaintance.

The CHAIRMAN. Before you sit down I would like to ask a few questions. Is there any scientific result achieved by the Coast and Geodetic Survey to-day which is not achieved by the Navy in its coast surveys on the west coast of Mexico and elsewhere?

Prof. WOODWARD. Yes, sir.

The CHAIRMAN. What are they?

Prof. WOODWARD. The surveys, if they were properly conducted on the west coast of Mexico, would be done by means of triangulation, and done with accuracy. I had occasion this morning to read a report of the work they have carried on on that coast, and in that report there was a note saying in the measurement of a base line they had a discrepancy of 3 yards. That is what we would call a gross error, and is a disgrace to any sort of scientific work.

The CHAIRMAN. What report is that?

Prof. WOODWARD. I can not give you the report, but I can get it for you, however.*

The CHAIRMAN. I will be much obliged.

Prof. WOODWARD. I will take pains this afternoon to send you the quotation.

The CHAIRMAN. Let me ask you another question. Is not it true that we employ Navy officers in the Coast and Geodetic Bureau?

Prof. WOODWARD. Yes, sir; to a very minor extent. They are employed almost entirely——

The CHAIRMAN. I am speaking of the Bureau; they are employed?

Prof. WOODWARD. A few such officers are employed for short periods of two or three years. They stay there two or three years as commanders of vessels and have charge of this or that sort of work, but the officer is never permitted to enter into the details of that sort of work that gives character to it; the character of the work is derived——

Mr. MONEY. What is the officer's special duty?

Prof. WOODWARD. To command the steamer. His business is commanding the vessel.

Mr. RANDALL. They make soundings?

The CHAIRMAN. I find there were 41 officers employed in the Coast and Geodetic Survey last year, and you say they are only employed in running steamers?

Prof. WOODWARD. That is substantially the only work they do, sir.

The CHAIRMAN. Do you remember the Mosquito Inlet, Florida; that was under the Coast and Geodetic Survey?

Prof. WOODWARD. Yes, sir.

The CHAIRMAN. I certainly saw a great many naval officers at work there.

Prof. WOODWARD. Undoubtedly; but did they have their coats off?

The CHAIRMAN. They did, and they waded in the water.

Prof. WOODWARD. I never saw any such thing.

Mr. RANDALL. In my district, on the coast of Massachusetts, that is done. When a coast survey steamer comes there the young officers, cadets, midshipmen, etc., are out there working at the soundings, etc.

Prof. WOODWARD. Did they do the work of triangulation? Let me tell you the work of triangulation of the State of Massachusetts has been done by civilians, and——

Mr. RANDALL. Attached to vessels?

The CHAIRMAN. Who appointed you to the Coast Survey?

Prof. WOODWARD. The Secretary of the Treasury, in 1890, at the request of the present superintendent.

The CHAIRMAN. Mr. Mendenhall?

Prof. WOODWARD. Yes, sir.

The CHAIRMAN. What were you to do?

Prof. WOODWARD. He assigned me to geodetic work in the development of those forms of base apparatus, of which I spoke a short while ago, and subsequently I perfected these forms of apparatus and measured two bases.

The CHAIRMAN. That was the special work to which you were detailed?

---

* The Methods and Results of the Survey of the West Coast of Lower California, by the officers of the U. S. steamer *Ranger*, during the season of 1889 and 1890, p. 31.

Prof. WOODWARD. Hardly; you could hardly call it special work, because it was an integral part of the work of that survey.

The CHAIRMAN. Do you know by what authority the appointment was made?

Prof. WOODWARD. Yes, sir; by authority of Congress.

The CHAIRMAN. What was the salary?

Prof. WOODWARD. Three thousand dollars per annum is carried in the appropriation bill.

The CHAIRMAN. Did you do any hydographic work before you went there?

Prof. WOODWARD. Yes, sir.

The CHAIRMAN. Did you ever do any geodetic work?

Prof. WOODWARD. Yes, sir; I was employed eleven years in the U. S. Lake Survey doing geodetic work the most of the time. A part of the time I did hydrographic work, and I had six years of experience in geodetic work for the Geological Survey.

The CHAIRMAN. That is all the work of the Coast Survey, either hydrographic or geodetic?

Prof. WOODWARD. You could hardly confine it to that. There is the tidal work, which requires a collection of tidal observations and a discussion of them by elaborate theories, which I may say were not devised by naval officers, but by La Place.

The CHAIRMAN. Are naval officers competent to do that work?

Prof. WOODWARD. There is not known in history a naval officer who has written a paper on tidal theories. Those theories are due to La Place and Sir William Thomson. There was a man who is now dead, formerly in the Coast and Geodetic Survey, Mr. William Ferrell, who also perfected tidal theories, and wrote a memoir which has met with commendation throughout the scientific world.

The CHAIRMAN. Did you ever do field work for the Coast Survey?

Prof. WOODWARD. Yes, sir; I measured two base lines.

The CHAIRMAN. What has been the result of the work you have done in the Coast and Geodetic Survey? Give us an idea of its value.

Prof. WOODWARD. I suppose I can give a fair idea. The first practical result was the perfection of these two new forms of base apparatus that served not only to expedite but to cheapen the work. I should say we could measure a base line now with sufficient accuracy for one-fourth of the expense it cost before the perfection of these methods.

The CHAIRMAN. That was something new?

Prof. WOODWARD. Yes, sir; that was something new. These two base lines I measured are in the so-called transcontinental triangulation, which furnishes a large number of latitude and longitude points in the country. The Geological Survey has already used much of this information in their map work.

The CHAIRMAN. Now, can you give us any idea of the time it would take for the Coast and Geodetic Survey to complete its work?

Prof. WOODWARD. Yes, sir; I can give you a definite statement about that if you will let me rise from my seat. I would like to elaborate a little upon that. I will say that so long as the earth turns, so long as you can see stars, so long as we have navigation and tides and phenomena of nature, such work will continue. It arises, not from the machinations of scientific men, but out of the phenomena of nature, and as long as we have these phenomena of nature scientific men will be found and governments will be found to prosecute that work so long as man is a civilized being.

The CHAIRMAN. That is, it will stand as long as the Republic stands? Prof. WOODWARD. Yes, sir. It will stand as long as the Republic stands. Whatever you may do you can not stop this work any more than you can dam the Mississippi River. It is a part of civilization. Look at the geodetic maps of Europe and you will find the whole country is covered with triangulations. Go to India, or look at the map of India, and see what the British Government has done there. That is practically an unknown country, a vast area of unknown lands that has been covered with triangulations. They have done ten times as much geodetic work in India as this country. Look at the continent of Europe. It is the same way. A part of Asia is already covered with such geodetic work which determines accurately the latitudes and longitudes of points, differences of heights, the forces of gravity, magnetic forces, and all of those things interesting and useful in a country's civilization. I would like to make that very emphatic, because the Secretary of the Navy, in his learned argument, seems to have entirely left out of sight the fact that these bureaus arose out of the phenomena of nature. He seems to think they might just as well be dispensed with as not. You might, gentlemen, just as well talk about dispensing with railroads and electric lights. You might just as well talk about abolishing gravitation as to talk about abolishing these bureaus.

Of course you can cut down and limit the expenditures and lop off here and there, and stop them for a few years, but scientific men will never be content—never, sir, as long as there is any such thing as civilization—scientific men will never be content with that sort of retrogression. Look at the maps of the French and German governments, and look at the millions of money they are spending in educational and scientific institutions. Look at the great institution at Berlin, established a few years ago, the *Physikalisches Reichs-Austalt*, which is administered under the direction of Prof. von Helmholtz. Why, gentlemen, it is astonishing in this part of the nineteenth century we should have a bill looking toward the destruction of such an institution as the Coast and Geodetic Survey. The German Parliament and German Government did not look amongst their naval and army officers to find a man to administer this function of scientific work. They looked to the leading scientific men of their country. A few years ago, also, there was a change made in the administration of what is known as the Geodetic Institute of Prussia. Did they look about in their army or navy for a man who might be furnished with an *ex officio* scientific reputation? No. What did they do? They looked about in the scientific profession and secured Dr. Helmert, a man who had written an elaborate treatise—a learned and scholarly treatise—on the subject of geodesy, the greatest treatise on that subject, and he was put at the head of that work.

There seems to be an opinion current in Washington that one only requires to invest a man with authority to make him a scientific man. It is preposterous. A scientific man must go through a period of remorseless drudgery and work before he can become recognized as such. I tell you the competition among scientific men is something frightful, especially in Germany and France. I read only yesterday an article in the Forum, written by Prof. Stanley Hall, president of Clark University, in which he details the amount of money spent by the French Government since the Franco-Prussian war and the amount of money spent by the Prussian Government since the Franco-Prussian war in founding institutions for scientific researches. It is enormous; it goes up to $30,000,000 or $40,000,000 since the time of the Franco-

Prussian war, and yet we find men in Congress who seem to be utterly ignorant of the state of modern science. No, gentlemen, do not destroy these bureaus, perfect them; take what is good of them and make it better; that is the true line of statesmanship.

The CHAIRMAN. Then I understand that the work of the Coast and Geodetic Survey will never be completed?

Prof. WOODWARD. No, sir; that sort of work will never be completed so long as the tide ebbs and flows and there is rotation of the earth.

The CHAIRMAN. I want to ask this question; you have been in the Geological Survey, does that apply to the Geological Survey as well?

Prof. WOODWARD. Yes, sir.

The CHAIRMAN. One more question and then I am through. You tell me you were opposed to turning the Naval Observatory over to the scientific men, to outside professors?

Prof. WOODWARD. No; you misunderstood me. I say I was opposed to turning the Naval Observatory over to that particular body of men who came before you a year or so ago.

The CHAIRMAN. Were they not scientific men in their way, the same as Prof. Mendenhall is in his?

Mr. GEISSENHAINER. You mean Prof. Boss, for instance?

Prof. WOODWARD. Yes, sir. If you will permit, I will go into that.

The CHAIRMAN. No; what I wanted to inquire was this: If you hold that the Navy was perfectly competent to handle the Naval Observatory, why would not the same line of argument apply to the Navy in regard to hydrographic work and geodetic work?

Prof. WOODWARD. I do not think the Navy is perfectly competent to handle the Naval Observatory, and the history of the administration shows it; but fortunately they have permitted a line of staff officers or professors of mathematics to retain their positions long enough to enable them to do a large amount of creditable work, but at present they are degenerating in that work, and it will not be long before the scientific public will say to Congress, you must have a different form of administration for the Naval Observatory. The trouble at present is that there are no successors to the learned professors who have distinguished themselves in astronomical science during the last thirty years. They are now passing away. Only a few years ago one was retired, and in a few years two or three more will go out; where are their successors? I can tell you, sirs; some are clergymen appointed as professor of mathematics in the United States Navy. Do you know that? Some few years ago there were two clergymen appointed.

Mr. GEISSENHAINER. Do not clergymen make very creditable scientific men?

Prof. WOODWARD. They might, but the point is that they were not in this case.

The CHAIRMAN. Is it not a fact that line officers of the Navy frequently resign for the purpose of being appointed professors?

Prof. WOODWARD. I have heard of only one case. In line with this, Mr. Chairman, if you will permit me to call your attention to another point which I omitted. I would like to call attention to another fact. In a rather considerable correspondence I have had with you, Mr. Chairman, you seemed to have labored under a misapprehension——

The CHAIRMAN. No; I answered you on the spur of the moment without looking at the bill, that is all, in regard to transferring the work belonging to the Geodetic Survey and the Hydrographic Survey to the Navy Department and the geological part to the Geological Survey.

Now, let me ask you one question before you leave that. I should judge from what you have said here, professor, that you hold that the scientific education given to the naval cadets at the Naval Academy at Annapolis is entirely useless as far as the Navy is concerned?

Prof. WOODWARD. No, sir; I have made no such proposition as that.

The CHAIRMAN. You seem to think they should confine themselves to fighting and to nothing else?

Prof. WOODWARD. That is their principal business and that is what they are educated for; but if you will allow me, let me say, if you permit them to stay long enough in the business, stay undisturbed and devote their time and attention and lives, they may become competent scientific men as well as anybody else. The *sine qua non* of scientific work is the same as the *sine qua non* of any other work; a man must devote his interest to it; but it is the policy of the administration of the Army and Navy to shift the men about from place to place.

Mr. GEISSENHAINER. That being conceded and time being given, do you claim they would be just as efficient?

Prof. WOODWARD. I could hardly say they would be just as efficient, because they would be liable at any time to be called out from this work and put in the Army, just as during the recent civil war.

Mr. MEYER. Before you proceed with that, admitting the force of your eloquent and forceful remarks as to the value of scientific progress, etc., what reason is there that the work of this Bureau could not be as well done under the Navy Department as it is now done under the Treasury Department? On board of the Coast Survey vessels there is no civilians at all. You stated awhile ago they are on shore and in tents; are they not under the direction of the officer on board the ship?

Prof. WOODWARD. No, sir; they are under the direction of the Superintendent of the Survey.

Mr. MEYER. They receive orders from the officers of the ship?

The CHAIRMAN. The officers themselves are under the orders of the Superintendent.

Mr. MEYER. Why could not the scientific work be better advanced under the existing administration of the Navy Department as under the Treasury Department?

Prof. WOODWARD. There is no particular reason why the Bureau should be under one Department rather than another so far as the maintenance of the Bureau is concerned. It might be under the Interior Department or any other as far as the real work is concerned, but ——

Mr. MEYER. According to that, you admit that it is rather material, as far as scientific results are concerned, whether it is control of one Executive Department, the Navy Department, or another?

Prof. WOODWARD. Exactly.

Mr. MEYER. On that point of view, as far as scientific results could be obtained, as far as scientific results go, it is the same, whether it is under one Department or another?

Mr. TALBOTT. If men were assigned to this special work and should be permitted to remain there ten or fifteen years without being interfered with, you say it would be remedied?

Prof. WOODWARD. In the course of ten or fifteen years, perhaps; but in the meantime it would be very expensive to the Government, and science would suffer.

Mr. MEYER. What is the position of the scientific men, whom I presume you represent, in regard to the transfer to the Navy Department; do they think it will have a deleterious effect?

Prof. WOODWARD. It would have an immediate deleterious effect. It would take ten or fifteen years to get a proper corps of men. As I explained before, the result of the action contemplated in this bill would be that the Navy would simply do the work of administration and hire civilians to do the real work. Now, they will necessarily have a low grade of civilian service, because no man who feels his liberty, as you and I do, will be content to work under an Army or Navy officer and be called "a damned computer," as I have been called.

Mr. MONEY. Let me call your attention to one of the provisions of the bill. "And such of the records, materials, and employés of the Coast and Geodetic Survey as may be necessary in order to carry out the purposes of this act," etc. It says that they shall be retained.

Prof. WOODWARD. Yes, sir; but you do not mean to infer that this bill will carry all of these men over bodily?

Mr. MONEY. Oh, no, sir.

Mr. ENLOE. Do you think they will resign if they are transferred?

Prof. WOODWARD. Many will.

Mr. ENLOE. And could their places be filled?

Prof. WOODWARD. They could be filled by an inferior grade of men, because it is only a low grade of men, devitalized men, who will subject themselves to the scorn and contempt of a naval officer.

Mr. MONEY. You are assuming what I think is a very violent assumption, that this competent corps of men who are to-day employed with such fine results as has been shown will resign if they are transferred to the Navy Department on account of some supposed assumption of their inferior position.

Prof. WOODWARD. I should assume they would; I should resign at once.

The CHAIRMAN. Why did you resign?

Prof. WOODWARD. I should be quite pleased to tell you why. I resigned because I could do far better outside of the Government service than I could in it. My services were worth more to me.

The CHAIRMAN. You say they would resign because they could do better outside?

Prof. WOODWARD. Quite possibly, but that does not end the matter at all. You recollect I called your attention to what would be the practical result. I say we could predict with practically absolute certainty. You are not going to remain in Congress continually——

Mr. MONEY. Yes, sir; we propose to stay here a good while.

Prof. WOODWARD. I suppose you do, but the people would say no——

Mr. MONEY. They will not let us off.

Prof. WOODWARD. At any rate the people will have something to say about this. Just as soon as you degrade our scientific work the scientific public of this country will become strong enough to change all that back again.

Mr. MONEY. But we do not propose to do that; we propose to continue the same work with identically the same men by the same methods.

Prof. WOODWARD. No, sir.

Mr. MONEY. Yes, sir; see the language of the bill. That is what we are going to do.

Mr. TALBOTT. And if we find some idlers we will get rid of them.

Prof. WOODWARD. I hope you might; I would be glad to see any idlers gotten rid of.

Mr. MONEY. And we propose to retain the satisfactory men.

Prof. WOODWARD. You propose to put the superintendent of this work where? Are you going to have the same superintendent? It

seems to me that one of the prime objects of this bill is to remove him.
Mr. TALBOTT. But suppose he was to die?
Prof. WOODWARD. Then the scientific men of this country would see
to it that no man but a scientific man would be placed in charge of it.
Mr. TALBOTT. So does the Government.
Prof. WOODWARD. I want to say to you in confidence and in all
honesty, gentlemen, that the scientific public would not commend you
for putting this sort of work under the charge of the Navy Depart-
ment.
Mr. MONEY. That might be.
Prof. WOODWARD. And I will say that you can not find 5 scientific
men out of 1,000 in this country who would vote in favor of this bill.
Mr. GEISSENHAINER. They would condemn it without a trial?
Prof. WOODWARD. Yes, sir; they would.
Mr. TALBOTT. What is the standing among the scientific public as
to the professors who teach the young men of West Point and the Naval
Academy; do not they rank well?
Prof. WOODWARD. Certainly; as a rule they rank well.
Mr. MONEY. I ask you, as a good, fair specimen of a scientific man
in every way, do you mean to say there is such an *esprit de corps* in
your body that these men will not continue in this service, to which
they have devoted practically the best years of their lives and the best
energies of their minds and bodies, and to which they must be, to some
degree, devoted; do you mean to say there is such an *esprit de corps* as
they would resign their life-work because the mere head of the administration has been changed?
Prof. WOODWARD. Yes, sir.
Mr. MONEY. With no disturbance of their work or their methods of
work, but simply because the scientific head has been changed; do you
mean to say that those gentlemen would resign, that the country would
lose their valuable services?
Prof. WOODWARD. That is precisely what I mean to say.
Mr. MONEY. Was that the fact before when it was transferred from
the Treasury Department to the Navy Department; did they resign
in a body, or any considerable number, or any of them?
Prof. WOODWARD. You could hardly say any considerable number,
because there were only a few of them.
Mr. MONEY. Did any man resign before when this Bureau was transferred from the Treasury to the Navy Department?
Prof. WOODWARD. I think a considerable number did.
Mr. MONEY. I ask your opinion because I am unprejudiced in regard to
this matter. The bill is new to me, and I am simply inquiring for information, because you are here to give us the information, and so you
will please excuse the questions I am asking you.
Prof. WOODWARD. Perhaps you will excuse me for being somewhat
earnest in this matter, for I have been so.
Mr. MONEY. I am very glad to see it.
Prof. WOODWARD. I have been under Army and Navy domination,
and had them, as I said, call me "a damned computer."
Mr. MONEY. You seem to be somewhat aggrieved ——
Prof. WOODWARD. I am, and every man would. No man who is not
undervitalized could feel otherwise, and I say these men who have been
trained for this service do not like the prospect of being placed under
the charge of a naval officer, or under the charge of an *ex officio* scientist.
The CHAIRMAN. Have you read the report of the testimony taken

before First Auditor Chenoweth in 1885 in an investigation of the Coast and Geodetic Survey?

Prof. WOODWARD. No, sir; I have not, and probably for very good reasons. Would you like me to tell you the reasons?

The CHAIRMAN. Yes, sir.

Prof. WOODWARD. That report, I believe, was never made public, and let me tell you, the First Auditor made a report concerning the survey, and Mr. Thorn, who was then in charge of the survey, reviewed the testimony and examined the facts and found that the charges in most instances were wrong. He exonerated the men, many of them very industrious and efficient men.

The CHAIRMAN. That would be decided by the testimony taken?

Prof. WOODWARD. Certainly, it was decided by the testimony taken, and that was the decision arrived at by Mr. Thorn, the man put in charge of that Bureau by President Cleveland, and he exonerated those men. Let me say to you, gentlemen, that I think it is a great wrong that this great nation has never publicly exonerated those eminent and industrious servants of the Government from the charges brought against them. It is a great wrong.

Mr. ENLOE. Why did not they make public that report?

The CHAIRMAN. I will say I have not had time to examine this report, as I have been two weeks getting it.

Prof. WOODWARD. I would like to have that made public and look over it myself.

Mr. ENLOE. I have been trying for three or four years to get a copy.

Prof. WOODWARD. Why did not you appeal to Mr. Cleveland and Mr. Thorn?

Mr ENLOE. Mr. Thorn I had no right to appeal to, and Mr. Cleveland has no jurisdiction of the report. They were not in office. I suppose if I had made my appeal properly to the Superintendent of the Coast Survey I might have gotten it as a matter of grace and not as a matter of right.

Prof. WOODWARD. Do you suppose he has authority to give out that report?

Mr. ENLOE. It seems that he thinks not, as he refused to give it to me or allow me to examine it.

Prof. WOODWARD. I think you will find the case as I have stated. It was a disgrace to the administration that made that investigation, and that is why that report has not been made public.

The CHAIRMAN. Is there a copy of that report in the Coast and Geodetic Survey Office?

Prof. WOODWARD. I understand there is, but I can not speak from personal information.

The CHAIRMAN. I asked Mr. Enloe's information.

Mr. ENLOE. I was advised by the Secretary of the Treasury under the former administration that the testimony and report was in the possession of the Coast and Geodetic Survey Office, and I went there and asked for it and was refused access to it and that is all I know about it.

The CHAIRMAN. On what ground?

Mr. ENLOE. On the ground that Mr. Thorn left it there in a desk and that it was not a public report, that it was his private property.

The CHAIRMAN. I want to say I found a copy of the report and testimony in the Treasury Department, so that there must have been two copies. It was just handed to me this morning and I have not had time to look over it.

Prof. WOODWARD. My opinion is the reason that report was not made public is this: Simply the examiners found the charges which were brought were not sustained and they did not feel like saying so. I hope sometime this country or our governors will be honest enough to say so and bring out the facts and exonerate the men of these charges that were brought against them unjustly.

The CHAIRMAN. Mr. Enloe was absent when Prof. Woodward made his statement in regard to what he considered the animus of the present bill.

Mr. ENLOE. I was before another committee, and I would have been very glad to have heard his statement.

The CHAIRMAN. The professor thinks you were animated somewhat from personal motives.

Mr. ENLOE. Then the professor makes that statement without any facts whatever to justify it.

Mr. GEISSENHAINER. The professor did not elaborate upon that point.

Mr. ENLOE. My motive in introducing the bill was to try, if possible, to prevent employing two sets of men to do the same kind of work. I do not know what the professor thinks about it or what he has said about it. An investigation of the work done by this Bureau and an investigation of the work done by the Geological Survey will show, as far as work on shore is concerned, that there is duplication to a very large extent, and that for all practical purposes they are going over the same ground, and that there is no justification for it. I introduced this bill for the purpose of avoiding the unnecessary expense of employing two sets of men virtually to do the same work. I believe it will be a better system, and I believe the hydrographic work will be more responsive to the demands of the Government if put under the control of the Secretary of the Navy than it is at present. I can see no necessity for having a superintendent here to superintend the work of a few men on the shore, practically doing the same work on the shore that is done by the Geological Survey. The work that is done on the water is done by naval officers, and the supervision is exercised by the Superintendent of the Coast and Geodetic Survey.

Prof. WOODWARD. Will you allow me for a moment, Mr. Chairman, to refer to the question of the duplication of the work. I have been employed in the two bureaus and I have seen how this work goes on, and I think I know all about this question of duplication, and I would be willing to assert, if you can figure up the cost of the work done, that you would find that the amount of duplication that has been done in the United States would not amount in value to $2,000. It has been merely accidental. The Geological Survey is not doing geodetic work of refinement. They are doing geodetic work which is sufficient for their map purposes, and that leads me to the question concerning which your chairman seems to have labored under some misconception.

Mr. ENLOE. Before going on that, allow me to ask you a question.

Prof. WOODWARD. I want to keep on this subject for a moment. Your chairman seems to have labored under a misconception that the Coast and Geodetic Survey is doing geological work, and he says they have been doing geological work for years. Not to make a false quotation, I will read from his letter——

The CHAIRMAN. Is it not a fact that their work in some cases extend several miles back in the country?

Prof. WOODWARD. Certainly, in geodetic work.

The CHAIRMAN. Do they not use men from the Geological Survey to do that work?

Prof. WOODWARD. Yes, to do geological work, certainly. First, let me quote from your letter, because it would seem there was a rather serious misconception——

The CHAIRMAN. I told you I wrote the letter before the bill was before the committee, that first letter.

Prof. WOODWARD. Here is a letter dated April 18.

The CHAIRMAN. What I wanted to convey to your mind was this fact, that the proposition was to transfer the hydrographic part to the hydrographic part of the Navy Department and the geological part of the Survey to the Geological Bureau of the Interior Department.

Prof. WOODWARD. The Coast and Geodetic Survey is not doing geological work, and it has never done geological work.

The CHAIRMAN. Then, why do you employ men of the Geological Survey to do the work?

Prof. WOODWARD. The Coast and Geodetic Survey does not employ men from the Geological Bureau.

The CHAIRMAN. You said they did.

Prof. WOODWARD. No; I say they do not. I say the Coast and Geodetic Survey has never done any geological work, but it does geodetic work.

Mr. ENLOE. What is the difference between geological and geodetic work? Define it for the committee.

Prof. WOODWARD. Geodetic work comprises the work of triangulation from precise bases, and it comprises the determination of longitude and latitude by astronomy. It comprises the measurement of the forces of gravitation and terrestrial magnetism. You know it is very essential in many surveys to know what the variation of the magnetic needle is, and the Coast and Geodetic Survey has carried on that sort of work. Another important and difficult branch of the work is that of the tides, especially the elaboration of the tidal tables which furnish the state of the tide, say at New York City.

The CHAIRMAN. Let us get down closer; we have heard all of that before. What I want to know is this, if the map that Mr. Enloe exhibited in the House during the discussion of the sundry civil bill—a map on which work was done 10 miles from the shore in one case——

Mr. ENLOE. I do not know the exact distance from the shore, but I exhibited maps there, and amongst them a map of the Chesapeake Bay and going east all along the Atlantic coast, and the survey extended back into the country, and it is the most absolutely detailed map I have ever seen of the city of New York, Staten Island, Boston, and other cities and towns and various watering places along the Atlantic coast, giving the streets, street car lines, roads, railroads, trees, and houses, and everything in detail for a distance back in the country which can not serve any purpose that I can see.

Prof. WOODWARD. Let me answer that question, the Coast and Geodetic Survey is authorized by law to do that sort of work.

Mr. ENLOE. But what is the practical purpose of that?

Prof. WOODWARD. The practical purpose for these maps, according to the original plans, was for offensive and defensive purposes as well as for the purposes of navigation.

Mr. ENLOE. That is called cadastral work?

Prof. WOODWARD. Let me read you the opinion of Gens. Wright and Smith.

Mr. GEISSENHAINER. Will you please confine yourself to the definition of the distinction between a geological and a geodetic survey?

Prof. WOODWARD. That is what I sought to do.

Mr. MEYER. Does the geological force of the Geological Survey do geodetic work.

Prof. WOODWARD. They do geodetic work of an inferior order, only just sufficient to afford a basis for their maps. The more refined geodetic work, the determination of latitudes and longitudes and the precise determination of bases and triangulation, are relegated to the Coast and Geodetic Survey.

Mr. ENLOE. They do not do work of triangulation, then?

Prof. WOODWARD. They do what is called secondary and tertiary work of triangulation.

Mr. MEYER. Why is it that they are confined only to the secondary and tertiary work, to inferior work? Are not they competent to do first-class work?

Prof. WOODWARD. They are confined to that because they do not wish to trespass upon the province of the Coast and Geodetic Survey. It is authorized by law to do that work, whereas the Geological Survey is not authorized by law to do that sort of work.

Mr. ENLOE. But you admit they are capable?

Prof. WOODWARD. Certainly; you can build up a corps that will do it, but, as I said to this committee, there is a strange incongruity in putting in charge of that sort of work a geologist and anthropologist in place of a geodesist and a mathematician. Maj. Powell is a distinguished gentleman, but, as I said, he does not pretend to have studied geodesy and the sciences which are allied to that. I will tell you the difference between geological and geodetic work. Geodetic work comprises the work of precise triangulation and a precise determination of astronomical positions of latitude and longitude. It comprises also a determination of magnetic forces, a precise study of the phenomena of the earth's magnetism. It comprises also a precise study of tidal observations whereby they are able to predict the state of the tide several years ahead. Geology explores the crust of the earth, it goes into the crust, while geodesy stays on the outside. It is necessary for the delineation of geological conditions to have maps, and hence they make maps, and the Geological Survey makes maps which are useful for their special purpose, but there is no conflict between the Geological and the Geodetic Survey. I know that, for I have been connected with both, and if there had been a conflict I would have run against it. Now, the Geological Survey makes use of much of the geodetic work, especially of the triangulations, because that is done on a very precise basis, and it suffices for the geologist when he wishes to make a map to have one point on the map whose latitude and longitude are determined; then, on the minor surveys, he can construct a map which is good enough for his purpose. Understand, the maps of the Geological Survey are geological; they are not carried to a special degree of refinement, but they are sufficient for the geologist. I am not at all disposed to say anything against the Geological Survey.

Mr. McALEER. In other words, one department keeps on top of the ground and the other goes underneath?

Prof. WOODWARD. That seems to be the tendency of this bill. This bill would keep them all the time in hot water, and the result will be anything but creditable to American science and American statesmanship.

STATEMENT OF PROF. GEORGE H. WILLIAMS, OF JOHNS HOPKINS UNIVERSITY.

Mr. WILLIAMS then addressed the committee. He said:

Mr. Chairman and gentlemen of the committee, at the request of a member of the committee it was desired a representation of Johns Hopkins University, of Baltimore, should be here, and as time elapsed President Gilman, who endeavored and would have liked to have been here, was detained by an important meeting, and he designated my colleague, Dr. Clark, and myself to represent him, and to represent the general feeling of the entire scientific faculty of Johns Hopkins University. President Gilman was at one time professor of physical geography of Yale College, and it is one of the subjects in which he has most special knowledge and has special interest, and he wishes me to say that every man of our colleagues of that faculty, and I myself, firmly believe it would be, as Prof. Woodward says, a great scientific calamity to this country to have this transfer made.

I have listened with great interest to Prof. Woodward's very able and detailed statement, and I can only say that I and all scientific men I know of would most heartily indorse it in the main. It does seem to me that if one thing is plainer than another it is that a scientific man to be a success must be able not to give up fifteen or twenty years but his entire life, from the time he starts in his career until his death, in attempting to accomplish some one idea. Now, if the competition is as great as it is certainly becoming in order for a man to compete, he must do this because competition, being as it is, the number of men crowding into scientific careers in this country, increasing as rapidly as it is increasing, it does seem to me that any man who is not able to do this will be left far behind in the race. There are enough very able men who are going into these careers which will render any competition by able men who are hampered by the time they can devote to this subject practically out of the race altogether. Furthermore, it seems to me that it is of great interest for scientific purposes that an independent bureau should conduct this work. As I understand from the bill, it is not the intention, as I hear reiterated by members of the committee, in any way to interfere or abolish the work, but merely to divide it, a part going to the Navy and a part to the Geological Survey. I have been for eleven years myself an active member of the Geological Survey, doing work for them each year, and I use the maps of the Geological Survey all the time, and have also had occasion to use the maps of the Coast Survey, and I must say there is no comparison between them. The Coast Survey maps are much better.

Mr. Enloe suggests that there is an amount of duplication. The Geological Survey at the present is only too glad to make use of the Coast Survey results, but where Coast Survey data is employed it is of a higher quality than the work that is done by the Geological Survey, but there is no time for me to enter into a discussion of that subject, and I am here to say that among every body of scientific men the feeling is certainly united, very sincere on their part, in the opinion that this would be a calamity, and we desire if possible to enter our protest most emphatically against it.

I thank you gentlemen for your kind attention.

Thereupon the committee adjourned.

COMMITTEE ON NAVAL AFFAIRS,
Friday, May 4, 1894.

The Committee on Naval Affairs this day met, Hon. Amos J. Cummings in the chair. The committee had under consideration II. R. 6338. Hon. B. A. Enloe, a representative from the State of Tennessee, and Mr. R. C. Glasscock, of Washington, D. C., appeared before the committee.

The CHAIRMAN. We will now hear Mr. Enloe in favor of his bill for the transfer of the hydrographic portion of the Coast and Geodetic Survey to the Navy Department, and the geodetic portion to the Geological Survey.

(To Mr. Enloe): Are you ready to proceed?

Mr. ENLOE. I believe I will ask you to hear Mr. Glasscock first.

The CHAIRMAN. Then we will hear Mr. Glasscock.

STATEMENT OF MR. R. C. GLASSCOCK, OF WASHINGTON, D. C.

Mr. GLASSCOCK then addressed the committee. He said:

Mr. Chairman and gentlemen of the committee, I am here to-day to represent the other side of this question with reference to the transfer of the Coast and Geodetic Survey to the Hydographic Office of the Navy Department and to the Geological Survey. This is a question that is not new. It has been officially agitated for more than ten years past. Secretary Chandler, Secretary of the Navy during President Arthur's administration, recommended this, and President Cleveland so far back as ten years ago had this to say in his message to Congress:

> The work of the Coast and Geodetic Survey was during the last fiscal year carried on within the boundaries and off the coast of thirty-two States, two Territories, and the District of Columbia. In July last certain irregularities were found to exist in the management of this Bureau, which led to a prompt investigation of its methods. The abuses that were brought to light by this examination and the reckless disregard of duty and the interest of the Government, developed on the part of some of those connected with the service, made a change of superintendency and a few of its other officers necessary. Since the Bureau has been in new hands an introduction of economies and the application of business methods have produced an important saving to the Government and a promise of more useful results. This service has never been regulated by anything but the most indefinite legal enactments and the most unsatisfactory rules. It was many years ago sanctioned apparently for a purpose regarded as temporary and related to a survey of our coast. Having gained a place in the appropriations made by Congress, it has gradually taken to itself powers and objects not contemplated in its creation, and extended its operations until it sadly needs legislative attention.
>
> So far as the further survey of our coast is concerned, there seems to be a propriety of transferring that work to the Navy Department. The other duties now in charge of this establishment, if they can not be profitably attached to some existing Department or other bureau, should be prosecuted under a law exactly defining their scope and purpose, and with a careful discrimination between the scientific inquiries which may properly be assumed by the Government and those which should be undertaken by State authority or by individual enterprise.

That is President Cleveland's message of ten years ago. Now, sir, there has never been a case which has been prepared for consideration that has attracted more authoritative consideration than this question you are now about to consider. In 1884 a joint commission was appointed by both branches of Congress to consider this question, and my duty to-day will be to refer you particularly to the testimony taken before that joint commission, and also to the minority report, which favors the transfer of this Bureau to the Navy Department, signed by the present Secretary of the Navy, Mr. Herbert, and Senator Morgan. There was also a majority report, signed by Mr. Allison, Mr. Hale, and Mr. Lowry, against transferring it.

Now, gentlemen, I do not propose to do much else than refer you to this testimony, for anything I can say in my individual capacity, I imagine, will have very little weight, but it is only the testimony; and I will say that, in collating this testimony, we not only go to the Secretaries of the Navy, to the Hydrographic Office of the Navy Department, and the Geological Survey, but we go to the Coast Survey itself, and we will produce before you here to-day evidence of Coast Survey officials to sustain the recommendations that this work ought to be transferred.

Now, gentlemen, I wish to say right here that the question was raised the other day by Prof. Woodward, when he appeared before your committee, as to what should be done with the weights and measures department, which is also in the Coast Survey. When I come to the proper place I shall have something to say upon that subject.

The following are some of the reasons why the hydrographic part of the Coast and Geodetic Survey should be transferred from the Treasury Department to the Navy Department and the geodetic part to the Geological Survey:

(1) All the coast surveys are completed and have been virtually so since 1879, except a small portion (about one-tenth) on the Atlantic Coast and two-fifths of the Pacific Coast.

(2) All the hydrographic work that the Coast Survey has been credited with for more than twenty-five years has been done by naval officers, and is to-day being done by naval officers through a hydrographic inspector stationed in the Coast Survey building.

(3) The geodetic work being done by the Coast Survey is duplicated to a great extent by the Geological Survey, and the cost of it done by the Coast and Geodetic Survey is $100 per square mile, while the cost of that done by the Geological Survey is on an average of about $3 per square mile.

(4) The Coast and Geodetic Survey, while technically under the Treasury Department, is virtually an "independent bureau;" consequently, in its efforts to cover up decrease of work and to maintain a steady increase of salaries, it has grown foul and corrupt, which culminated a few years ago in an investigation that proved disgraceful to the management and disastrous to the work. Since then it has been regarded with more or less suspicion, and to-day is not free from adverse criticism. In order to meet the political complexion of any administration that happens to come into power, the combination that "runs it" is composed of Republicans and Democrats, and the alliance is "offensive and defensive." "Offensive," as has already been shown when you recall the attack made on the Secretaries of the Navy and Treasury and on the naval officers the other day by Mr. Woodward, and "defensive," as will appear by testimony later on.

(5) "The Hydrographic Office in the Navy Department is established by law (says Secretary W. E. Chandler, Senate Mis. Doc. No. 82, vol. 4, p. 64) for the improvement of the means for navigating safely the vessels of the Navy and the mercantile marine by providing, under the authority of the Secretary of the Navy, accurate and cheap nautical charts, sailing directions, and manuals of instructions for the use of all vessels of the United States and for the benefit and use of navigation generally. The Coast and Geodetic Survey, whose geodetic branch overlaps the work of the Geological Survey and whose hydrographic branch overlaps the work of the Hydrographic Office, has no connection whatever with the Treasury Department, under which it is placed."

 (6) One-tenth of the survey of the Atlantic coast is kept in an unfinished condition in order to influence appropriations and to perpetuate the Coast and Geodetic Survey.

To sustain these reasons I will call your attention to the testimony taken before joint committee commissioned under an act of Congress July 7, 1884, and continued again on March 3, 1885, to consider the present organization of the " Signal Service, Coast and Geodetic Survey, Geological Survey, and the Hydrographic Office of the Navy Department, with a view to secure greater efficiency and economy of administration of the public service." (Senate Mis. Doc. No. 82, first session, Forty-ninth Congress, vol. 4.) I also commend to your careful consideration the minority report of the said Commission to be found in vol. 7, first session, Forty-ninth Congress, Senate Reports.

The Coast Survey was originally organized by an act of Congress in 1807 for the purpose of surveying the coast within 20 leagues of the shore, the work to be illustrated by maps showing islands, shoals, roads, or places of entrance, together with such other matters as might be deemed best for completing an accurate chart of the coasts within the extent of the United States.

Mr. ENLOE. That is within 20 leagues of the shore on the water, or is it 20 leagues on land, I only want to know?

Mr. GLASSCOCK. I am only quoting the law.

Mr. TALBOTT. You must go waterwards.

Mr. GLASSCOCK. I am simply giving the law authorizing this. Secretary of the Navy W. E. Chandler says, in a letter to the joint commission (Mis. Doc. No. 82, vol. 4, first session, Forty-ninth Congress, p. 64):

This survey might with proper diligence have been completed in seventy-five years. As the time must sooner or later arrive for its completion, it became necessary to delay the completion of the hydrographic charts until some new branch of work to justify the continuance of a separate organization could be firmly established.

Accordingly, in the sundry civil bill of March 3, 1871, appeared an appropriation of $15,000 " for extending the triangulation of the coast survey so as to form a geodetic connection between the Atlantic and Pacific coasts."

From this minute beginning dates a complete revolution in the (original) purpose of the Treasury Bureau then known as the Coast Survey. By carefully drawn and unobtrusive provisions in the annual estimates, which have been followed in the appropriation bills, the change has been brought about by imperceptible changes, until now a large part of the appropriation which was formerly devoted to coast work has become absorbed by labors in the interior.

When this last work was securely established the organization took upon itself the name of " The Coast and Geodetic Survey," which name was officially recognized in the appropriation act of 1879, and in the year 1881–'82 the expenditure for triangulation and topography amounted to $132,000, while for those for hydrography was only $36,000.

I wish to say here, in respect to a gentleman I am about to mention, that he is one of the few men in the Coast and Geodetic Survey who has stood the test of all the scandal and has come out unscathed and stands to-day pure and perfect, so far as any scandal is concerned; and I regard him, although he might be mentioned as one of those " damn computers" we heard about the other day, as an estimable gentleman and a gentleman of high learning and high ability, and I am glad to have an opportunity of saying so.

4561——3

Mr. C. A. Schott, chief of the "Computing Division," in the Coast and Geodetic Survey, in a letter to the joint commission, page 367, vol. 4, defined "geodesy" as a science which has for its object primarily the determination of the figure of the earth and, secondarily, the mathematical definition of the position of objects upon its surface, and, consequently, of their mutual relations." Do you understand this? Let me explain further. If I were a draftsman I would draw the earth showing the mountains and valleys, and on the top of one of the mountains I would draw a tree, and by some mathematical computation I would determine the "mutual relations" that exist between the earth, the mountain, the valleys, and the tree.

This explanation may be deemed as a little grotesque, but if you will look at it a little you will find it expresses as near as a man who is not an experienced scientific man can come to this matter.

Of what use can be made of this work when finished? In the first place, it is not admitted by anyone that it will ever be finished.

I think you had it verified the other day when the question was asked of Prof. Woodward when the Coast and Geodetic Survey intended to finish its work and he replied they never intended to finish, or it would never be finished, or something of that kind; and the use of it is beyond the comprehension of all who have tackled it, including the joint commission.

Maj. Powell, chief of the Geological Survey, testifies before the joint commission (vol. 4, p. 198) as follows:

> I am unable to state any useful purpose which this cadastral or artificial element in the coast charts subserve. First, because it is not executed so as to form a complete cadastral map. Second, because the artificial topographic features are ephemeral. That is, this culture changes from year to year in such a manner that the charts speedily become misleading.
>
> In illustration of this fact I may state that one of the commissioners of the Massachusetts survey informs me that he has lately examined certain charts made in Massachusetts on this plan, and he discovers that in the areas coming under his eye 50 per cent of the houses placed upon the charts twenty years ago have disappeared on the old charts, and that the confusion arising from these two causes renders the charts almost unintelligible. He also informs me that the same confusion arises from the delineation of fences, but to a greater extent, and that a similar confusion arises through the delineation of minor public or private roads, but not to so great an extent.

Now, gentlemen, we will come to the Coast and Geodetic Survey and take one of the officials there and see what he has to say about it.

Benj. A. Colonna, now assistant in charge of the office of the Coast and Geodetic Survey, ranking next the Superintendent as second in authority, was before the joint commission and was asked this question concerning this work (vol. 4, p. 868).

> Q. But for purposes of map-making it would be of no use?—A. Of no use in map-making, so far as the delineation of separate sheets, but of much use to make these sheets join.

We confess we can not comprehend this [says the minority report of this joint commission, vol. 7, p. 71]. But we can understand this great arc of triangles, and indeed we consider it quite intelligible and entirely consistent with all the facts, when we regard it as a part of the system which the Coast Survey, without authority of organic law, and by what have been aptly called "unobtrusive provisions" in appropriation bills has undertaken for the survey of the whole United States.

Now we want to know how much this geodetic work is going to cost?

Prof. Hilgard, who was Superintendent of the Coast Survey at that time, testified before the joint commission (vol. 4, p. 157) that he estimated "to make a skeleton of triangles over the United States on a basis of $4,000,000 will require fifty years."

Herbert G. Ogden, now chief of the Engraving Division of the Coast Survey [says the minority report], gravely testified before the commission (vol. 4, p. 620) that as the Coast Survey maps were admitted to be accurate and were said to cost $100 per square mile, and as the topography of the Geological Survey was said to cost only $3, therefore the latter was only 3 per cent of the correct survey. We cite this reasoning simply because it seems to us to illustrate the extravagant methods of this Bureau.

As there is about 3,625,000 square miles in the United States, this would make the work cost over $362,500,000.

Maj. Powell of the Geological Survey testified before the commission (vol. 4, p. 638):

That to do the topography of the whole United States as that of the coast is being done by the Coast Survey would require 400,000 sheets equal to a library of 8,000 large folio volumes, and would cost $350,000,000.

And on page 206 of the same book, he testifies that—

There is no substantial difference in the accuracy of the charts of the Coast Survey and Topographic maps of the Geological Survey as *maps*.

And on page 607 same book, he testifies that:

The cost of the Topographic Survey which is preceded by the Geological Survey, and which maps subserve the purpose above enumerated, is greatly variable in different portions of the country.

but he states the cost to be from $1.50 to $5 per square mile.

(To his son): Now, let me have those maps. Now, gentlemen, I want to show you the work of the two surveys [exhibiting maps]. Here is the Coast and Geodetic work across the continent that has cost, as these experts say, $100 per square mile. It takes two maps to show it all. This is the work of the Coast Survey that is costing $100 per square mile according to this testimony, and here is the map of the Geological Survey that is costing from $5 to $10 per square mile. Here is one which costs $5 per square mile [exhibiting same]. I got the prices that I have marked on it from the man who has charge of the maps at the Geological Survey. This map here is from the Geological Survey which cost from $5 to $10 per square mile, and this is from the Coast and Geodetic Survey which is said to have cost $100 per square mile [exhibiting same].

Mr. RANDALL. How do you explain the difference between the cost?

Mr. GLASSCOCK. I can not say.

Mr. RANDALL. Do they cover the same ground in the same localities, or is one on the ocean and the other on the land?

Mr. GLASSCOCK. Why they are both on land, the Coast and Geodetic Survey do only land work. If you will examine——

Mr. GEISSENHAINER. Is this entirely new?

Mr. GLASSCOCK. Yes, sir; I just got them a few days ago from the Geological Survey.

Mr. GEISSENHAINER. The work I mean?

Mr. GLASSCOCK. Yes, sir.

Mr. GEISSENHAINER. It is not based upon old work that is made a groundwork for this?

Mr. GLASSCOCK. I presume not, but I am not familiar enough with map making to tell you that.

Mr. ENLOE. I see from the dates on it that this is surveyed in 1882, 1883, 1884, 1887, 1888.

Mr. GLASSCOCK. I presume they have the dates. Your question can be better answered by examining the maps of the geodetic work and the maps of the Geological Survey.

Mr. TALBOTT. But do they do the same work in the same locality at different rates of cost?

Mr. GLASSCOCK. Well, the Coast and Geodetic Survey does not do any Geological Survey work. That is the question that was put and Prof. Woodward was very positive in answering it. The chairman, it seems, in some communication, had asked him the question if the Coast and Geodetic Survey did any Geological Survey work, and Mr. Woodward answered that they did not. That is true, but the Geological Survey does do geodetic work. You have got the question just reversed.

Mr. GEISSENHAINER. I notice that is a large map and it is outlined, while this small map apparently has the same outlines, but is worked out and filled in?

Mr. GLASSCOCK. I brought this here to demonstrate this is the work as it comes out in their reports, and it demonstrates that the very work as done by the Coast and Geodetic Survey is work done by the Geological Survey. Here is the way the work of both those bureaus gets before the public. This was cut out of one of their annual reports.

Mr. MONEY. I was about to ask you if it will not interrupt your argument——

Mr. GLASSCOCK. I would be pleased to answer.

Mr. GEISSENHAINER. If you will pardon me, Mr. Money, what I meant was this, was it not more a matter of mere details of shading than anything else?

Mr. GLASSCOCK. That is intended more for a geological map of that part of the country.

Mr. GEISSENHAINER. Would not this map cover the same ground, the outlines being the determining lines?

Mr. GLASSCOCK. If you are able to determine that fact——

Mr. GEISSENHAINER. I asked you; we are seeking the information.

Mr. GLASSCOCK. I do not know; as I say, what use is all of this?

Mr. GEISSENHAINER. That is another point.

Mr. GLASSCOCK. What use is it, as the joint commission further say they are unable to comprehend the use of all of this work?

Mr. ENLOE. They sometimes demonstrate an error of probably an inch in a mile in surveying.

Mr. GLASSCOCK. I know that is given in some testimony as probably coming within a fiftieth part of an inch or an inch in so many miles of the correctness of the survey. What I brought these maps here for, gentlemen, was to illustrate to you the different kind of work done by the two surveys. Here you have it by the Geological Survey in these maps, and here you have it in the Coast Survey. This map costs the country $100 per square mile, according to their own testimony, and this is costing the country $5 to $10 per square mile according to their own testimony, all of which is referred to in this book.

Mr. MONEY. The question I was about to ask you is this, you say that this map cost $100 per square mile and this cost $5 per square mile?

Mr. GLASSCOCK. Yes, sir.

Mr. MONEY. What do I understand by that; does that include the cost of labor in the field, of the bureaus here, of officers here, of the whole outfit, and everything? Is everything of that kind included to make up this cost?

Mr. GLASSCOCK. I presume it is the work in the field.

Mr. MONEY. It does not convey any meaning to my mind at all.

Mr. GLASSCOCK. I can only tell you as far as I know, and I confess I am not very well versed in these matters, because I am not a map maker, but I guess this is the cost of the work in the field, not the work in the office.

Mr. MONEY. Do we understand this map we have here cost $100 per square mile?

Mr. GLASSCOCK. That is what the testimony shows.

Mr. MONEY. You know that is not true, because here is a map that includes hundreds of thousands and millions of square miles?

Mr. GLASSCOCK. But that is not worked all over, that is only worked to a certain extent.

Mr. MONEY. Only this that is mapped out here?

Mr. GLASSCOCK. That is all they have worked out.

Mr. MONEY. Then what does all this mean [illustrating on maps]?

Mr. ENLOE. They have primary, secondary, and tertiary triangulations. That is what this work here represents, and it is completed here [illustrating].

Mr. MONEY. Then this map shows nothing that an ordinary geological map does not show?

Mr. GEISSENHAINER. You do not mean there is no notice taken of the area?

Mr. GLASSCOCK. I mean this, that these maps represent work done; these lines here represent the triangulation done.

The CHAIRMAN. Do these maps represent that 20 leagues?

Mr. GLASSCOCK. That is geodetic work; I am speaking of the work across the continent.

Mr. ENLOE (to Mr. Money). They have started here to survey a line to connect the Atlantic with the Pacific ocean, as I understand, and they have completed the line there and they have got here to Colorado and done some work along here [illustrating], and then they have done some work in Kansas. In other words, they are doing it by sections. They have done a little in connection with that line there, and are proceeding to complete this map in this manner to cover the entire area of the United States, and when they cover the entire area of the United States it will cost $100 per square mile to the Government.

Mr. GEISSENHAINER. This map is really intended to show the public the general progress of this work, and it is of no utility or value whatever to anybody, but simply designed to show the progress of the work of the Geodetic Survey and nothing else?

Mr. GLASSCOCK. That is, all their work that they have done through the interior of the country. It is not a map at all, and the testimony goes to show that it is of no use as a map.

Mr. GEISSENHAINER. It does purport to be so. It purports only to be a sketch of the general progress——

Mr. GLASSCOCK. Of their triangulations across the continent. Now, let me read what this commission——

Mr. ENLOE. Just one moment; there is this point in there. It shows that if Congress attempts to keep up the appropriations to complete this work according to the design of the Coast and Geodetic Survey, that when it is completed it will cost $100 per square mile for the entire area of the United States. Do you understand that?

Mr. GEISSENHAINER. An aggregate of $350,000,000.

Mr. ENLOE. That only shows the progress they have made in this work. It shows what part is completed, what part is primary, what is secondary, etc.

Mr. GLASSCOCK. This is a thing that is absolutely astounding, and it has not struck you any harder than it did this commission. I want to read you what this commission says about this thing.

The CHAIRMAN. That is the minority report.

Mr. GLASSCOCK. This is the minority report of the joint commission.

There you have it; you are not the only parties that have confounded by this matter. Parties who have given this investigation
months after months have been obliged to acknowledge that they did
not comprehend it, except that it is an unobtrusive provision in the
appropriation bills to perpetuate the Coast and Geodetic Survey. That
is all it is. And you must in forming your opinion come down to the
testimony taken in this thing and you must consider what such men
as Maj. Powell and Mr. B. A. Colonna say when they tell you it is of
no use for map-making. Now, Mr. Colonna testified——

The CHAIRMAN. One minute right there. It seems to me we can
draw a little plainer the point I am trying to make in regard to the
Coast and Geodetic and the Geological Survey. I understand you to
say that the Geodetic Survey has undertaken to make a map, a geodetic map, I will call it, of the United States?

Mr. GLASSCOCK. The Geodetic Survey, no, sir. You did not understand me to say anything of the sort.

The CHAIRMAN. Then I do not know what you mean by saying they
are attempting to make a connection between the Atlantic and Pacific
ocean in a map; I understood that was their work?

Mr. GLASSCOCK. That is what they said, and nobody is able to understand it, so far as I know, unless some scientific man we have not heard
of yet. It is intended to make a connection between the Atlantic and
the Pacific coast——

The CHAIRMAN. Is that not the same that the Geological Survey is
doing?

Mr. GLASSCOCK. To a certain extent wherever they go along.

The CHAIRMAN. Is not the Geological Survey going over the work
the Geodetic Survey has marked on that map?

Mr. GLASSCOCK. Well, I do not know about that.

Mr. ENLOE. Here is the point about that, Mr. Chairman, I think.
You understand, of course, the object of this base line. This is the
base line from which they are to triangulate the entire United States.
Well, I do not understand that the Geological Survey has ever
attempted to do the work in as complete a form as the Coast and Geodetic Survey is doing this geodetic work. They are doing it, I suppose,
as far as I know, with absolute accuracy as nearly as it can be done.

The CHAIRMAN. They claim that it is.

Mr. ENLOE. Yes, sir. Now, the question is what utility is there in it?
The Geological Survey, I understand, does a line survey—for it is
nothing more than a line survey in simple terms—and it does that survey with sufficient accuracy to answer all purposes, and if the States
want any more detailed maps than the Geological Survey can furnish,
that is a matter that ought to belong to the municipalities and States.

Mr. MONEY. The Geological Survey establishes lines upon which
these surveys can be completed?

The CHAIRMAN. The Geological Survey is doing work under specific law, whereas the other is not doing the work under specific law?

Mr. GLASSCOCK. There is no organic law.

Mr. MONEY. What do you understand by an organic law?

Mr. GLASSCOCK. By any special act of Congress.

Mr. MONEY. That is not organic law at all. This provision in an
appropriation bill is just as much law as if a specific law was passed.
Organic law relates to constitutions strictly.

Mr. GLASSCOCK. I am only quoting from what Mr. Herbert said.

Mr. MONEY. That has no meaning there at all.

Mr. GLASSCOCK. They do it, but they say this, that they get this permission through an appropriation bill.

Mr. MONEY. That is the law.

Mr. GLASSCOCK. Of course it is law but it is not organic law. The Coast and Geodetic Survey was not created by organic law.

Mr. MONEY. That is very true, but organic law refers strictly to constitutions and not to the statutes.

Mr. ENLOE. That term has no meaning except that it seems to carry this idea, that this concern is acting without authority of law.

Mr. MONEY. As a matter of fact the word "organic" simply misleads.

Mr. ENLOE. Let me call attention to this suggestion. I observe here in discussing matters before Congress relating to a resolution, in speaking of legislation in an appropriation bill it is treated as being of a different character of legislation from legislation in a separate and distinct bill organizing a bureau for a purpose. Now, I suppose the term "organic" is used in this minority report referred to by Mr. Glasscock in that sense; of an act creating and outlining work and specifying its objects and purposes.

Mr. MONEY. But it does not make a particle of difference, and the word itself is simply misleading.

The CHAIRMAN. As far as these bureaus are concerned, the Geological Survey and the Coast and Geodetic Survey, you will find that they both originated in a paragraph making an appropriation for such work in an appropriation bill.

Mr. MONEY. The word "organic" seems to be misleading, you might go to almost any department on that proposition and question their right to exist. That is a thing where they are all exactly on the same footing.

Mr. ENLOE. Before going away from the subject of maps I will state I had occasion to investigate that matter to some extent and tried to understand exactly what the objects and purposes of this Geodetic Survey were. We have maps made by the Geological Survey, and all maps which are printed by the U. S. Government are printed upon surveys made by the Geological Survey. Now, that for all practical purposes it seems would be sufficient, but they have bureaus—and these gentlemen are simply doing as we do in other things, imitating European governments—and in the various ends of science they make what are termed cadastral maps, which are made for military purposes, and they go into detail with so much accuracy that they have located everything, so that a military officer in possession of one of those maps if he were to invade this country and make a landing in the neighborhood of New York, Staten Island, or Boston, or wherever this work has been followed, would know every obstruction in the progress of a military force, he would know the exact location of every house, of every prominent building, etc., so that in proceeding with military operations he would know exactly how to move round.

Mr. MONEY. Let me ask you a question. Does the Geological Survey in making topographical survey do exactly that work?

Mr. ENLOE. Not with that degree of accuracy; it makes a general outline but it does not go into detail. You never saw a map of the Geological Survey which attempted to locate houses and streets, and street railway lines, ditches, fences, and trees, and all that sort of thing, but that is exactly what this geodetic work is when it is completed.

Mr. MONEY. A few years ago——

Mr. ENLOE. That is what it is to be when it is completed. If they go on with this triangulation that they have here, that is, of course, the basis for this cadastral map work.

Mr. MONEY. A few years ago the Geological Survey were making exactly that kind of a map; they were making what was called a topographical map for the use of the Army. They had every creek, every ditch, every hill of any sort of eminence, or house, or road, or cross-road, or by-road, or anything of the sort.

Mr. ENLOE. And if you give them the money they will now. That, of course, is just as Congress wants it.

Mr. MONEY. I will tell you how I happen to know. My son is a boy, 18 years of age and he had charge of one of the parties, being a draftsman, to make the survey and to make a drawing of everything of that sort.

Mr. GLASSCOCK. Here is one of the maps which shows all that now.

Mr. MONEY. I say the Geological Survey does that.

Mr. GLASSCOCK. Except that they do not do it on such an expensive scale. According to the testimony here their maps cost from $1.50 to $10 per square mile, and while this work is not map work yet it costs $100 per square mile.

Mr. RANDALL. How is that difference in cost explained?

Mr. GLASSCOCK. Why they say that is owing to the accuracy of the geodetic work. They profess that it is not for map making.

The CHAIRMAN. Let us try to get at an understanding of it, if we can. If I understand you correctly you assert that this Coast and Geodetic Survey is doing the same work as the Geological Survey has done or is doing, claiming that they are doing it more accurately and more thoroughly. Is that it?

Mr. GLASSCOCK. No, I say this. That the work the Coast and Geodetic Survey is doing is not geological survey work at all, but the Geological Survey does do geodetic work, and the work that the Geodetic Survey does (which is this triangulation all over the country) is costing $100 per square mile.

The CHAIRMAN. Does it not go over the same ground as the Geological Survey?

Mr. GLASSCOCK. The Geological Survey goes over some of the ground that the Coast and Geodetic Survey does, sometimes.

The CHAIRMAN. The Geodetic Survey is doing work in the interior of the country?

Mr. GLASSCOCK. Yes, sir.

The CHAIRMAN. Is not the Geological Survey doing the same?

Mr. GLASSCOCK. Yes, sir; but——

The CHAIRMAN. The only difference is that the Coast and Geodetic Survey goes over the ground more in detail than the Geological Survey; is that it?

Mr. GLASSCOCK. Yes; but the Coast and Geodetic Survey is doing this triangulation for some purpose, we do not know what, but the Geological Survey, of course, are doing their work for the purpose of making maps. That is the point you all must understand, that this Coast and Geodetic Survey is of no use for map making. That is the testimony piled up——

The CHAIRMAN. And the Geological Survey is?

Mr. GLASSCOCK. And the Geological Survey is for map-making, and as the Commission says and everybody else says, we do not know what this geodetic work is for except to give points for State surveys, if they choose to ask for them. That is one of the reasons they give for the work, but these authorities that I have quoted here say that they can

uot understand it. Now, that is the point that you all must understand, that they can not understand, and that I can not make you
understand for what purpose it is.

The CHAIRMAN. Does the Coast and Geodetic Survey itself understand?

Mr. GLASSCOCK. Well, I do not know. Mr. Colonna says it is of no
use for map-making, but of great use for connecting the sheets. They
are expending $100 per square mile for work that is of no use except
for connecting the sheets.

The CHAIRMAN. Connecting sheets of what?

Mr. GLASSCOCK. I do not know what kind of sheets, whether they
are sheets you sleep on or whether——

Mr. MONEY. If you will refer back you will find that he says taken
separately they may be of little utility, but when taken together in a
great map they will be of great utility.

Mr. GLASSCOCK. That is the astounding question.

Mr. MONEY. On this line of argument it would be like asking these
gentlemen for an excuse for their existence in the Navy Department or
anywhere else.

Mr. GLASSCOCK. It is all defined here in these few words which are
underscored here. Now, gentlemen, are there any further questions
which you desire to ask at this point?

Mr. MONEY. I want to say one word, professor.

Mr. GLASSCOCK. Did you call me "professor"? I am not a professor.

Mr. MONEY. You have offered no reason to us to support the bill for
the transfer; you have simply presented reasons for abolishing the
whole thing.

Mr. GLASSCOCK. I will get to all that, but I have not got to it yet.
I am new in my argument. It is geodetic work that I have been talking about.

Mr. MCALEER. The abolition of it?

Mr. GLASSCOCK. Well, I should think the abolition of it is what
ought to be. So much for the geodetic work until a little later on. Mr.
Colonna testified——. I beg to introduce again Mr. Colonna, who is
to-day assistant in charge of the office of the Coast and Geodetic Survey, the second in command there. Mr. Colonna in 1885, gentlemen,
you must recollect, was posing before this commission as a kind of a
reformer. It is true that he had just been raised from an $1,800 position
to a $3,600 position, and the Coast and Geodetic Survey was at that time
having a good deal of trouble at the Treasury Department, so much so
that its very existence was threatened, and Mr. Colonna was a little
more liberal in his testimony, perhaps because he wanted to concede
something; he wanted to save the Coast Survey, and he wanted to do
the best he could to try and save it, and consequently he was liberal
in giving his testimony. Now, we will see what he had to say upon
that point. It turned out that the Coast Survey was saved, and that
Mr. Colonna, to a very great extent, ran it for the next four years after
that. It was true that Mr. Thorne was Superintendent, but he was a
civilian, and not a scientific man as they call them over there, and Mr.
Colonna, having been long in the service, knew all about it and virtually
ran the Coast and Geodetic Survey. Now, let us see who does the
hydrographic work of the Coast Survey. Mr. Colonna testified (p. 605,
vol. 4) as follows:

Q. I understood you to say a moment ago that the bone of contention was the
Hydrographic Office?—A. The hydrographic work of Coast Survey is what the Navy
has been striving after for a long time. They virtually do all the work as it is.

The CHAIRMAN. Colonna says this?

Mr. GLASSCOCK. Says this in 1885, that they virtually do all the work as it is.

The CHAIRMAN. That does not agree with Prof. Woodward's statement?

Mr. GLASSCOCK. No, sir. They bound him up a little tighter, too.

Q. Are your opportunities for observation sufficient to tell us whether or not that work is being well performed? What is your opinion about that?—A. Yes, sir; I think the work is well performed in the main, in some instances with distinguished ability; for instance, the steamer *Blake's* past season's work, directed by Lieut. Pillsbury, is something that all may be proud of.

Commander John R. Bartlett, chief of the Hydrographic Office of the Navy, testifies (p. 73, vol. 4.):

That substantially all of the Coast Survey work is done by naval officers, and substantially all the civilian assistants of the Coast Survey are engaged on geodetic work.

"Objection is made to naval officers doing this work," says Mr. Woodward, "because they remain only three years," and this is answered on p. 76, vol. 4, by Commander Bartlett:

With regard to the employment of the naval officers at the Coast Survey, objection has been made to the fact that they are allowed to remain there only three years at a time. The Coast Survey goes on, and their surveys go on even if this rotation does exist, and there is a constant demand on the Navy Department for officers of this service——

The CHAIRMAN. Whose testimony is that, Colonna?

Mr. GLASSCOCK. No, Commander Bartlett.

One point to be considered in this matter is the fact that we now have a Naval School at Annapolis which has been conceded by graduates of West Point, by members of the National Academy, and by prominent civilians who have examined it, to be one of the best scientific schools in this or any other country. The young officers of the Navy are there taught thoroughly all the branches that relate to surveying, and it is only the young men that are wanted in the Coast Survey. The hydrographic work of the Coast Survey is under the immediate direction of, and is done entirely by, naval officers. There are no civil assistants of the Coast Survey doing this work.

On p. 65, vol. 4, will be found the following testimony, submitted by Secretary Chandler:

In the annual report of the Navy Department for 1882 (twelve years ago), the Secretary of the Navy makes the following statement: For the past fifty years the Coast Survey has required and received the support and assistance of the Navy. Thirty naval officers a year, on an average, have been engaged in the work, and during the last ten years the number has steadily increased. The annual report of 1883 says: The Coast Survey, originally established for the purpose of making hydrographic charts, has of late years extended its functions in a totally different direction, that of geodetic surveys in the interior. In making these extensions, it has gradually abandoned the water surveys of the Navy, until now the actual work in this field is done almost exclusively by naval officers, withdrawn for the purpose, from the direction and control of their own department.

- Mr. GEISSENHAINER. What is the date of that?

Mr. GLASSCOCK. This is the report of the Secretary of the Navy of 1883.

Mr. GEISSENHAINER. This is 1894; have the conditions, as far as you know, changed at all?

Mr. GLASSCOCK. They have changed to this extent, that this work ought to be this much more concluded.

Mr. GEISSENHAINER. I mean in regard to the number of naval officers employed?

Mr. GLASSCOCK. There are more naval officers employed now than then, according to the last report I have, which is of 1889; then there were 312 seamen employed as against 250.

Mr. GEISSENHAINER. In that service?

Mr. GLASSCOCK. In this service now. The average number of officers for the year ending was 56, I think. This was the year 1889, two or three years later than that, so you see the naval force has increased. It was only 250 seamen and 30 odd officers, and now it has 56 officers and 312 seamen.

The CHAIRMAN. Before you go on with that I want to give you a list of officers of last year so as to give it exactly. This is according to the report to the Fifty-second Congress.

The CLERK. The report of the Coast and Geodetic Survey to the Fifty-second Congress shows, officers and men of the Navy attached with annual pay from appropriations for the Navy received by them, to be 39 officers and 250 enlisted men.

Mr. GLASSCOCK. This I see is House Report 847, first session Fifty-second Congress.

The CLERK. Yes, sir.

Mr. GLASSCOCK. I did not have this later report; consequently I gave it for 1889.

By an extraordinary anomaly in legislation the U. S. Hydrographic Office, an indispensable branch of the Navy Department, is allowed to survey and make charts of every coast in the world but that of the United States, while the best naval surveyors are claimed by another department to perform this work under its supervision. Sixty-seven naval officers are now directed in this manner from the direction of the Navy, and 280 seamen out of the 7,500 allowed the Navy, are now on board Coast Survey vessels.

Mr. MONEY. In other words, instead of transferring that Bureau to the Navy, they have transferred the Navy to that Bureau?

Mr. GLASSCOCK. That this is it exactly, so far as the hydrographic work is concerned, and it is all done under the supervision of the Coast and Geodetic Survey, and it is testified to all the way through that not a civilian assistant of the Coast and Geodetic Survey does any of this hydrographic work. That is what Secretary Chandler says, and I ask you all to read his whole report. You will find it here in this testimony—but I will quote a little further:

For such an arrangement there might be some show of reason if the work upon which the officers are engaged were especially connected with the Department under which they are placed, and remote from the subjects of which their own Department has cognizance.

Mr. GEISSENHAINER. The Treasurer does not know anything about it?

Mr. GLASSCOCK. The Treasurer does not pretend to direct the work. He says in a letter, which I will quote you, that this work ought to be under the Navy Department. He can not know anything about it, and he has nobody to advise him about it, but the Navy Department has; but, in view of the fact that no part of this work has the faintest traceable connection with the general purpose of the Treasury, that its effectual performance is of vital importance to the Navy, and that an office exists to-day in the Navy Department where similar work is necessarily carried on, it is inconceivable why so inconvenient, artificial, and indefensible an arrangement should be perpetuated.

For further and latter testimony on this point I beg to refer to letters from the present Secretaries of the Navy and Treasury—Messrs. Herbert and Carlisle—under date of March 13 and 14, 1894, to Hon. B. A. Enloe, and also an extract from President Cleveland's message, first session Forty-ninth Congress, all to be found on page 3664 of the Congressional Record.

The Coast Survey is an independent bureau, because it is under the Secretary of the Treasury, who officially knows nothing about hydrography or geodesy.

What does the Secretary of the Treasury officially know about hydrography or geodesy?

Mr. GEISSENHAINER. What does he officially know about the Life-Saving Service?

Mr. GLASSCOCK. That is a question I am not considering, and I do not think he knows much about it.

Mr. ENLOE. He does not need to have much scientific knowledge about it.

Mr. GLASSCOCK. Nor is he supposed to have in his Department any-one who can officially advise him on these subjects, consequently this Bureau runs itself, and this is the one great reason why the efforts of Congressmen, Secretaries of the Navy, the Treasury, and the President himself have so utterly failed to put it under the Navy Department, and this "independence" has been the cause of all the scandal, irregularities, and adverse criticism that have originated there.

Now let us look into this independent record and see what it has been and is to-day.

In the Democratic campaign book of 1886 you will find on page 143 that—

evidences of irregularity and possibilities of fraud in this institution (Coast and Geodetic Survey) were so strong as to warrant an official investigation, which was ordered by the President, and began on the 23d of July, 1885, before Auditor Chenoweth. The development of fraud and corruption made by this investigation are astounding, the more so from the fact that the Coast Survey is a Bureau of the Treasury Department and under immediate direction of Treasury officials. The "personnel" of the institution was known as the "silk-stocking" gentry. The Superintendent held a chair in the National Academy of Sciences, and the scientific satellites of the Bureau included among them products of many of our celebrated institutions of learning.

Congress has made liberal appropriations for this Bureau, amounting to about $1,000,000 annually. An investigation developed that about $100,000 of this sum was yearly diverted from a legitimate purpose by theft and careless administration. In fact, the "scientific results" of the Coast Survey appear to have reached the acme of perfection in robbery and jobbery. It was developed that the chief of the Bureau was the prime mover in consummating frauds, and had actually grown rich at public expense, as well as several of the smaller "fry" who basked in the sunshine of his favors.

Mr. MONEY. Who was he?

Mr. GLASSCOCK. Mr. Hilgard. Now, this is a fact, for I was property clerk there myself after this.

Hundreds of thousands of dollars worth of Government property belonging to this Bureau was found to be scattered broadcast over the land with no intelligible idea of its whereabouts. Scientific instruments ordered and paid for by the Survey were never delivered, and it was a common thing to see expensive chronometers, purchased with moneys appropriated for the Survey, sported in the pockets of the Superintendent's office favorites; the pay rolls were burdened with a list of "pensioners" who never rendered a day's service to the Government.

Mr. MONEY. Where is that from?

Mr. GLASSCOCK. From the Democratic campaign book of 1886.

The CHAIRMAN. You say that comes from the Democratic campaign book?

Mr. GLASSCOCK. Of 1886; yes, sir.

The CHAIRMAN. Does it purport to be information given from that report of Auditor Chenoweth?

Mr. MONEY. It must have an official base.

The CHAIRMAN. And that is what I want to know, if it has an official base.

Mr. GLASSCOCK. Yes, sir; that testimony was taken before Auditor Chenoweth, and that testimony—I have never seen a line of it, although I have tried hard and hard——

The CHAIRMAN. I wish to suggest to the stenographer that he leave that out for the reason I have all the papers of that Chenoweth matter now, and hereafter the committee will examine it.

Mr. GLASSCOCK. The testimony will show it.

The man who was found with a chronometer in his pocket is still in the Coast Survey as chief of the miscellaneous division, at a salary of $2,200 per annum, and has charge of the sale of all charts, and purchase of supplies for the office; so that if he is still inclined to appropriate Government property to his own private use his opportunities are all that he could ask for.

Benjamin A. Colonna, second in authority at the Coast Survey to-day, posed before the joint commission as a great reformer, when he testified (p. 608, vol. 4) as follows:

The nature of the services are such that necessarily a very large part of the amount appropriated is expended for pay of employés, and if we compare the number of men in the normal force and their aggregate pay with the amount to be expended in the execution of the work, this is very evident. I have frequently con n sidered the matter, and I know that if the normal force was scaled one-third in numbers, and the office force one-tenth, and the aggregate of the appropriations kept at the present figures, under a new distribution, more work could be done.

This statement was duly sworn to, and I have no cause to alter my opinion. But it might be modified perhaps by substituting "costs" for "numbers" in the scaling of the field and office force.

Q. That is, you think it can bear a reduction of 30 per cent or more, and not impair its efficiency?—A. I think so.

This was in 1885 that he proposed this reduction of 30 per cent in the "costs" of these employés, and on the 17th of October, 1887, we find in his annual report, p. 114, that he recommends that E. Hergesheimer (then getting a salary of $2,400 per annum) should receive at least $3,000; that the services of H. G. Ogden, chief of engraving division (then getting $2,000), are worth $3,000; and his chief clerk deserves better compensation than he receives, and that Mr. Braid's pay (then getting $1,800) be placed at $3,000.

Then again it will be found by referring to Ex. Doc. No. 180, first session, Fifty-second Congress, p. 2, that in 1890 the pay of just one-half of the normal force was increased from $100 to $500 each per annum, on the recommendation of B. A. Colonna, and since he testified before the joint commission in 1885 that the cost of this normal force ought to be decreased 30 per cent, nearly every member of it have had their pay increased from 10 to 20 per cent on his recommendation.

Mr. GEISSENHAINER. In the meantime had anything occurred in the service to make them more valuable?

Mr. GLASSCOCK. On the contrary, the work was nearing completion and it ought to have been scaled more. If it ought to have been scaled 30 per cent in 1885, in 1887 it ought——

Mr. GEISSENHAINER. Was there any extra work?

Mr. GLASSCOCK. There was no extra work that I know of.

Mr. MONEY. Was there any decrease in numbers?

Mr. GLASSCOCK. Yes, sir; there was in numbers, but not in pay.

The CHAIRMAN. You say there was a decrease in the number?

Mr. GLASSCOCK. Yes, sir; but whenever they die or resign, they divide-that pay up; and that too in the face of the fact that the field work is completed, and the normal or field force of the Coast Survey is to-day virtually out of a job.

Congress has been very patient, but it has occasionally inquired when the survey will be completed.

In 1857 Superintendent Bache said that it would be completed within fifteen years.

Now you heard something on that the other day from Prof. Woodward when he said it would never be completed. Now, I propose to give you some other authorities.

Mr. MONEY. I do not think he alluded to the geodetic part of it.

Mr. GLASSCOCK. I think that is the very part he did allude to.

Mr. MONEY. He said as long as the currents and tide operated to change the configuration of the coast it would be necessary.

Mr. GLASSCOCK. The testimony of Commander Bartlett is that when this work on the coast is done it is done for all time. You will find that in his testimony. Of course rivers and such things as those some-times change owing to floods.

Mr. ENLOE. These surveys of changes after the survey is once made are made by naval officers.

Mr. MONEY. I am not talking about who will do it. The fact is there is a necessity of making charts. Here is the harbor of Greytown which has been filled up by bars in the last twenty years.

Prof. Hillgard testified before the joint commission (p. 58, vol. 4, December 5, 1884) that it would take about five years yet to finish the work on the Atlantic coast; and, on page 140, that the work on the Pacific is about three-fifths done, and that it will require about nine years at the present rate of appropriation. Colonna says, 1885, in his testimony, twelve years.

All this time has expired except Colonna's, and yet we find the Super-intendent of the Coast Survey coming to Congress and asking, and getting, within a small fraction of the amount of appropriation that he received ten years ago.

Commander Bartlett, on page 76, testified before the commission in 1884 as follows on this point:

Now the primary triangulation and the secondary triangulation has been com-pleted on the Atlantic and Gulf coast, except about one-tenth. That one-tenth is on the Florida coast and on the coast of Texas, and the Coast Survey is not attempting to finish it. They are holding on to that one-tenth so as to have the work of the Coast Survey continued.

"Never to be finished," says Prof. Woodward.

Does this not confirm what Commander Bartlett says about the one-tenth? Are the dangers of an unsurveyed coast to remain forever unfinished in order to perpetuate this Bureau?

How these Coast Survey officials have bamboozled the Committees of Appropriations of both Houses of Congress, and Congress itself, by their scientific technicalities can easily be attested by referring to the appropriation bills. Observe the deception they have practiced about this.

Senator Allison signed the majority report of the joint commission in 1885 "against transferring." Here is what he said in 1887:

Mr. ALLISON. I believe that this Coast Survey, composed, as it is, of scientific gen-tlemen who have given their lives, many of them, to this service, has men capable of carrying on the operations of the Survey, and it is perfectly well known to those who have investigated the subject that if we will give them proper appropriations they will be able to carry on the field work substantially as they have been carried on for three or four years, and the work will be completed, with the exception of Alaska, within from six to seven years, certainly not exceeding nine years.

Is it reasonable to suppose that he would be willing to perpetuate this Bureau for all time?

In consequence of having nothing to do this normal or field force is maintained to a great extent in an inactive condition, and Superintendent Thorn, on page 284, Book of Estimates, 1886-'87, speaks of the winter months spent at home by these employés as a " period of comparative idleness."

Mr. GEISSENHAINER. Can they work during the winter time; is there not a great deal of ice, snow, and inclement weather?

Mr. GLASSCOCK. Not in the Southern countries.

Mr. GEISSENHAINER. They can go to other portions of the country naturally?

Mr. GLASSCOCK. Oh, yes; but they can not work up North.

Mr. MONEY. Field work can be done in Mississippi, Texas, and Florida, and they do a great deal of it.

Mr. ENLOE. I do not think they do much work except in the spring and summer.

The CHAIRMAN. I know that some years ago they were at work in Florida during the winter.

Mr. GLASSCOCK. The pay, however, never gets inactive, and one man drew a salary of $3,000 per year for over five years and was not at the office but once during that time, nor did any work for it, but he did render valuable service by appearing before the joint commission in favor of maintaining the Coast Survey intact.

Mr. GEISSENHAINER. Who was that?

Mr. GLASSCOCK. Mr. Pierce, of New York.

The appropriations are made for this force as the field force, and they are supposed to do field work, but out of 28 assistants whose salaries range from $2,000 to $4,000 each, only about 10 are engaged in the field, and the remainder are utillized in the office as chiefs of divisions, and those that can not be supplied with a chief's place, are required to report from day to day with virtually no duty to perform, except to draw their salaries.

Prior to 1878 there was but one assistant employed in the office as chief, and chiefs were made by promotion for merit from those skilled workmen employed in the office. Then, efficiency was stimulated and developed by competition; now, work performed by skilled labor is presided over and passed upon by green surveyors taken from the field, who know absolutely nothing about that kind of work.

One of the first acts of Mr. Mendenhall in 1890, after he was appointed Superintendent, as will be disclosed by referring to this Ex. Doc. 180, first session Fifty-second Congress, and House Report No. 2017, Fifty-first Congress, first session, page 25 (both of which he wrote himself), was to convene a board composed chiefly of B. A. Colonna and these chiefs. This board revised the estimates for the first session Fifty-first Congress, and increased their own pay of all (except two), from $100 to $400 each, and further manipulated the bill by decreasing the pay of some of the workingmen and clerks under them from $100 to $565 each, so as to make it conform with the bill of the previous Congress.

All these irregularities, and many others (too numerous to mention), arise from this independent position of this Bureau, and are the causes that produce scandal. Under the Secretary of the Navy all this could be reformed, and this office force, composed, as it is, of intelligent skilled laborers, and experienced clerks, would become a valuable adjunct to the Navy Department to mature the data brought in by naval officers, and save an annual expense to the Government of $250,000.

Why is it that the Coast Survey officials are so solicitous about this change from one Department of the Government to another Department equally interested in doing what is best for the good of the whole country? Why is it that they resist so strenuously every effort of the Secretary of the Treasury, who himself declares that it should be transferred to the Navy Department? It is because they know they can befog and overwhelm him with scientific technicalities, and because they know they can not deceive the Secretary of the Navy with scientific technicalities, as he is protected by advisers who can fathom the sea, and can also measure the value of scientific technicalities, and compute what they are worth in dollars and cents to the country.

The Coast Survey officials have endeavored to create the impression all over the country that this change is to destroy the Coast Survey. You heard Prof. Woodward say that colleges and scientific organizations have been implored to forward petitions (that owe their origin to the Coast Survey) to members of Congress, protesting against this change because it will work destruction to that Bureau. But such is not the case.

Mr. B. A. Colonna, if I may be permitted to refer to his testimony again, testifies on page 635, vol. 4, as follows:

Q. (By Mr. HALE.) I want to ask you one or two questions, Mr. Colonna. You have evidently given a great deal of attention to the practical questions arising from the work of these different surveys. Now, I would like for you to state whether you believe that if these different surveys, viz (the Coast and Geodetic, so far as its land work goes, and the Geological Survey), were put under a common head under the same department of the Government there would be any difficulty in the way of that one governing head so arranging the work that there would be not only no clashing of interests, but no duplication of work, and that out of it we would, in the speediest and most economical way, get complete surveys of the country?—A. That I believe, sir. If the whole thing were subordinated to one head, no matter what that head might be, the directors left at the head of each particular class of work to operate under that chief head, call him a Secretary, or a Commissioner, or whatever you please, we would then get the best results for our outlay in money,

Q. Should you think such an arrangement as I have indicated would be of great value in this service?—A. It would be of great economy.

Q. Well, of great value; you think they would get along much better than now, do you?—A. Yes, sir; better than now, and the results would be as valuable as they are now. Of course the value of the work would depend on the way it was done.

They call themselves a scientific bureau, but the country has never been startled by the announcement of any scientific result obtained by the Bureau, certainly not in the last twenty-five years. If there is any bureau under the Government that can be termed a scientific bureau it is the Geological Survey.

How, then, can the scientific work in the Coast Survey be destroyed by uniting the two, especially when it is shown conclusively that geodetic work is done in the Geological Survey on a more useful scale than in the Coast Survey, and is shown and illustrated by useful maps that are eagerly sought after by the public, while it is admitted by the testimony of Mr. Colonna "that the geodetic work of the Coast Survey is of no use for map-making?"

The only perceptible result of this geodetic work appears in the annual reports of the Coast Survey in the shape of what they term sketches, and is about as much use to and as much sought after by the public as the water of the Potomac would be if Congress were to order it all bottled immediately after a flood for the benefit of the poor.

The Secretary of the Treasury, the Secretary of the Navy, and the President of the United States are all on record, on page 3664 of the Congressional Record, as saying in effect that the transfer would secure a service fully as efficient in all respects as that now existing, and result in a large saving of money to the Government.

Now, here is one other point to which I wish to call your attention, which was raised by Mr. Woodward, and that is in regard to the bureau of weights and measures. I refer you to page 370 of volume 4, of Senate Miscellaneous Documents. Now, sirs, before that investigation they had this gentleman, Mr. Pierce, who drew so much unearned salary, and he was at the head of this bureau of weights and measures, and this is what he says about the weights and measures.

By Mr. LYMAN:

Q. What position do you hold under the Government?—A. I am assistant in the Coast Survey, and have charge of the office of weights and measures, under the Coast Survey. I have charge also of the gravimetric survey.

Q. Will you, if you please, give the commission a short sketch in your own language of your work as the person in charge of the office of weights and measures?— A. The office of weights and measures at present is a very slight affair, I am sorry to say. It only exists in law, because Congress many years ago directed the Secretary of the Treasury to supply the different States and Territories, etc., with standard weights and measures, and that provision was afterwards extended to the agricultural schools, so for that purpose it has been necessary to have standards and balances made and the States and schools have been supplied with these articles. We have our office there to keep up the supply of these various things, and we take occasion to verify any standard that is referred to us.

Now, I understand something was said the other day about verifying the polariscopes. I do not know, but I do not suppose that that work is very immense?

Mr. MONEY. That has no reference to weights and measures?

Mr. GLASSCOCK. I suppose it might, but, gentlemen, that bureau can stay right where it is. It is an insignificant affair, anyway.

The CHAIRMAN. Is that bureau under the control of the Coast and Geodetic Survey?

Mr. GLASSCOCK. It is under the control of the Coast and Geodetic Survey. Now, there is another thing ——

Mr. ENLOE. Before you pass away from that—in discussing this matter with the Secretary of the Treasury, before I offered the amendment in the House and before the introduction of this bill, the Secretary of the Treasury suggested that in making a division of the work that was proposed by this bill that the bureau of weights and measures could very properly remain in the Treasury Department and be organized as a separate bureau. That is the reason why this bill does not contain any provision for the disposal of it, and it will not be necessary, in order to keep up that bureau, to retain possession of these buildings over there, because it has been carried to the Treasury Department and organized there as a bureau of the Treasury Department.

The CHAIRMAN. This bill does not propose to transfer it?

Mr. ENLOE. It leaves it with the Treasury Department to be organized as a separate division by the Secretary of the Treasury.

Mr. GLASSCOCK. It only employs two or three men. Of course one of the assistants of the Coast and Geodetic Survey is chief of that bureau, and it has a verifier, a laborer, and a mechanician. That is all it amounts to, and occasionally they have some verifying to do. There is no amount of State work to do unless it is for some of these new States, as all of the old States have had this work done. They have been supplied with standard measures. New Jersey was supplied twice; that was destroyed by fire.

Now, gentlemen, in conclusion, I would like to read, if you have the time to hear me, it will take five minutes, the five or six reasons given here in this minority report why this bureau should be transferred.

First. The prime purpose of such a survey is to make maps to be used by the mariner. Sailors best know what is needed to be sketched upon such a map; how frequently the soundings should be made, and how noted; how much topography is necessary; what objects on the shore should be sketched, and what should be omitted. They also understand better than civilians upon what projection a map should be made.

Second. By doing such work upon their own coasts, naval officers familiarize themselves in time of peace with every bay, harbor, inlet, and possible landing place of the shores they are to defend in time of war.

Third. The work falls naturally within the scope of their profession. By exercising their faculties in useful activities they will keep themselves bright.

Fourth. Navy officials who feel reasonably secure in their positions, and whose official life does not depend upon favor to be acquired by assuming unauthorized functions, will not be so easily allured to depart from the work they are set to do as civilians often are by the prospect of gaining éclat among scientists or favor among politicians with the hope of thus prolonging their official existence.

Fifth. However it might have been formerly, the personnel of the Navy since the operation of our excellent Naval Academy has had full effect is in capacity and education fully qualified to conduct this Survey. The claim that young men educated at Annapolis are not competent to do geodetic work is not worthy of notice, when coming from an official who is shown frequently to have put in charge of triangulation parties professors who are utterly without experience in the field.

It is insisted by one of the officials of the Coast and Geodetic Survey that one of the purposes of employing college professors here and there to do triangulation is to enable them better to instruct the youth of the land. If this be true it is another glaring instance of departure from the purposes of the law. But the undersigned can see in this application of public moneys only an intent on the part of the Coast and Geodetic Survey thus to fortify itself against any attempt Congress may make to correct abuses or retrench expenditures.

Sixth. As naval officers are already in the pay of the Government, it would be more economical to utilize their services than to pay civilian employés for doing the work of this Survey.

Gentlemen, I think that is about all I have to say, unless you have some further questions to ask.

Mr. GEISSENHAINER. Have you any estimate of what the increase of force in the Navy will be under this transfer?

Mr. GLASSCOCK. What the increased force would be under the Navy?

Mr. GEISSENHAINER. Yes; what would it necessarily be?

Mr. GLASSCOCK. There would be no increased force under the Navy; the same naval officers who are doing it to-day will continue to do it.

Mr. ENLOE. I understand there will be a reduction of force instead of an increase.

The CHAIRMAN. If the committee does not desire to hear Mr. Enloe to-day, we will adjourn and hear him on Tuesday next.

Thereupon the committee adjourned.

COMMITTEE ON NAVAL AFFAIRS,
Tuesday, May 8, 1894.
The Committee on Naval Affairs this day met, Hon. Amos J. Cummings in the chair.
The CHAIRMAN. We are here to-day to hear Prof. Mendenhall in regard to the bill proposing to transfer the Coast and Geodetic Survey to the Navy Department and to the Geological Survey. Mr. Mendenhall, we will hear you now.

STATEMENT OF PROF. T. C. MENDENHALL, SUPERINTENDENT OF THE COAST AND GEODETIC SURVEY.

Prof. Mendenhall then addressed the committee; he said:
Mr. Chairman and gentlemen of the committee: The Coast and Geodetic Survey, the disruption and transfer of which is proposed by this bill, is not strictly, and in fact not approximately, even a scientific bureau in the real sense of the word. It is rather a bureau of applied sciences. That is to say, it is a bureau in which the practical results are reached by and through the application of the best results of modern science. Of course it happens in the execution of practical work of the character which is undertaken by this Bureau that problems are met with which have not hitherto been solved, in which case it becomes the duty of the Bureau to solve those problems, and to that extent the Coast and Geodetic Survey has in its history extended the domain of our knowledge considerably along the line of work in which it has been engaged. But I wish to emphasize the fact that it is a bureau of applied sciences, and that it is not fair or just to speak of it as a purely scientific bureau; that is, a bureau engaged in pure scientific researches, as the scientific researches in which it is engaged are only incidential to its practical work. However, the nature of its work is such that it is not at all surprising that there are not a very large number of people in the country who understand the operations of the Survey.
Although the results are quite clear and have been, as everybody knows, I think, very valuable and very useful, yet the methods and means by which those results have been reached are things that have come less prominently before the public, and, in fact, there are few persons outside of perhaps a comparatively limited circle who have had an opportunity, or by actual contact with this work have had opportunity, of knowing and understanding the methods and means by which these results are reached. This Bureau, which has been complimented, as I presume you all know, as being the most perfect illustration of applied sciences of any Government bureau in the world, and I think justly so, therefore has labored under the disadvantage always that it has not been fully understood; it has not been understood as to the methods and means which are actually necessary in the production of its results.
I, therefore, Mr. Chairman, would ask the kindly indulgence of the committee in a presentation as brief as I can give it, but still I am bound in justice to do this thoroughly, of the methods which are employed by the Coast and Geodetic Survey in the production of these results, and particularly of the relations that the several parts of this work sustain to each other. I may not be able to complete that in a single hour, but in consideration of the great importance of this work

of a bureau which has existed to the honor and credit of the United States for sixty or more years I trust the committee will not be unwilling to allow me opportunity to present this side of the case.

Before beginning an explanation of these methods I wish to remind you of a few points historically, and I will present a very brief sketch of the history of this Bureau, simply saying that it was organized first in the year 1807 and had its origin in the intelligence and foresight of President Jefferson, combined with the wisdom of Albert Gallatin.

Gallatin had come to this country after graduating at some of the best institutions of learning in Europe, and was one of the first to recognize the importance of having a survey made of the coast of the United States, and also of the necessity of having that survey carried out on a systematic plan. At his request, therefore, the first superintendent of the Coast Survey was brought to this country, one Ferdinand Hassler, also a Swiss, being, I think, a fellow-student or classmate of Gallatin, at least he was his intimate friend, and the work of making this survey and the plan and organizing and executing it was put in his hands by President Jefferson in execution of a law passed in 1807. This work proceeded, unfortunately, very slowly during the first ten or twelve years, owing to two or three causes which everybody will at once recognize.

In the first pla e, very shortly after the passage of the bill war broke out between the United States and Great Britain, and at the time it so happened that the superintendent, Mr. Hassler, was in London, where he had been sent by President Jefferson for the purchase of instruments and appliances for the execution of this survey, and he was quarantined, so to speak, in that country and for several years did not return to this country. The result was therefore an interruption in the early operations of the Coast Survey, so that for one reason or another it was transferred to the Navy Department in the year 1818 by act of Congress and this work was taken out of the hands of Mr. Hassler, and the plan of Mr. Hassler, Gallatin, and President Jefferson in organizing the work of the survey of the United States was transferred to the Navy Department in 1818. It remained in the hands of the Navy from that time until ten or twelve years later, during which time it was, as a very high authority has stated, fitfully and irregularly carried on. In 1828 the Secretary of the Navy, in reply to a communication from the then Committee on Naval Affairs, specially urged the transfer of this Bureau to the Treasury Department, and at that time made the following remarks, which I will read. The Secretary of the Navy, then the Hon. Samuel L. Southard, said in regard to this survey that they—

do not furnish a satisfactory survey of the coast for the following reasons: (1) They exhibit detached parts unconnected with each other. (2) They are generally confined to the shores and do not extend sufficiently far into the ocean. (3) Were many of them made by incompetent men with incompetent means. (4) They were governed by no certain and fixed principles or guides in ascertaining the latitudes and longitudes of the principal points and positions. (5) They do embrace the whole coast. For these and other reasons they are unsafe, and in many instances useless and pernicious.

Secretary Southard furthermore in his report—what I have just read is in reply to a communication from the Committee on Naval Affairs— but in his report for 1828 he further remarks:

They do not afford materials for an accurate chart of the harbors and approaches to them, and they assist but little towards a perfect knowledge of our coast, which can only be acquired by that scientific survey of the whole, the importance of which I have ventured to urge and would again respectfully suggest.

And he added that—

These surveys with others, which from time to time have been made under the direction of the Department, have to a certain extent been useful, but they have also been very expensive in proportion to their usefulness.

I invite the attention of the committee to this emphasis of the necessity of carrying on what you might call a systematic survey of the coast of the United States as distinguished from a survey of detached portions, which proved to be very objectionable.

However, a retransfer to the Treasury took place in the year 1832 in response to this action of the Secretary of the Navy. That is to say, during a period of about fourteen years at that time the Survey was under the direction of the Navy Department. However, it only remained in the Treasury Department about two years, when it was again recommended by the Secretary of the Treasury to be retransferred to the Navy. This was by Mr. Taney, Secretary of the Treasury under President Jackson, afterward Chief Justice Taney. I am unable to find any reasons given for this transfer, but the transfer was recommended, and in response to that recommendation President Jackson transferred the Bureau back again to the Navy Department. It had scarcely reached the Navy Department again before Mr. Woodbury, who was Secretary of the Navy when it was transferred to the Navy Department, became Secretary of the Treasury. Mr. Taney, as you all know, on account of his action in connection with the United States Bank dropped out of the secretaryship of the Treasury, and Mr. Woodbury, the Secretary of the Navy, became Secretary of the Treasury, and as he had had a year or two of experience in connection with the management of this Bureau in the Navy Department, he made a recommendation that this be retransferred to the Treasury Department, so that it was brought back to the Treasury Department, and finally, in the year 1836. Thus you will see it had two periods—one very long one, and one very short one—of administration under the Navy Department, and in both cases that it came back it came back on a recommendation of the Secretary of the Navy and the Secretary of the Treasury, and——

Mr. MONEY. Would it interrupt you if I ask a question right there; do I understand from what you say that it was moved by Executive order?

Prof. MENDENHALL. It was moved by Executive order because under the first law providing for the Coast Survey it directed that the President should be instructed to make this survey.

Mr. MONEY. Then the transfers were made under Executive orders?

Prof. MENDENHALL. As I understand it, it was by Executive order, because the President was directed by the law to make this survey, and it was specifically provided it should be under his direction.

Mr. RANDALL. The last change was made in 1836 and it has remained where it is since then?

Prof. MENDENHALL. It has remained where it is since that time.

The CHAIRMAN. Do I understand it was transferred the first time by act of Congress?

Prof. MENDENHALL. No, sir; I think not—yes, it was by act of Congress the first time, that is to say the first time the organization of the Survey, as planned by Jefferson, Gallatin, and then by Supt. Hassler, was entirely set aside and a new organization constituted under the Navy Department. The next time it was transferred by Executive order after two years' existence.

Now, in 1843—I may say the superintendent, Mr. Hassler, very vigorously prosecuted this Survey during the succeeding years, but he died, I think, in 1843, and then it became necessary to appoint a new superintendent and establish the organization of the Survey under which it has ever since been conducted, which was accomplished at that time, and it was accomplished by means of a board, which was organized by President Tyler, and in order that all sides of the question involved might be represented, that board consisted of nine persons, four of whom were Army officers, two of whom were naval officers, and the remaining three were civilians.

Those 9 persons constituted a board which reorganized the Survey. I think that the action of this board was before the death of Supt. Hassler, and it was a reorganization under which the work has been conducted from that time to this. That board was in session many weeks and gave very careful consideration to the whole question. It was in the first place, of course, quite competent to give a careful consideration of the question; and, secondly, I would remind the committee that it was a board organized, not in favor of the civilian control of the Coast Survey, as only 3 out of 9 members of the board were civilians, the others being officers of the Army and Navy. The report of that board, which perhaps is quite well known to the most of you, was very decidedly and positively in favor of continuing the execution of the work of the survey of the coast in accordance with the plan originally devised by President Jefferson and Gallatin, and to continue the work of this survey under the control of the Treasury Department. Congress, therefore, took action to carry out that recommendation, and from that time to the present the survey has continued along those lines with only such modifications as have been made from time to time by acts of Congress, one or two of which I shall refer to as I go on.

In 1848 an attempt was made to retransfer this Bureau again to the Navy Department, but it was defeated by a very large majority. This was a resolution or bill introduced in the House of Representatives. In 1849 a bill was introduced in the Senate to provide for the retransfer of this Bureau to the Navy Department, which was defeated also by a majority of more than two to one at that time.

Mr. ENLOE. If it will not interrupt you there, I would like to know. when the authority was taken from the President to transfer this Bureau by an executive order?

Prof. MENDENHALL. Well, I can not answer that question. I think it must have been done in the act following the organization of 1843. That is my judgment; indeed, I could not say positively that authority does not still exist to make that transfer, but that would require an examination of the statutes on the question, and that I have not made, but I think there has never been any assumption of authority, or there has never been any suspicion that that authority exists, because of the fact that several attempts have been made to bring this about by act of Congress.

After 1849 the next attempt to accomplish this was in the year 1882, when a bill was introduced which provided not only for the transfer of the Coast and Geodetic Survey to the Navy Department, but it provided also for the transfer of the Life-Saving Service, the Light-House Establishment, the Bureau of Navigation, and the Revenue Marine, but in fact all the bureaus of the Treasury Department which are in any way related to the operations of commerce upon the seas. The history of that bill is probably well known to many of you gentlemen; it did not become a law. Again, in 1884, the question was brought prominently forward, and I have not been quite able to know, but I have suspected, the action in 1882, in connection with the proposed transfer of several bureaus, gave rise to the establishment in 1884 of the joint commission for the investigation of the several scientific bureaus, a body which is well known to all of you and which published a very voluminous and full report; I believe some selections have been read of that report to this committee, and I need not refer to it at any length.

I will say that that joint committee, composed of members of the Senate and House, investigated the matter for two years, and gave a great deal of time and study to this question, and at the end of that time the report of the commission, as has been presented to you, I think, was that the Coast and Geodetic Survey should retain its autonomy as it had during the many previous years of its history. As this is a public printed document, and the evidence is accessible to everybody, I will not refer at length to anything in the report, but I would like to emphasize the fact that a careful study of the question, through two years of all the relations of the scientific bureaus to each other, resulted in this conclusion.

The next attempt I refer to was in 1888, when a resolution or bill was introduced to disrupt the Coast and Geodetic Survey and transfer part to the Geological Survey and part to the Navy, and that also failed. So you will see the history of this Survey up to the present time has not been one entirely free from ripples of inconvenience arising from attempts which have been made to disrupt it by transferring one bureau to another, but I think the history of the transfers that have been made constitutes a very strong evidence for maintaining the existing condition of things.

Now, without going further into historical mattter, to address myself to the merits of the question, I would like to say I think you will all agree with me that such a change as this one, which upsets the traditions of nearly three-quarters of a century and which destroys a bureau which has produced work the excellence of which has not been rivaled anywhere in the world, that such a change as this should be made in response to a strong demand from some source or for very good reasons. I discriminate between demand and reasons, because it is quite true we might have a demand for a change when no particular good reason exists. As to the demand, I have not been able myself to learn of the existence of any demand for this change. There is not a newspaper in the country that has referred to the subject, and many have, that has not referred to it adversely, and which has not been opposed to the change proposed by this bill. There is not an institution of learning where there are men particularly competent to understand the merits of this work that has not spoken adversely to this change. There is not an engineering society which has spoken, and many of them have spoken, that has not spoken adversely to this change.

The Geological Survey does not want this; I speak with the authority of the director of that Bureau in saying so. And of all the naval officers I have spoken to, and I have talked with a great many in the last year or two on this subject and several in the last few weeks in which th e matter has been agitated, I have not found one in favor of this disru ption of this Bureau. Hence, I may venture the assertion that as far as I have been able to determine I am unable to find any demand for ths action. Hence, action should only be taken on account of good reasons. Are there any good reasons for this transfer? There may have been no demand, but still good reasons. I will, therefore, examine the reasons which seem to be against the passage of this bill. That is, I believe all the reasons are altogether on this side; I have not yet heard of one single reason for the transfer of this Bureau and the disruption as proposed that can not, in my judgment, be very fully and completely answered. I will attempt to present these reasons and then I will be happy to answer any questions which any of the committee may wish to ask me in regard to those reasons.

First, let me say that the object of the organization of this Bureau is distinctly stated in the law over and over again. The object is "for commerce and defense and to furnish points for State surveys." If you will examine the law you will find those three things are distinctly brought out, and those are the three points for which the Bureau is in existence; not merely for commerce, but for defense. The very earliest law upon the subject, and that has been repeated continually since, stated that these surveys must be "for commerce and defense." I emphasize that because some criticism has been made, to which I will reply later, as to the character of the work of the Bureau, that it has been too refined and too accurate, and possibly that may be true, although I will try to show in that connection it is not true as far as commerce is concerned, and certainly we have the best of evidence to show that the work of the Bureau has not been too refined and too accurate for purposes of defense; hence I invite your special attention to the fact that the law provides for those things.

Also now for a number of years, I can not quite remember, perhaps twenty years, there has been continually a provision in the law providing that the work of the survey shall be directed to furnishing points for State surveys, and this we have been trying to comply with and have done without any very large expenditure of money. But in order that the argument which I wish to present may be fully understood I will ask you to consider the actual operations of the Bureau; that is, I will go a little into details of the work of this service, which I trust you will not find uninteresting. I waive for the present two of these questions—that is, I will waive the question of the production of a map for purposes of defense and the operation of furnishing points for State surveys, and I will consider solely in the beginning the production of the chart for purposes of navigation.

Let us suppose that is the only problem that is before us, and then I will ask your attention to some of the method—show this work is done and the actual necessity for it. I will say that, very unfortunately, the work which has been pushed most prominently before the public, the hydrographic work of the Bureau—and I say this because I shall show you proof by and by—is the very simplest and the very easiest of all the work which this Bureau does. It happens to be work which appears on the surface just as the roof appears to be the last part which is put on the house, but it does not by any means represent the work and the great foundation upon which that all rests is not shown upon the chart, and sailors do not see it, and the men who use these charts do not come in contact with the fact that a very great mass of work is necessary before ever the chart can be produced or attempted—and I hope to show you something of this work. Now, if Mr. Wainwright will give me one of these charts I will exhibit it to you. I will ask your attention to this chart, which I have selected as one covering a locality with which everybody is familiar, and I will try to trace from it as rapidly as I can the methods resorted to in our work.

This chart covers Long Island, Long Island Sound, a portion east of this point here, the entrance to New York Harbor, New York City, and a little of the east shore along there [illustrating]. This is one of the sailing charts. Now, the question I want to answer is, how do we make a chart of this kind? That is the point. It is perhaps very different from what a great many people expect. The first operation, in a logical order, and in the practical order of this case, is the execution of what we know as triangulation, a scheme of triangulation. That is the same chart here, and I have sketched out here the actual figures of triangulation which were executed and which were absolutely necessary for the production of this chart. A great deal has been said about triangulation and excessive refinement which was perhaps not necessary, and all that sort of thing. In regard to that I hope to demonstrate to everybody it is absolutely essential. At this point down below, on Fire Island, we have the first base line ever measured in the United States. That was a base line of Mr. Hassler.

He began the work of first developing the coast survey of the United States from that base, believing of course New York Harbor and its environments constituted the most important part of the coast. They made a study of it and began work on the Fire Island base. This is the base line here [exhibiting]. A base line is simply a line of several miles in length; we have base lines varying from a little less than 3 miles in length to a little more than 11 miles. But a base line is a line which is measured with the utmost degree of precision possible to modern devices. I would like to say here that the U. S. Coast and Geodetic Survey, as is acknowledged in Europe as it is everywhere I am sure, has carried that base line measurement to the highest degree of accuracy possible. The base lines which have been measured in the last two or three years for accuracy exceeds anything in Europe or any other country in the world. Why, you may ask, is it necessary to have this done with such a great degree of refinement?

It is because, as everybody will see from these figures, if any, even a very small error was made in the base line, it becomes magnified as you proceed away, and an error of an inch, which we do not permit, would become many inches, and by and by many feet the farther you go up or down the coast, and hence the necessity of having the first line upon which the whole system rests of the highest degree of precision, as has long ago been recognized; and it was for the purpose of getting an exact standard measure that Mr. Hassler went to London in 1810 or 1811 to obtain a yard of the highest degree of precision with which this base line could be measured. I would like, if you have no objection, to say a few words in regard to the degree of precision in measuring a base line. A base line is measured by laying off in the locality selected a line as nearly horizontal as possible. It is then measured usually by using bars which may be 12, 14, or 15 feet long, the length of which is determined with the highest degree of precision at the office by comparison with the standard yard or meter. These bars are used in pairs or singly with microscopes, and their length laid off along the line with the greatest care.

Great attention is paid to the question of temperature. Of course, that enters into the question of these bars as other matters. They vary with different degrees of temperature, but in the end we have a result that is accurate within a degree that is apparently incredible to those who are not accustomed to measurements of this kind. In the very earliest work we obtained results on a base line nearly 7 miles long, measured in 1847, and the possible or probable error of that line was not more than 1 single inch in that whole length of 7 miles, and we have progressed from that until lately, in the Colorado base line, measured in 1879, we got it down to seven-tenths of an inch on a base line 7 miles long, and on a base line recently measured by the most refined process which modern science and art has produced, we have reduced that error to two-tenths of an inch; that is to say, one-fifth of an inch, which is a very minute quantity. We know the length of this base line several miles long within that error, and, as I say, the importance of that is, if we do not know the length as accurately as that, when we proceed from that base we magnify the error constantly in these minor triangles, until it becomes entirely too great to produce satisfactory results. Having established this base line, we proceed by a system of triangulation, which I will refer to briefly hereafter.

The CHAIRMAN. What is the length of that line, beginning at Fire Island?

Prof. MENDENHALL. It is about 5 miles long; I do not know whether I have it here or not. (Examining papers.) Eight and seven-tenths miles it is; I have it exactly.

Mr. HULICK. What is the variation?

Prof. MENDENHALL. I am not sure I have that error here. (Examining papers.) It does not seem to be here. It would be, perhaps, a little more than an inch, or something like that; less than 2 inches certainly. It is one of the first bases measured and we were not exact as we are now.

Now, having established the base line, we next make what is known as a reconnoissance, and this is one of the most difficult operations we have to do, requiring especial skill. It requires an examination of the whole country with a view to the selection of points which are intervisible and properly related to one another. We can not use an ordinary map of the country, for it would not be accurate enough for this work, nor would it show the relative heights of the several points.

This is an important problem, and the man who does this work must examine all the country, utilizing information from the best maps available, the best county maps or whatever maps he may have, and ascend the prominent elevations, climb trees, and all that, until he finally perfects what is called a reconnoissance scheme. And having the reconnoissance scheme completed, a man with an instrument, a theodolite, goes into the field and commences a series of observations for what we call triangulation work. This work here [exhibiting] we call primary work. This is a term that has been used a great deal, and I want to be permitted to say that the primary triangulation work is the largest triangulation work that it is possible to make over any area of country. That is to say, in a very flat country, such as we have in the West in the transcontinental line across the Mississippi Valley, the primary triangulation lines are not more than 25 to 30 miles long, because it is impossible to have a longer line than that without building extremely high signal towers.

We have built observatory towers 156 feet high, but in the mountainous country the lines become very much longer, and we always make them as long as possible, because we get over the country in that way much more rapidly by the use of the longer lines than we do by the shorter lines. For instance, in the great triangulation of the mountains west of Denver, the most magnificent system of triangulation which has yet been executed in the work is the system from Denver west to the Pacific coast where we have lines, many of them from 100 to 140 and 150 miles long, and where we have some lines nearly 200 miles long, one observation being 211 miles in length, which is the longest distance seen in the world from one point on the earth to another. We make our lines as long as possible, because we get over the ground faster and it takes less time. The observer occupies this station with his theodolite and takes care of observations of these angles, not only of a single series of observations, but of many others.

Now I would like to refer to what I think will be interesting to everybody here, and that is to the internal evidence of the accuracy of this work. Sometimes, when we say that the triangulations of the Coast and Geodetic Survey are, as a whole, better than any ever executed by any other country in the world, it seems to some people as though we were boasting, but I would like to say that this will be admitted by competent authorities among the geodesists of Europe and of India, where such surveys have been made on a great scale covering the entire area of the country.

This claim is justly and safely made on account of the internal evidence of the correctness of the work. It is a great advantage that we can take the work and turn it over to anybody who can estimate the value of a thing of that kind. The internal evidence of accuracy depends on a simple geometrical principle with which everybody is acquainted. That is to say, in any triangle the sum of all the angles is equal to two right angles, or 180°. Take, for instance, this triangle; if observations have been absolutely accurate, barring a little excess owing to the curvature of the earth, the sum of these three angles must be 180°.

But we have never absolutely accurate observations, and consequently the error of closure, as it is called, is a very good measure of the value of work of this class. If the error is two minutes or three minutes or four minutes, we call that very rough and very bad work; that is, if the sum of the angles is greater or less than 180° by such quantities, we would call it very bad work. Now, as I say, there is an error of closure, and the portions of our great system of triangulation that have been reduced and published have been studied by European geodesists as well as our own, and these errors have been found to be, on the whole, less than that of any piece of work executed by any other country in the world, so we feel naturally proud of the accuracy and the precision of that work.

Now, in addition to what we call the primary system, I have also put on this map the secondary and tertiary triangulations. which are necessary to enable us to execute typography and hydrography. Suppose we have in view a survey of this water here in the neighborhood of Stonington. Here is Fire Island [illustrating] and we shall take in the water between that and the mainland [illustrating], and in order to do that we reduce the triangulation gradually until we get a system of very small triangles as you see. The next smallest system of triangulation is known as the secondary system, and the next, or the third, the smallest we have, we call the tertiary system of triangulation. When this is reached, we have certain points along and near the shore, whose relations to other points and to the base line are known or can readily be computed.

But the exact geographical positions of these must be determined. Determined how? By the connection of these triangles with the primary base line, also by determinations at various points as indicated by these dots of the latitude and longitude, to which I will refer later on. As declared by the Secretary of the Navy at an early period in the history of the Bureau, surveys made in detached fragments and not properly connected with one another or to principal points in the interior, so as to form a complete whole, would result in absolute failure, so a complete system of primary, secondary, and tertiary triangulation is necessary. The triangulation alone is not sufficient to give us material for making this chart; some other things must be done.

A certain kind of astronomical work must be done, which, as you can understand, in the Coast and Geodetic Survey is restricted very closely to the absolute necessity of the case. The Coast and Geodetic Survey has never done astronomical work unless it related absolutely and necessarily to the construction of charts. Astronomical work in the Survey means the determination of latitude and longitude and azimuth; that is to say, we must determine for a number of points on the chart—of course not a great number, because we connect these points by a system of triangulation—but for a certain number of points we must determine accurately the latitude and longitude and also the azimuth, or the direction of the lines which go from this point, or the bearing of those lines with the meridian. The determination of latitude and longitude has been perfected by the U. S. Coast and Geodetic Survey (I will read you, later on, some testimony to that effect), and such men as Humboldt, Schumacher, the great German scientist, and Arago, and European astronomers generally will support me in the assertion that this work has been perfected by the Coast and Geodetic Survey.

The methods that they use now, and have for many years, for the determination of latitude and longitude are known everywhere as the "American" methods. We were the first to invent and apply the electric telegraph to this work. The first device for using electricity in the determination of latitude and longitude I saw many years ago in a little garret room in the city of Cincinnati, where the first chronograph was devised by Mr. Mitchell, an astronomer well known to all of you. The Coast and Geodetic Survey very quickly took advantage of all the scientific investigations available in this country in this direction, and began at once to use electricity in the determination of longitude. It perhaps may not be without interest to refer briefly to just what that means, and how it is done. You know the difference in longitude between two points means the difference in time between two points, local time. If it is known here at this moment, east or west of here it will be later or earlier than it is here. If we can find out the exact difference in time between two points we instantly find out the difference in longitude.

Now, the question is to determine the difference in time. This was an important problem previous to the introduction of the electric method, and the principal means we had for its solution was by the use of chronometric methods; that is, by carrying a chronometer from one part of the country to another. In like manner, when you carry a watch which is an accurate timekeeper, in traveling from one place to another and find the local time at any town does not agree with your watch you can quickly determine the difference in longitude between the town where the watch was set and those towns where any difference of time was noted. In navigation this is a very important matter, and Great Britain recognized that fact, and in the latter part of the last century a reward of £100,000 ($500,000) was offered by Parliament for the greatest improvement in the construction of chronometers. That reward was earned by a gentleman who devised a very simple method for correcting errors in rate due to variations in temperature, which, strange to say, was very shortly discarded by the discovery of another within a year or two after he received his reward.

The error arising from variation of temperature is still not perfectly eliminated and is to-day a serious difficulty in accurate time-keeping. Now, the telegraph came and it became at once possible to reproduce local time at different points almost instantaneously, so that immediately it was introduced into the determination of longitude. Suppose we want the difference in longitude between this city and New York. We have a telegraph line between here and New York and we have our little observatory here and a little transit instrument for observing the stars and getting the local time, and we have the same thing in New York. Now, the observer at New York touches a key, and the instant he touches that key the fact is recorded in Washington on a cylinders, which is covered with a sheet of paper—we have one of the sheets here—and that mark shows the instant at which that signal is made in New York City.

Now, let us suppose when it is precisely 9 o'clock here it is later in New York than 9 by so many seconds, the chronograph record instantly shows the difference in time. The telegraph method is one which enables us to reduce the error to a very small quantity. Here is one of the sheets we have showing the records made [exhibiting same]. It is a very interesting record. This was made a few years ago on the Hawaiian Islands, and Queen Liluokalani, who had some scientific and astronomical tastes, visited the observatory there and made an observation of several stars, and the records of her observations are recorded on this sheet, which she signed and wrote in her own language to the effect that she had observed the stars at the observatory of the Coast and Geodetic Survey. These marks here show the beats of the clock. So accurate are these that the error of longitude is reduced to a few hundredths of a second in time. Long ago the Coast and Geodetic Survey determined the longitude between Europe and America by means of the cable with great precision, and although it has been done since by the English across to Montreal, I very much regret to say they have not yet published their observations. I infer from what I have learned that their results are not better than those we obtained many years before.

Latitude work is of a similar degree of precision and is executed by a method known everywhere as the American method, which was introduced by the Coast and Geodetic Survey. We know it as the "Talcott method," because devised by Capt. Andrew Talcott; but it is elsewhere known as the "American method."

Besides work above referred to necessary for the construction of charts, we must go further before being ready for hydrographic work; for instance, we must have tidal observations. I have been rather surprised that so little has been said, in the discussion which has taken place on this subject and the arguments which have been introduced in favor of the passage of this bill, of the great importance of tidal observations.

I need not explain this in detail to you, who are accustomed to the movement of the tides; but it goes without saying that where the tide rises and falls several feet, as it does on all of our coasts, and in some places more than 20 feet, it is impossible to determine the depth of the sea without observing the tide, because the depth varies at different times. It is therefore necessary to have accurate observation of the tide. There are two classes of tidal observations, one of which is employed by all hydrographic parties, including those directed by naval officers now detailed to the Coast Survey. I may as well remark here, as I have touched upon this point for the first time, that I do not wish, in anything I shall say, to be understood as disparaging in any way the excellent performance of the naval officers connected with this work. It has been my pleasure to be brought directly in contact with them for the past few years, and many of them I have known for a long time. Many very excellent officers have devoted themselves

in the most unselfish way to the success of the work'of the Coast and
Geodetic Survey and have been thoroughly loyal to us under all circumstances, having spoken in the strongest way against the wisdom of such
dismemberment and consequent destruction of the Survey as is proposed in this bill.

Whatever I have to say that may appear to be in any way a criticism of their work or rather to be a criticism of the wisdom of throwing
the whole of this work upon them, must be understood to refer to the
conditions by which they are surrounded and not to them because
if they were to devote their lives to this work without any question
they would do as well as others, and I simply refer to the conditions
under which the work will necessarily be executed if this bill should
pass.

As I say, tidal observations must be made, and they are of two kinds.
In one method there is employed a simple tide staff showing the feet
and inches, which is erected at any place where the water rises and
falls, near a wharf, and the height of the tide is read by an observer from
a convenient place. He makes a record of these observations and these
tidal records are kept in books known as tidal books, and brought back
to the tidal division of the office.

The other kind of tidal work is of the utmost importance, and is of a
somewhat different type—that is to say, it is a prolonged observation
of the tide at a given point. For instance, at New York Harbor we
have maintained a tide gauge there for many years, and are still maintaining it and shall continue to do so, I trust, for many years to come, as
it is of great importance to fully understand the tides of New York Harbor. The same thing has been done at a few other places. The fact is,
the full period of tidal observations should not be less than 19 years at
a single point. We do not depend upon a man to read the stage of the
water at various hours, but we have a tide gauge which is a self-regis-
tering apparatus, making its own records. We have a man who looks
after the clock and keeps it in order, but this tide gauge itself keeps a
continuous record of the rise and fall of the tide. This is an actual sheet
[exhibiting same] from one of the tide gauges, and it gives you an idea
of the kind of record that is made. This is from Fort Hamilton, New
York Harbor. This curved line is a line actually traced by the pencil.
These vertical lines are hour lines, and this shows the rise and fall of
the water at Fort Hamilton. Of course the rise and fall is greater than
this, as this has to be reduced in scale. This is reduced to one-ninth of
the real size. The tide at Fort Hamilton is nine times as great as here
shown.

Mr. ENLOE. Let me ask if this record is made by a mechanical
device?

Prof. MENDENHALL. Yes, sir; it is recorded by a mechanical device
which is constantly under inspection. I would like to invite the attention
of those of you who are familiar with New York Harbor that in connection with this gauge there is an arc 20 feet in diameter, and on that
arc are the figures 1, 2, 3, 4, 5, etc., of large size, so that it can be seen
across the Narrows, and any vessel going in or out of the harbor of
New York by looking at that arc can see the exact state of the tide,
which is shown by an index hand pointing always to the figure showing the height of the tide. There is an arrow below this, and as long
as the tide is rising it points up, and when it begins to fall it points
down, so that a vessel coming in or going out can see precisely what
is the height of the tide and whether the water is rising or falling.
We have been urged by the Chamber of Commerce and other maritime

organizations in New York to reproduce this in the Chamber of Commerce by means of a small model. That will be possible, I think.

The necessary work on the reduction of these tidal tables requires mathematical talent of a very high order. The ablest physicists, the ablest scholars that the world has ever produced have given a very large portion of their time to the study of tidal problems. The necessity for mathematical and scientific attainments of the highest type in operations like those of the Coast Survey is well illustrated by this tidal question.

Sir William Thompson, now Lord Kelvin, one of the greatest physicists of the age, devoted many years to the study of tidal problems, and he evolved a machine for interpreting these curves. The complete reduction of a record of this kind is very laborious, and Sir William Thompson devised a machine for doing this. One of our own officers, at one time an employé of the Coast and Geodetic Survey, now dead, Prof. Ferrell, invented a machine for the same purpose, by which these curves are utilized and the state of the tide predicted.

The CHAIRMAN. The hour for the meeting of the House has arrived, and as the naval bill is expected to come up to-day we will continue your hearing on Friday next.

Thereupon the committee adjourned.

COMMITTEE ON NAVAL AFFAIRS,
Friday, May 18, 1894.

The Committee on Naval Affairs this day met, Hon. J. A. Geissenhainer in the chair.

The CHAIRMAN. Gentlemen, Prof. Mendenhall is with us this morning and will continue the address which is of so much interest both to him and to us.

STATEMENT OF PROF. T. C. MENDENHALL—Continued.

Prof. MENDENHALL then addressed the committee. He said:

Mr. chairman and gentlemen of the committee, before beginning at the point where I left off at the last hour I was here I wish to call your attention to a little drawing I have had made here in representation of the accuracy of the triangulation to which I referred the other day without being able at that time to give any very tangible example of that accuracy. This, however, will represent it, I think, very fairly. This green line on the outside, and including this square surface, represents the exact scale of signals which was used in this particular case. It was a piece of timber 4 inches square, on the top of which at right angles was an iron gas pipe, a section of which is represented here, the diameter being about the same as that of a half-dollar.

These arrows, the ends of which are drawn on this sheet of paper, represent lines that are drawn from distant stations, the scale, as I have said, being in fact the actual scale, not a reduced scale. The accuracy of the work is shown by the nearness with which these arrows come to the iron gas-pipe here [illustrating]. This indicates to you the great precision that is reached in this work. This line [illustrating] is from a station about 7 or 8 miles distant; here is a line from a station about 25 miles distant; and here is one from a station about 16 miles, and here is one from one about 7 miles, and one from 8, and so on; all of these being, as I might say, shots which were made at that slender iron pipe from distances varying from 25 to 6 or 7 miles, and when these results are all combined they are found clustered around the real position of the iron pipe in that way, and, as will be seen, three of them actually going through it, and the others coming within a very small distance of it. That illustrates there better than I did on a previous occasion the degree of precision that is actually reached and which is necessary for this class of work.

Mr. MONEY. If it will not be any interruption to your remarks——

Prof. MENDENHALL. I will be very glad to answer any question.

Mr. MONEY. You say that precision is necessary?

Prof. MENDENHALL. Yes, sir.

Mr. MONEY. I can understand the value of accuracy, but as to this nicety of precision, will you please tell us the necessity or utility of it?

Prof. MENDENHALL. Of course upon the degree of accuracy or precision at any one of those points—I referred to that briefly very the other day, and I intended of course, to take it up as I go further along—depends and affects the final relative precision of all points widely separated——

Mr. MONEY. I recollect the explanation.

Prof. MENDENHALL. That is to say, that is only a part of the chain; this particular figure, or this particular instance, is part of a chain which is being carried across the continent to connect San Francisco with the Atlantic coast, and that chain being more than 3,000 miles in length and going across a mountainous region, and all that sort of thing, of course, if we were to allow any error which was at all serious or noticeable to creep in any part it would become constantly magnified.

Mr. MONEY. I understand that; but what I wanted to know was simply to bring out the idea as to what was the practical utility of having that degree of precision. Suppose it does vary, in a distance say of 3,000 miles a few feet or yards?

Prof. MENDENHALL. It will vary a great deal more than a few feet or yards if these errors are kept up. Perhaps I can answer your question better by calling attention to this fact. The question has often been raised why is not the slender line of coast triangulation which we have run around the Atlantic coast sufficient for determining the relative location of these positions, and why is it necessary, as it has been deemed necessary, to connect the extremities of this slender line with what we call our "oblique arc," which runs practically across the eastern part of the continent, and the question is asked why that oblique arc is necessary, and why is not the slender line of triangulation sufficient to satisfy the demand? Now, the answer to that is that any line of triangulation of that character must necessarily be suject to cumulative errors, and when you get around to the Gulf coast, or even to the South Atlantic, you will find that when you compare your distances there with the distances as they ought to be, as a matter of fact you will have errors not of a few feet, but of several hundred feet.

That we know to be a fact, and when we complete our oblique arc, which will be completed in one more season, and would have been completed in fact before this if we had not been driven out last year owing to the absence of a law in a State in which work was being done to protect the monuments of the survey. We had those laws in almost all the States, but there was no law in this State and some of the landowners objected to some of the signals, and so we had to leave, and an effort has been made to have a law passed by the legislature. Aside from that the oblique arc would have been completed, and only a few days ago I asked Mr. Schott, who is chief of the computing division, and who keeps these things well in mind, and he said the error of the slender line of triangulation would unquestionably be found to be several hundred feet; the result of all these positions located on this eoast here [illustrating] will be found to be several hundred feet out of the way, and these corrections will be made when this arc is completed. That correction would be absolutely impossible without maintaining this high degree of precision through the whole work.

Mr. MONEY. I did not desire to interrupt your argument, but you must not take it for granted that this committee is as familiar with these things as you are, and occasionally you may think it is impossible for us to be ignorant of a fact which is very familiar to you, when in fact we are absolutely ignorant in regard to it.

Prof. MENDENHALL. It is my object, and my only object, to inform the committee, and I shall be only too glad to have you ask any questions which may occur to you at any time.

Mr. ENLOE. Will you tell the Committee what effect these corrections will have upon the safety of navigation; does it make any difference in the charts?

Prof. MENDENHALL. Yes, sir; it will make a very decided difference. Some of these put on a chart of a small scale, say a small sailing chart, the difference will not be important, but when you prepare a chart which is larger then it will be noticeable; but I think everybody knows the location of a danger when it is actually several hundred feet out of the way is a very essential matter in navigation, and it would not do to allow locations of that kind. If I may further illustrate this: A vessel coming in from the sea depends almost entirely for its position upon astronomical observations which they have been able to make during the last days or weeks previous to sighting the shore, and assuming these observations are of the best quality possible, which of course we must assume and always do assume, then the question is, what will be the error in the position of a particular danger which this vessel first meets with.

It is no more safe to allow that to go into a chart 200 feet, 300 feet, or 400 feet out of the way than to allow a very much greater error in the case of a vessel hugging the shore and able to pilot its way by objects which it can pick up on shore; but vessels at sea do not do that, but are obliged to locate their positions by actual latitude and longitude, and when a vessel comes in and after the captain has determined the latitude and longitude is so and so at this point, now according to the chart there is a danger to navigation at this point, so if that danger to navigation is located several hundred feet out of the way a very serious result might take place, and such a serious error as that ought not to exist, and it has never been allowed to exist in any foreign government. Everything is done to prevent any errors of that sort from creeping into charts in order if possible to prevent such accidents.

Mr. ENLOE. But you say it does exist?

Prof. MENDENHALL. Yes, we believe that such errors exist, and they must, and that can not be avoided until our triangulation is perfected. I might remark here that I endeavored to present the other day, and my intent this morning was to present, the order of these operations logically considered, but in the actual practical working of these operations they have not been taken up in every instance in their logical order, and the reason of that is of course very plain when we come to examine the circumstances. Just as a man in going out on the plains or into a new country does not begin to build a stone foundation first, but puts a roof on first, that being the most essential thing because he must have something to protect himself in that way; but Mr. Hassler, the first Superintendent of the Survey, did begin in the logical order, as I showed the other day through this base line beginning on Fire Island.

He continued that triangulation from that point, and he very quickly carried it on until he reached New York Harbor, and he then began the topography and hydrography with reference to New York Harbor, because the commerce of the nation demanded that that should take precedence over the logical order of extending this triangulation across the country and up and down the coast in order to reach these points. That is the only reason the slender line of triangulation is run first, because it was an absolute necessity. That is to say, it is much better to have charts even imperfectly prepared than to have none at all. That is the plan Mr. Hassler followed continually, really beginning in the logical order with the measurement of the base line on Fire Island, and all the time planning for the more complete system which has been consistently carried out from the organization of the Survey under the Tyler report in 1843 up to the present time.

Mr. ENLOE. If it will not disturb you, I would like to know if you can not reach that accuracy before you complete this transcontinental line to which you have referred?

Prof. MENDENHALL. We can reach the accuracy required of any particular combination when that particular combination is completed. For instance, when this oblique arc is completed that will give us the accuracy necessary for the combination of the extreme South Atlantic, including the Gulf coast and North Atlantic coast, and the relative parts of that will be brought together. The object of the transcontinental line as far as it relates to this particular thing—it has another object which I will take occasion to speak of later—but as far as this particular object of the transcontinental arc, it is to tie together the Atlantic and Pacific coasts, because that is a very great necessity.

Mr. ENLOE. Does that object relate more to geodesy than to navigation?

Prof. MENDENHALL. The object of the transcontinental arc is—the word "geodesy," I would like to say at this point, does not strictly apply to the particular operation; it is a word that is very greatly misunderstood. Every operation of a survey is geodetic in its nature whenever it assumes that the earth is round, or rather that it is not a plane. That is a geodetic survey. Any kind of survey that is made, even on the assumption that the earth is not a plane, is a geodetic survey, and that is all there is to it. Now, the ordinary survey of the country surveyor, and to some extent Government-land surveying, are based on the assumption that the earth is a plane, and, the areas covered being small, the rotundity of the earth is not noticed; but even in our land survey its importance was recognized by President Jefferson, and he was desirous of passing laws regulating that survey, in order to have what is now called a "geodetic survey." The history of the organization of the present line surveying shows that at that time he was unable to do so, and the consequence is that the line surveys to-day contain many marked contradictions and irregularities with regard to that fact.

Mr. ENLOE. Am I to understand from that the transcontinental arc survey relates particularly to the land surveys——

Prof. MENDENHALL. If you will pardon me, I will complete the answer to the question which you asked me a moment ago, and that will perhaps be best. The object now of the transcontinental arc—this is leading me to state in regard to which I wished to state further along in order, but perhaps it will be well to take it up—the object of the transcontinental arc is to tie together the Atlantic and Pacific coasts for the purpose of construction of charts for the navigator, because we must know these relative positions with great accuracy, which can not be obtained in any other way than that, and this tying together of the continent must be made between one part of the continent and another, and it must be made between one country and another. You are probably aware of the fact that we have tied our country to Europe by means of the cable in determining longitude. However, this is not the only object of the transcontinental arc. The law of Congress has long provided, besides the function of the Coast Survey in providing charts for the navigator, as I referred to the other day, one of its functions shall be to furnish points to State surveyors, and that is one of the most essential and valuable features of the transcontinental arc that is now being extended. Every State in the country will eventually, must eventually, prepare an accurate map. In my judgment, that should be done by State authority and not by the Government of the United States.

Mr. ENLOE. Will you please tell us how many States have applied for those points?

Prof. MENDENHALL. Perhaps a dozen or more; I can not give you now the number exactly, but if I am allowed to continue in the line on which I am I would like to explain the value of that. As I say, every State must eventually construct a map, and as I said in my judgment it is best to be done by an appropriation of its own money and not by the National Government, but the National Government must do what the States can not do; and that is the States can not carry on this system of triangulation which would enable them to relate themselves to each other. If you make an independent map of the State of Ohio and of the State of Indiana and of the State of Illinois, such maps made independently can not be fitted into each other; they will not properly join each other. There will be and there has been an inaccuracy, and if I should take up the time of the committee to consider it, I could point out many maps made in such a way.

I could cite numerous examples of boundary lines run in this way by independent action which have been found many miles out of the way. Within the last three years the Coast Survey has been called upon to settle disputed boundary lines, and they still exist all over the United States. There are some disputes in regard to boundary lines that have been in existence a hundred years or more which have not been settled. One important one was settled in the last year by the work of the Coast and Geodetic Survey between the State of Delaware and the State of Pennsylvania, a controversy existing ever since the days of Lord Baltimore and William Penn, which was finally settled by the application of such methods as the Coast and Geodetic Survey uses and no one else uses. These questions can be forever and definitely settled, so that no future dispute can arise, when this transcontinental line is completed; and I may say that it is now nearly completed, there being but a short break between the two links, one of which came from the west toward the east and the other of which started from the east going to the west, and the States through which it passes will be able to hang their own maps on it. They have recognized that long ago.

We are carrying on now in several States of the Union these opera-

tions and furnishing points to the State surveyors to be arranged whenever we can establish the transcontinental line so as to attach each to
the general system. I might mention work which is going on in the
State of Minnesota, where the State itself has made an appropriation
for the topography of this work, and that is right. My own judgment
is that the United States Government ought not to pay for interior
topography, and it never has been the object of the Coast and Geodetic
Survey to make this interior topographical work, and that has been
greatly misunderstood by many people. It has been thought that we
are ambitious to go into details of an interior topographical survey of
the whole country. That is not the case. The Coast Survey as constituted can do for the United States what no State alone can do, that
is, to carry out this scheme of triangulation, and that is one of the most
vital and most important features of the work.

Now, I have been led into some remarks upon triangulation which, if
they had come regularly, I am glad to say I would have wanted to
take up a little later on the work on this character that has been done
by other nations of the world, and you will there see that the United
States has not done one-fifth of this character of work that has been
done by European nations. Take India, which is a poor country, and
is of very large area, yet the whole surface of it is covered by a network
of triangulation of the very highest degree of precision. It is considered
a necessary detail of a survey of the country. England, Germany,
France, Italy, and all of those countries, all European countries practically, have been covered in this way. I have some maps of those
countries showing that fact which I will at some later time show you,
in order that you may see that the criticism which has been made
against this work is not well taken. We have a single slender line of
triangulation across the country, an oblique arc, that is necessary
for the correction of the shore line, and that is all we have done. I
must say honestly, because I wish to be honest in all these matters, it
is by no means all that ought to have been done. The U. S. Government must eventually extend this triangulation extensively. This is a
subject which must some time or other be taken up again——

Mr. ENLOE. If it will not interrupt you at that point, before getting
away from the subject of the foreign surveys, I would like to know
whether that is done through the coast survey in the foreign countries
or through the engineer officers of the army?

Prof. MENDENHALL. Mr. Chairman, may I ask to be permitted to take
up this question rather systematically in the way in which I started,
because i can not answer questions so satisfactorily as I can if I am
allowed to take up the subject in its regular course?

Mr. MONEY. I suggest the propriety of allowing Prof. Mendenhall to
go on in the line which he desires, and any gentleman wishing to inter-
rogate him upon any point can make a note of it and ask those questions at the conclusion of his remarks.

Prof. MENDENHALL. I will be very glad to be interrupted with questions on any topic bearing on the question which I have in hand; I do
not object to being interrupted by a question of that kind, but I have
been led, as you see, to the consideration of subjects which come later
along and which can not, of course, be brought in at this point as intelligently as ——

Mr. ENLOE. I want to beg the pardon of the committee, but I have
not asked questions on a subject about which the gentleman was not
talking; I thought I was asking questions pertinent to the matter under
discussion.

Prof. MENDENHALL. All of these questions suggested as to the way in which the work is done abroad I have down in my notes and I wish to take it up at the proper time, but I think it will be impossible for me to present it intelligently and clearly until the present plan of the work and the relations which each part sustains to the other is explained, so if you will permit me I will go on in that way.

Leaving then the subject of triangulation and astronomical work which we do and of which I spoke at the last session of this committee, I had then taken up the matter of tidal observations and explained to the committee some of the work of the tide registers, showing the way in which the tides were recorded. I wish to say briefly farther with regard to that, that when these tidal curves which I exhibited to you the last time are studied the outcome of this study is the means of forecasting or predicting the tide. Now, this is one of the most important operations in which the Coast and Geodetic Survey has ever been engaged. I am sure no one who is familiar with navigation at all will doubt that a knowledge of the state of the tide at any time is of the greatest importance to the navigator. Of course, if one is on shore he can go and measure the state of the tide by observation, but the navigator is not on shore, he is afloat, and he must know if he wants to enter a harbor safely, and if that harbor has not very much more water than his vessel carries, he must know the state of the tide.

For instance—we have many harbors—take Charleston Harbor, where just now the bar carries 17 feet at low water and at high water it stands either 22 or 23 feet; therefore a vessel drawing 22 feet of water has been able to go safely into Charleston Harbor, but it can only go in there by taking advantage of the precise moment when the tide is at its highest point. Therefore, it is necessary for us to predict and publish a tidal almanac, and I have one of those tidal almanacs here which is one we issued some months ago for the year of 1895. We issue, of course, for a year or two in advance, so that they may be distributed to vessels wherever they happen to be. By the use of this the navigator can tell at any time of the year at just what hour there is high water in the ports of the United States. If he wishes to know what the state of the water will be at any harbor, he looks at the almanacs and discovers when it will be high water and when low water, and thus he can control his entering the harbor in that way. It is needless, I think, for me to remark that such a book as that predicting the tides must be the means of greatly facilitating the commerce and thereby adding many millions of dollars to it which would be lost if they were not able to make these harbors.

The production of that book requires the exercise of mathematical talent of a high order and requires a study of the subject of tidal problems for years, and we have at work on this book all the time men who are graduates of our best technical engineering colleges and universities of the country and who are especially remarkable for their mathematical attainments, and they are all the time employed in that work. The old method of computing or predicting the tide by computation was a very laborious method, so that we were very much gratified a few years ago when one of the officers of the Coast and Geodetic Survey, who is now dead, Prof. Ferrell, devised a machine for gauging the tide. There are several constants obtained from these curves, and these constants are set on the machine and by turning a crank (it is a little more than that), certain other constants are made to appear by means of which the prediction is made; but of course the existence of this machine does not by any means make it unnecessary to have connected with this tidal work men of long experience and understanding and of a high order of mathematical attainments.

The forecasting of the tides is much more difficult than the forecasting of eclipses by astronomy. We know much less about the real operation of the tides than we do about the heavenly bodies, and therefore that point is to be considered in considering the importance of this work which we are doing. The tides, while due, of course, in general to the influences of the sun and moon, yet they are modified so much by the conformation of the coast and by the varying positions of the sun and moon that they are constantly varying month by month and year by year, but by means of very careful study that has been given to this subject we are able to publish this almanac and predict the tides a long time in advance.

Another very important operation in which we have been engaged for many years, and which is of most vital importance to navigators, not relating especially to geodetic work, is the magnetic work of the survey. Almost all sailing to-day is done by the compass. It is true that the captain of a ship will correct his compass as often as he can get an astronomical observation, but there are many days at sea when he can not. There are very few coasters who are able to take an astronomical observation with any particular accuracy at sea, so they must depend for position upon the compass. Now, the compass is also a very erratic standard, almost if not quite as erratic as the tide, and the old saying in relation to truthfulness, "as true as the needle to the pole," is a very mistaken one, because the needle is about as false to the pole as it very well can be.

In the first place, at only very few points on the surface of the earth does the needle point to the North Pole; and, secondly, it does not remain constantly pointing in any one direction for any length of time. It is constantly varying. Therefore it has been important to study this question, and for fifty years or more the study of magnetism has been one of the vital features of the Coast and Geodetic Survey, and we have probably to-day in our s rvice the best expert knowledge on the subject of magnetics that is available anywhere. The result of that has been the production of a series of magnetic maps which enable us to show and enable the mariner to see wherever he may be what the variation or declination of the needle is at that particular point. For instance, at this place [illustrating on map] the needle does not point north, but it points about 5° west of north. If you go east it increases and if you go west it diminishes until you get to a certain line through the United States where the variation at a given time will be zero.

Along that line [illustrating] the needle points due north. If you go west of that line it varies, and if you go east of that line it varies. Extending it to the sea this line here becomes of the greatest importance to the navigator. This chart which I have here is one of the charts published in the year 1885. These lines here show the variation of the needle at different places. [Exhibiting same]. These lines run in a crooked way. For instance, this heavy line starting where my finger is, and running in that crooked way down here, in 1885 was the line of no variation. That is, any man living on that line, wherever he was, his needle would point to the north; and if he lived on this line here [illustrating], wherever he was, the needle would point 5° west of north or 10° here, or 15° here, or 20° here, and so on, as you will see on the map. So you see the variation is of no small quantity and it is not a small thing.

Now, anyone can appreciate the value of that information to the land. Surveyors and engineers everywhere over the country are constantly applying to us for these charts and for these facts and by them they are able to solve problems of the utmost importance in the older States of the Union by being able not only to predict forward as we are by our knowledge of the magnetic problem, but to predict backwards, being thus enabled to tell what the variation of the needle was in the early days before it was recognized or known by surveyors, and thus we can straighten out surveys made one hundred and one hundred and fifty years ago. We have settled a great many cases of property disputes, and boundary line disputes, and that sort of thing by being able to go back to the year 1770 and showing at that particular point the needle must have been so many degrees east or west of the meridian. That has only been possible by a study of the laws of magnetic forces. This is not simply from observations, but of course we make many observations, many thousands of them scattered over the country, but it requires ability of a high order and long-continued application to the study of this one subject in order that we should be able to solve the problems in the way we have.

Mr. ENLOE. If it will not interrupt you, I would like to ask if this variation is not in obedience to a regular law or whether it is erratic?

Prof. MENDENHALL. I am just coming to that fact. This is a chart of 1890. Now, if I should compare the chart of 1885 with the chart of 1890, which you can do, you will find the lines of 1890 are different from those of 1885, and this makes it necessary for us to publish the map, which we do about once in five years; and in a rough way I will say these lines swing perhaps 25 miles in five years——

Mr. ENLOE. Always in the same direction?

Prof. MENDENHALL. I will come to that. This swing has been studied for many years. In various parts of the world they have been studied one hundred and fifty years, perhaps a little longer than that. That was known in Europe probably very soon after the discovery of the magnetic needle, which was about 1000 or 1200. The fact that it varied in error in different places on the face of the earth was first discovered by Columbus on his voyage of discovery, as you doubtless remember. That was the occasion of one of the critical periods of the history of that voyage when he discovered the needle did not point astronomically as it pointed when he left. He made the discovery that in different parts of the world the needle did not point in the same direction. At a later period it was found that the variation was a variable quantity and that these lines of variation were constantly moving or swinging backward and forward. Now, to answer the direct question. We do not know the law of movements of these lines; although we have been studying them one hundred and fifty years or more, yet it is an unsolved problem. It will not always be an unsolved problem; we shall solve it sometime, but the best we can do now is to trace the course of these changes, and our predictions are based upon what the variation of the needle will probably be, backward or forward, and a continuance of the same law of variation which the needle has during the present time.

The observations in Paris seem to show that there is a great cycle of these variations and the cycle seems to vary in different parts of the world. The observations in London show a cycle in some perhaps one hundred and fifty or two hundred and fifty years. The observations in this country show a continuous movement, but yet not of a cyclical character; that is to say, we know it is going on, and we know tolerably well the lines it is following. It is like following the curves of a railway; you see it bending around a curve, but you do not know if you go on that road and travel you are coming back to the same point, and that is the trouble with this problem.

Now, the great importance of this magnetic work has been emphasized by, and I could get the testimony of, thousands and thousands of engineers. As important as this is on shore, how much more important it is on the sea, because I say when a navigator is afloat he is obliged almost invariaby to sail by compass.

Now, if he goes from one part of the sea to the other, the variation of the needle is constantly changing, and he must know this variation wherever it is. Here, for instance, is a chart showing the Alaska line of variation. To simply show you to what extent this varies here. Here [illustrating] they have the line of no variation which runs on through Japan, and here it is at that point [illustrating] and that variation changes on this curve until we have a variation of minus 35. The change in going from Unalaska to the Pribilof islands means a change of variation very decidedly, and on this chart the variations are all given. Therefore, I think it will be easily conceded that this is of the utmost importance to the sailor.

Now, it would be impossible to have developed that work at sea. That, I think, can be seen, because the sea is not a good place to make observations, the vessel is not steady and it is often difficult to get the meridian by observations of the stars and sun, so that we have had to depend mainly upon observations made upon the land and on some observations made at sea by navigators, upon quite a number of them, for our understanding of the question of magnetics to-day. We have had to make use of observations which they make at sea, but still they are not of very high character. The only solution of this problem has come from a careful study of the law as prevailing on the land as shown on these charts, and then the extension of that out to sea. That is the way in which we have done this, by studying these problems from the curves and then extending the lines out to sea by means of mathematical processes, and we have succeeded in solving the problem in magnetics as far as we have thus far gone.

Mr. ENLOE. Allow me to interrupt you there; I would like to know how is it possible to project a variable line from land observations?

Prof. MENDENHALL. That we do. We project a variable line with very marked curvature from one point to another simply because no natural phenomena ever makes a sharp turn; that is, it never makes a sudden turn.

Mr. ENLOE. How can you tell the point at which it does turn?

Prof. MENDENHALL. But I say it never makes a sharp turn.

Mr. ENLOE. I am trying to get information——

Prof. MENDENHALL. And I am trying to give it to you, if you will pardon me. The way in which we do, as I illustrated a moment ago in a railroad, if you see a railroad curve and it disappears around a hill you know perfectly well it does not turn at a right angle because no railroad does that.

Mr. ENLOE. But how do you know it turns at all?

Prof. MENDENHALL. We are justified in assuming that curvature extends because, of course, we check that. We always check our work by observations, and if they do not differ materially from those indicated by this theory, we assume that our theory is correct. I admit what is called in scientific work "exterpolation," that is, interpolating, if you please, outside, is not a good thing to do, and if we could get the facts we would not do so, but we are forced to do this; as a matter of fact, we have had to do it, and I think with great success, as can be shown.

Mr. ENLOE. Do you use the observations made on the water for the purpose of verifying these lines?

Prof. MENDENHALL. Yes, sir. We make a theory of the variations on land and we extend these lines out to sea and then there are observations made at sea. If our theory is far wrong that will show it, and if not we will follow it. Most of this work, of course, has been land work. We have had perhaps a thousand stations carried through the United States at which the observation of the magnetic constant is made. I do not mean that we keep men at these magnetic stations, but to each one we send a man out who spends two or three days at one station, after a few years he goes and makes the observations again, and a few years after that either he or another man goes there and makes observations, and only by doing that repeatedly have we found out at each one of these stations the change, and by applying that change we get these results.

Mr. ENLOE. As I understand you have not arrived at a point where you can say it is a law, but——

Prof. MENDENHALL. It is empirical, a law based on observations combined with, of course, a theoretical knowledge of magnetism.

Mr. ENLOE. You have not been able to determine what the law is?

Prof. MENDENHALL. No, sir; and we shall not be able to determine it until the work is continued for a great many years to come, and one of the important points involved in this is the question of the magnetic pole in the northern part of North America, and it would be a very important expedition which must sometime be undertaken, and the United States Government can well afford to undertake it now, to send an expedition to determine the magnetic pole. It would add very much to the solution of this problem we are considering.

Mr. ENLOE. Considering the number of years since the discovery of this variation of the needle by the scientific observers here and elsewhere, how long do you think it will be before they can ascertain what that law is and determine it definitely unless you make that expedition?

Prof. MENDENHALL. I wish I could answer that question.

Mr. ENLOE. Considering the degree of progress you have made here?

Prof. MENDENHALL. The progress of science is such it may be discovered to-morrow. We may know to-morrow, but of course I do not expect it, and it may be fifty or one hundred years, or ten years; but as every year goes by we are increasing the accuracy of the work with great precision.

It will interest the committee, probably, if I illustrate, as I have some curves which only came in yesterday, a very curious relation we are constantly finding between magnetic phenomena and some other phenomena. In the absence of a stationary observatory, which I was about to mention, this connection would not have been detected. On that sheet I have there a couple of tide curves. This is the tide at San Francisco on the 22d of March, and here is the tide at the Hawaiian Islands of the same date, and you will see there are some peculiar features in these curves. You will see that the end of the curve starts out smooth, and here it is quite rough, and here it is a little rough at this point. Usually the tide curve is nearly smooth, being affected but little by the motion of ordinary waves dashing against the wharf. These waves show that they were at least half an hour in length, that is, half an hour from the crest of one wave to the crest of another wave. Very curiously, on the same date and covering the same hours, we had some men making magnetic observations in an observatory in Texas, which we have had there for several years, and the observations show a series of curves distributed in the same way.

Thus you see now a very unusual disturbance [illustrating]; toward the latter end you can see the roughness of the curve. This curve is photographed. A very delicately suspended magnetic needle has a mirror so arranged as to reflect a beam of light which strikes against a sensitive sheet, and that sheet is kept in motion all the time, and if the needle is at absolute rest, of course, it makes a straight line on that sheet, but if the needle is waving at all the line of light is variable, and as the sheet moves it produces a curve like this [illustrating]. This is the way in which we get the history of the changes in magnetic forces at this time going on, and this is taken every hour, minute, and second. We have a record of just what has been done. When this came to us it attracted our attention that this happened to the tide at Honolulu and the tide at San Francisco at the same time, and also that there was at the same time a disturbance of the magnetic needle in Texas. What is the explanation?

The only explanation I know of is that it was a submarine earthquake; that is, an earthquake underneath the sea, that occurred at that time between San Francisco and the Sandwich Islands, which produced this wave, and this wave of course affected the tide registers. This is perfectly simple, and we have had it happen before, that a submarine earthquake has produced this effect. Now, in regard to its magnetic influence, this is not the first time we have had the same thing occur to the magnetic needle, and I had a suspicion a year or two ago of a precisely similar phenomenon. Now, the explanation of that is, and this is the only one that I am prepared to suggest, that the compression of the crust of the earth, due to the passage of the wave of that earthquake, altered the magnetic constant in the magnetic field and produced this variation of the needle. It is a simple fact, but it may be a fact that is filled with the utmost importance in the solution of these problems which are before us, and I bring it to your attention because it shows the value of keeping on doing this work without always being absolutely sure that every day's record is worth so many dollars and is going to accomplish some particular thing; because we can not tell what this may be worth in the next ten years; we can not tell how it will lend itself to the solution of this magnetic problem.

A study of the sun is another thing of the very utmost importance in the solution of that problem, but I presume if we were to devote ourselves in the Coast Survey to an observation of the spots upon the sun we would probably be subject to criticism because everybody would ask, what has that to do with the production of charts for the use of navigators, but as a matter of fact we should have been doing it for the last twenty-five years if it had not been that somebody else did it for us, because it has been the solution of one element of this problem of magnetics. It has been found, as many of you are aware, that the appearance and disappearance of the spots upon the sun is accompanied by a movement of the magnetic needle, not a small movement but a considerable movement, so by having a good knowledge of the coming and going and periodicity of the spots upon the sun, which we have now, thanks to the astronomers, particularly of Europe, we are enabled to put them into our knowledge of magnetics, and the magnetic constant from our own magnetic observations in Texas and elsewhere shows the appearance and disappearance of the spots upon the sun with perfect regularity and precision. Going back one hundred years if I had the magnetic constant I could predict the sun spots which appeared upon the sun. The value of this is very apparent.

Mr. ENLOE. I want to ask you if the Astro-Physical Observatory is not doing that work?

Prof. MENDENHALL. It probably will eventually, but it has not taken up the problem.

The CHAIRMAN. I would suggest, professor, that you suspend your remarks at this point, as some members of the committee are obliged to be upon the floor at this time.

Prof. MENDENHALL. Mr. Chairman, I hope that the committee will not only indulge me another hour, but more than that if necessary, because I am proceeding a little more slowly than I anticipated, but I am glad to have had these questions come up, but I wish to have full opportunity to present the work of the Survey.

Thereupon the committee adjourned to meet on Tuesday, May 22, 1894.

COMMITTEE ON NAVAL AFFAIRS,
Tuesday, May 22, 1893.

The Committee on Naval Affairs this day met, Hon. AMOS J. CUMMINGS in the chair.

The CHAIRMAN. We will proceed with this hearing informally until we get a quorum if Prof. Mendenhall is ready to proceed.

STATEMENT OF PROF. T. C. MENDENHALL—Continued.

Prof. Mendenhall then addressed the committee; he said:

Mr. CHAIRMAN AND GENTLEMEN OF THE COMMITTEE: I have already referred to the number of operations which are necessary to the actual construction of a chart, but do not actually appear on the chart, but are operations preliminary to its construction, namely, the operations of base-line measurement, triangulation, astronomical work, tidal observations, and magnetics. The chart usually contains a note, in which the results of tidal observations are given, and it also contains a note and at least one or two compasses drawn on the face of the chart, which give the result of the magnetic observations as far as it can be used on that particular chart. With these exceptions none of the work which I have thus far referred to, and which constitutes by far the greater part necessary to the production of the chart, appears, and I think I am justified in saying from 75 to 90 per cent of the whole work does not appear on the chart.

We come this morning to that which does appear on the chart, the first being the topography. The topography shown on the chart is restricted to the exhibition of the coast line, which is absolutely necessary, and to a certain strip of topography adjacent to the coast line, the width of which strip is regulated by circumstances and conditions. As I stated in the beginning, it is dependent upon two conditions, commerce and defense. For the purposes of commerce the strip of topography must be sufficiently wide to show all prominent features, so that the navigator, in case he is approaching a harbor, will be able to identify the prominent natural features, such as hills, valleys, and rivers, and also such artificial or "culture" features, as they are technically called, as will be of any use to him in guiding his vessel and determining his course, as, for instance, very prominent buildings, church spires, and all that sort of thing. Of course, in every kind of a harbor chart a very careful delineation of all these artificial features is required, as they are extremely useful to the navigator.

Some criticism has been made as to the extent to which the Coast and Geodetic Survey has carried this topography. I will not discuss that just at this moment, but I mention it to say that I will take it up a little later when I come to consider other criticisms upon the work of the survey, and will show, I think, beyond doubt, that the topography of the Coast and Geodetic Survey has been rather less in extent than might be expected, in fact rather less than the average of all other countries which maintain a coast survey, but I wish to call your attention as briefly as possible to the mode in which that topography is executed.

Suppose a harbor has not been surveyed at all, or a coast has not been surveyed at all. It is necessary to provide for the triangulation which I have already explained, and to establish points and their geographical relation to each other, and to other fixed points of the base line and datum planes.

The topographer is then sent to the field. Before going out. he receives what is called his "projection sheet," which I will merely show you here. (Exhibiting same.) This is the thing the topographer starts out with. It contains, as you see, lines crossing each other, which represent the parallels of latitude and the meridians of longitude drawn at the proper distances apart, according to the nature of the work. This is all he has, except certain points, which you can see here marked by small black dots scattered over the sheet, showing triangulation points, the geographical positions of which have been accurately determined by the previous work. Now, the topographer starts out with this sheet in his possession. He then, by various methods, which I can not well detail here, makes a topographical survey, the first essential naturally being the drawing of the shore line. This may be done in various ways, as I have said, but I will remark that the topographical method in general use in the Coast and Geodetic Survey has been the "plane table" method. That word defines it.

By means of this plane table he carries this sheet, of which a portion is exposed, and on this sheet is actually constructed the map of the country, the topographical map which he is drawing. This is not the method which is used universally in the world, but it is, we think, the cheapest method that is in use, and we think for excellence, combined with cheapness, there is no method comparable to plane-table work. The great ordnance survey of Great Britain was not made with the plane table, but was made by the use of a very much more expensive process, a process which, in the judgment of many topographers, is not nearly so good, and which did not give such accurate results as the plane-table method.

The completed work of the topographer is shown on this chart [exhibiting same]. This shows Fishers Island.

I began by showing a published chart of a portion of Long Island Sound containing Fishers Island. The sheet before you is actually the original sheet made by the topographer in the field in 1882, Mr. Hergesheimer, who is now dead. These points marked in red show the triangulation points, which were first determined in order that he might proceed with the plane-table method in the construction of the chart. Of course without these points the proper construction of the chart would have been absolutely impossible. So the first operation, the first thing embraced in the production of a chart, is the topography. Here, you will see, the whole island is surveyed, many of the charts only show a narrow rim of topography, but this scale is very large, being 1-10,000 of nature, and here, for the purpose of navigation, the whole area is actually required to be shown.

We give here all buildings, wharves, and all that kind of thing. This being a small island, that is thought to be necessary and desirable for the purpose of the navigator and also for the purposes of defense. This is the same thing [exhibiting] showing the north shore; and is also an original sheet. It will be only necessary to hold it up to let you see something of the nature of the work we have done, especially the topographical work. We do not extend the topography indefinitely. We only take a certain strip showing the coast and shore line, which in this case is exceedingly intricate.

Now, the next step, and the final step in the field in the production of this chart is the hydrographic work; and I would like to ask the special attention of the committee to the method of doing this which I will explain of course as briefly as possible. You will observe that we have now got the topographic work on the sheet and we are now ready for the hydrographic work, or even ready before, since whenever the shore line is completed it can be furnished for the hydrographic work. This chart shown here exhibits the same area, the same Fisher's Island, ready for the hydrographic work. When a hydrographer goes to the field this sheet is what he takes with him.

The hydrographic party may be either a party of naval officers or civilians who have undertaken to do the hydrographic work. A sheet like this [exhibiting same] is taken with him, necessary data being in this case the shore line, which shall be actually drawn on the sheet, and as many other artificial points, such as church steeples, prominent buildings, and particularly the triangulation points should be platted on the sheet as may be necessary to guide the hydrographer in the execution of the hydrographic work. This forms the original sheet of the hydrographic survey. With regard to the execution of the hydrographic survey, I may say briefly, it consists, as I am sure everybody knows, of running a line of soundings in a definite direction and in definitely located positions. It is of no use for a hydrographer to go out on the water and drop his lead and determine the depth of the water unless he knows exactly where that lead is dropped so he can indicate its position on the chart; consequently you will all see the absolute necessity for this preliminary topographic work in order that the positions may be located. Various methods of locating these soundings on the hydrographic maps have been adopted from time to time, and later on I will say something about the changes of methods which have taken place in the last twenty years, but now I will state how it is executed at the present time by us. If it is what we call inshore hydrography, that is, if it is not far from the shore and where points on the shore can be seen quite readily, the work is executed from a boat. If the vessel has a sufficient force there may be two or three boat parties, each of which will contain enough men to row the boat, and of course a leadsman who drops the lead and calls out the depth, and also a recorder who records the soundings, and two men, usually young ensigns if the work is done by a naval party, with sextants.

The use of the sextant is to determine the exact position of the boat at any given time, and the sextant of each man will determine the angle between two points on the shore, which may be high church spires or signals on hills, or any other features marked on the chart. One man determines the angle between two points, while at the same instant the other man determines the angle between one of these points and the third. This is known as the method of the three-point problem. By means of these angles they can quickly plat on the chart the position of the boat when the observations were made. It is not necessary and it is not customary to determine by angles the position of the boat at each dropping of the lead. ·

We find that when the boat moves at a uniform rate, soundings intermediate between two determined positions of the boat may be laid down with a great degree of accuracy, if the time is noted at each dropping of the lead, as well as at each point determined by angles. The practice is to start at a certain point and run a straight line out to sea as far as necessary, and then off a little distance to run a parallel line.

I have here a sheet which shows the exact results of soundings in this area, and which gives you a better idea of it, perhaps, than I can in words. This sheet shows a very complete piece of work and will give you a good idea of its nature [exhibiting same]. As far as possible lines are run parallel to each other, and all of these points show where the soundings were made. These indicate the depth of the water in feet; and these other lines are run across the first series in order that if any errors should occur in this work they may be detected by the cross lines. That is to say, where these lines cross the depth of water should of course be the same by each line, and if it is not, the error is thus detected. Sometimes we run diagonal lines which give a still greater check, so we have the ground gone over quite thoroughly by the sounding parties. This method which you see here is our present method of making soundings.

Here is a survey around the same island (Fishers Island), and this chart is of value for purposes of illustration because it shows a large number of points determined by triangulation of the plane table which were actually necessary in order that these soundings could be made. For instance, running along this line [illustrating] the parties using the sextant would determine the angle between this, that, and another point, three points, and in that way certain positions would be located. We sometimes determine the positions by having parties stationed on the shore with instruments at two points, theodolites in both cases. A signal being given on the boat by the dropping of a handkerchief or flag, the theodolite is used at each station on the shore and the sextant on the boat, and afterwards the position can be platted on the chart. But much more of the work is done by the previous method, and that is the method which is preferred. ●

This chart is a very good representation of the modern method of doing hydrographic work of this character. The tidal observations must be made constantly at some near point. That is to say, we must have the several stages of the tide read very frequently, every hour or sometimes oftener than that, so that we may know the tidal curves, as I explained the other day. To obtain the real depth of the water the state of the tide when the sounding was made must be known. Let us say the sounding is made at high water. Now, the datum plane to which soundings are referred is mean low water. That is, whenever you see on one of our charts that the water is said to be 19 feet, it means 19 feet at mean low water. At high water it may be 24 feet, but by knowing the state of the tide at that moment we can of course reduce it and find out the exact depth of the water. The mean low water does not represent the lowest of low waters which may occur during any period, but represents the average. So if the chart shows

19 feet of water at one point, you may perhaps find at low water 21 feet or 17 or 18 feet, because low water varies. Low water is not always the same, nor is high water.

This kind of hydrography of which I now speak is that which gives what is sometimes called the topography of the bottom of the sea. The topographer on land represents on our chart, as we have seen, all the elevations and depressions, etc. Unfortunately we can not see the bottom of the sea, and therefore the methods of determining the variations and topography of the bottom of the sea must be quite different, and they are different, as I have shown. The comparison has often presented itself to me in this way. If one were surveying the topography of this country from a balloon floating at a long distance from the earth and he should let down a measuring line and take different depths and soundings, he could get a fairly good idea of the elevations and depressions of the surface of the earth, but as that is accessible to us we do better than that. We get the topography of the sea by the methods indicated.

There is another kind of hydrography, however, which is of very great importance and to which I must refer very briefly, which we call "physical hydrography," which differs from the preceding perhaps more with regard to the object that is in view than the method of procedure. This hydography which I have described explains itself. It is to give to the navigator the knowledge as to the depth of the water over which he can sail. Physical hydrography is rather for the purpose of studying the laws of the movements of the currents and tides at particular places, and especially for determining the effect of these currents and tides on the physical features of the land. It is well known to all of youth at our Atlantic seacoast particularly is constantly undergoing changes. We have hardly a harbor in this country that is a constant harbor; that is, nearly all are being modified as years go by, and some of them very materially so. This does not mean simply a modification of the bottom of the sea, although that is very marked in some particular harbors towards the south. If you take Charleston Harbor and Brunswick Harbor, and some others that have been rather recently looked into and take the shoals off Nantucket, the charts which have been published a year or two are out of date.

These changes which take place are very material, and even the land itself has changed, as in the case of New Jersey, for instance, where the changes have been very marked. Our chart of Charleston Harbor, in the present instance, shows a considerable projection of land out into the harbor which does not exist at the present time at all. We have been at work but we have not yet been able to bring that chart up to date, to show all of these changes. We want to determine what these changes are, and for the purposes of the navigation and civilization and enlightenment we want to determine the causes of the changes; we want to find out what is going on and why those changes are being brought about. This is what physical hydrography means, and some of our studies in physical hydrography have been in the past of the greatest importance. I might cite New York Harbor, where many of the improvements which have been made have been the results of the study of physical hydrography by the Coast Survey.

The study of the movements of the currents of the harbor and the passage of the water from Long Island Sound into the lower harbor is of very great value to commerce and to the city of New York, but we have been prevented from continuing that in the last two years by the absence of the man who began it, and the only man perhaps in the

country competent to do it. Physical hydrography is that sort of
hydrography by which we investigate the laws and operations of the
currents and their effect upon the coast, and the final results that may
be expected from these effects. We have not spent much money (particularly recently) on that subject, but we have usually one or two
parties for a few months every year engaged in physical hydrography.
It is a much more difficult process than ordinary hydrography, as the
refinement of measurements is necessarily greater; in other words, to
be a good physical hydrographer requires very long training and very
great experience. I regret to say we have but very few physical
hydrographers in this country and I have been endeavoring for the last
three or four years to secure one who, by his experience and training, would be qualified to do that work which lies before the Coast Survey in that direction and which would be of indefinite and almost infinite value if it could be done; and although I have searched the country
very thoroughly, I have been unable to find any one who could be
employed by us for that purpose.

Now, I wish to refer a little further to the matter of interior triangulation and a few other points which are brought out in our work, to
complete the presentation which I have attempted to make of the character of the work of the Survey. In addition to this interior triangulation, we carry on in the interior a system of precise levels which has
been authorized by appropriations of Congress for many years and
which is working its way also across the continent, having reached just
a little bit beyond Kansas City. That means we are running a line of
precise levels across the continent with as high a degree of precision as
we can. This degree of precision is of course very much higher than
that of the ordinary engineer leveling process. I say as high as we
can because I feel myself, and I am sure that others do, that we have
not yet the degree of precision in the leveling which is absolutely desirable, but I think we are equally as far along as foreign nations.

Now, the question might be asked: What is the use of running a
line of precise levels across the continent? There are innumerable
uses. In the first place, any map of the country which may be eventually made—it may not be made now, but in fifty years—but whenever
an accurate map of the United States is made it must contain the differences of levels and therefore it would be important for that. Take
France, for instance. France has only recently laid out a scheme of
precise leveling, which is one of the smallest operations of our Survey—
that is, we pay the least attention to it—and the total cost of this in
France is calculated to be about $5,000,000, a sum almost infinitely
large compared to anything we have expended or contemplated expending, and that shows the importance in which it is held by the French
Government. But there are other uses.

Only yesterday I had a call from a gentleman from Denver, who was
very anxious to know how soon or when our precise levels would reach
that city. He had been investigating the railroad surveys at Denver,
and had found, which is an interesting fact, and shows the importance of the work being done with the greatest precision, that by following the levels of the several railroads which enter that city, although
the rails came in and ran side by side into the depot, so that they looked
to be of the same level, he found actually a difference of 50 feet between
levels; that is, if he followed the level of one line and then the other
when they came together there appeared to be a difference of 50 feet.
Whenever it became necessary for railroads to connect with each other
leveling of that kind must be regarded as very curious, and I have had

the greatest demand for these precise levels by railroad engineers all over the country. We have run along the thirty-ninth parallel and we have planted bench marks wherever we could, definitely, and every geological-survey party that goes into the neighborhood and every State survey has attached itself to this line of levels. It is required, for instance, in Missouri, by the State geological survey for the purposes of triangulation, and although it is one of the least expensive operations I think we have been engaged in, yet it has been considered as one of the most important, and I speak of it as representing a part of the necessary operations carried on by the Coast Survey, which, of course, could only be carried on by the organization such as we now have.

Mr. ENLOE. On that point, I would like to ask if that could not be done by the Geological Survey?

Prof. MENDENHALL. Yes, sir; if you make the Geological Survey what the Coast and Geodetic Survey is, but you can not unless you do that. That is to say if you have the same men and the same standard of accuracy, with the same disposition, and same power in any corps of men, of course the same kind of work can be done, and that is perfectly clear, and it is not necessary to call it one thing or another, but without wishing to reflect at all upon the character of the work done by the Geological Survey the Geological Survey knows perfectly well it has never done such a thing and that with the present organization it would be absolutely impossible to do such work. It never had the material or the men or the organization by which such work can be done, and they will tell you that just as frankly as I will.

The CHAIRMAN. Speaking about the difficulty in finding experienced hydrographers, are there not experienced hydrographers in the Navy Department?

Prof. MENDENHALL. None of the kind of which I speak. There is not a man in the Navy Department who can be considered a hydrographer of the type of man to which I referred, and there can not be in the case of a man who works for three years on one thing and the next three years on another and whose whole interest is necessarily that of a warrior, whose service is in the military department of the Government and must naturally be.

The CHAIRMAN. Then is it your opinion the hydrographic department of the Navy is worthless?

Prof. MENDENHALL. By no manner of means.

The CHAIRMAN. If you can not get a hydrographer there, why is it not?

Prof. MENDENHALL. I use the word in a different sense from what you are using it; I particularly distinguished between the two types of hydrographers which we are discussing, and I think the committee will bear me out in that. That one type of hydrography which consists of making these coast soundings is done with excellent results by our naval officers.

The CHAIRMAN. If you will bear with me, I am endeavoring to learn why it is. Your long lecture is about the work of the Coast and Geodetic Survey, which, of course, is very interesting, but I want you to apply it to the bill, and I understand your position is this, that it is utterly impossible for the Navy Department or for the Geological Department to do the work which the Coast and Geodetic Survey are now doing?

Prof. MENDENHALL. Under the present organization of those two departments; yes, sir. That is my position. If you will pardon me, a little later on I hope——

Mr. ENLOE. Before you get away from that I want to know if you take the position that the Navy Department could not procure just as competent men as you have employed in the Coast and Geodetic Survey, or the Geological Survey could not get the same character of service you are using there?

Prof. MENDENHALL. I think the Navy Department would have great difficulty in securing the services of competent men. A transfer of a part of the work to the Geological Survey would undoubtedly result in lowering the standard of accuracy of such work. I will refer more at length to that subject later on. I am prepared to discuss that question, but I simply want to present the character of work before considering the character of organization necessary for its execution. I think that is the logical order in which it should be presented. I refer to this triangulation as being of value and to the precise leveling as being of value in furnishing points and datum planes for State surveys. The topography to which I have just referred, as I said the other day, and which I anticipated in the course of my remarks, is naturally restricted by us to a narrow line and has always been restricted intentionally. The triangulation necessary for the construction of State maps must be executed by the United States; it should not, in my judgment, be executed by local authority, and I would like to show just now one or two maps which illustrate what other nations have done in the direction of this triangulation, so it may be seen that we have not certainly at the present time done what we would have been expected to accomplish in this Government as compared with others.

I referred also the other day, and I will not expand upon it now, to the use of these triangulations being made in the various States. In the States of Tennessee, New Jersey, Minnesota, and other States there is more or less activity in this direction, and they have been of great use in local surveys.

Now, pardon me for interrupting just a moment to show a map of India. I spoke the other day of the survey of India. That chart will show just what has been done there in the way of a system of triangulation, whereas we have run a certain line, which is almost completed now, which would correspond to this one line across the country like this [illustrating on map]. We have also run another shorter line called our oblique arc running along there, and that is all we have thus far done, and, as will be seen, that nation has done much more. Here is a triangulation map of the continent of Europe which is on a smaller scale, but you will be able to see it very well and all the red lines indicate the triangulation, and you will see that practically the whole of Europe, with the exception of Russia, is almost covered with triangulations, and Russia has begun its extensive arc east and west of this line [illustrating] and has planned for another arc in a north and south direction. I wanted to exhibit this simply to show that we were very far behind in our work of this character, as compared with European nations.

I referred the other day to the usefulness of this triangulation work in regard to the settlement of boundary lines disputes.

I will add this morning to what I then stated; I referred to the boundary line between Pennsylvania and Delaware, and I would like to add that the boundary line between California and Nevada, which has been for a long time in dispute, is now being determined for a certainty by the Coast and Geodetic Survey. This is a line of exceeding difficulty. It has been already surveyed three or four times and the amount of money that has been already expended in attempting to survey that line I think is more than twice if not fully three times the amount the Coast and Geodetic Survey will extend for its complete execution in a manner which will never need to be repeated. The difficulty of that line is such that all previous attempts have been failures, and we have been called upon to execute the work by our methods and by our processes and they are so rigorous that it will be done in such a way it need never be done again, and at a much less cost than already expended on previous operations.

In the case of Ohio and Indiana, I think probably I referred to that the other day. A boundary-line dispute which was supposed to affect 1,200 square miles arose between those two States, and a very short examination of the subject by methods which we use and which could not be used by local authorities, as was well recognized by local surveyors, determined that instead of there being 1,200 square miles erroneously taken from one State to another there were about 100 square miles, and that, therefore, leaves it to the States to settle, and the value of that survey was very great compared with the cost of it.

I will say at this point also that in the work of our survey it is necessary to know the figure of the earth, the shape of the earth. For instance, in this boundary-line dispute between California and Nevada the reason why the line never was correctly surveyed before was because those who attempted it have not properly understood the method of surveying an oblate spheroid; that is, a round body which approximates very closely to the real figure of the earth.

Heretofore the United States has contributed in a very small way compared with most countries to a determination of the figure of the earth. Several years ago there was organized in Europe an international geodetic association, the principal object of which was to determine accurately the form of the earth. The United States, some years ago, shortly after the organization of that body, was made by treaty a member of that convention. We have not had a delegate there for several years, but still the Coast and Geodetic Survey is a part of that international convention for the determination of the figure of the earth. The necessity for this determination is shown whenever you attempt to run any extensive line such as this boundary line to which I have referred.

The figure of the earth, its general form, its dimensions, etc., can also be determined and the form of it can be ascertained with great degree of accuracy by what is known as gravimetric work, so we have included in the Coast Survey a determination of the force of gravity at various points upon the surface of the United States. Sir Isaac Newton was the first to recognize the importance of the study of the force of gravity in relation to the form of the earth, and was the first to suggest that it was an oblate spheroid flattened at the poles, instead of being a sphere, and everybody knows that the further you go from the center of the earth the less the force of gravity is; so if we determine the force of gravity at Washington and also at New York, Montreal, and say a hundred or a thousand other points throughout the country where it is desired to make such determinations, and then by bringing all those facts together and comparing the relative forces of gravity at these points, we are able to obtain the form or figure of the earth; so the gravimetric work of the Coast Survey is one of the features that has been carried on for a number of years. It has not caused a large expenditure of money, but it is a kind of work that everybody who knows anything about it knows requires very high attainments of mathematical and physical knowledge, and for a man to be successful in such observations he must have long training and experience, and I mention it as being one of the important things in which long and continued training is necessary in order to accomplish results.

Now, in addition to these things which I have mentioned and which I have touched on this morning quite rapidly, because I wish to use no more of the committee's time than I am entitled to, we have a very important bureau in the Coast and Geodetic Survey to which I feel bound to refer at some greater length, and that is the Office of Weights and Measures. This bill, which provides for the breaking up and destruction of the Survey and its division into two bureaus, makes no provision whatever for the distribution of the office of Weights and Measures. There is nothing said about the Office of Weights and Measures in this bill. Now, what is the intention of Congress in case this action should be successful of course I can not know. I would like to call your attention to the great importance of that office, and to its original connection with the Survey, and to the fact that it must have an administration which can not differ greatly from the present administration. It has been suggested, I believe, by some person that it might remain a bureau of the Treasury Department. Of course it might remain a bureau of the Treasury Department, and I think it belongs more properly to the Treasury Department than to any other, just as I think all of this work belongs there more than anywhere else; but if it is disconnected from its present relations with the Coast and Geodetic Survey it would at once become one of two things. It would be either practically destroyed and its usefulness would be lost, ·or else it would at once become a source of very serious expense to the Government. It is now maintained, as I shall ·show, at a cost less than that of any similar bureau maintained by any other government in the world. This is solely on account of its relations to the Coast and Geodetic Survey. It became necessary, as I think I stated in the beginning, to have standards of the highest degree of precision in order to carry on the Coast Survey. The first superintendent, Mr. Hassler, was sent to London to obtain these standards and he brought over with him a standard 82-inch bar, a very interesting and curious historic relic which we now have in the Coast and Geodetic Survey. This bar was divided into inches by a prominent London instrument maker and it was supposed to represent the English yard and inch at that time, and it became the foundation for the standard of the Coast and Geodetic Survey operations.

Now, when the Government discovered, as it did very early, of course, that it was necessary to have a standard of weights and measures in order to collect customs properly, it gave attention then to the fixing of this standard, and it became important to know what a yard was in order to levy customs on the yard. It became important to know what a pound was, so that the weight of a pound might be properly used in the levying of customs, and the whole people of the United States were, of course, greatly interested in this. Now, it is known to all of you that the Constitution of the United States authorizes Congress to provide a system of weights and measures and coinage, but perhaps many of you do not recollect that with regard to weights and measures Congress has almost absolutely neglected that duty. Of course, in regard to coinage something had to be done, and that was done at an early day, but for a long period the U. S. Government had no legislation on the subject of weights and measures, and the consequence was there grew up all over the Union widely varied standards of weights and measures.

New York, for instance, had a different gallon and pound, and the other States had standards which were different. This was of course a very unhappy condition of things, and gave rise to the establishment of the Office of Weights and Measures, in Washington, in the Coast Survey, primarily for the object of furnishing to the Treasury Department the standards of weights and measures and adjusting them, and, secondly, for the object not of legislating, because the Treasury Department had no power to legislate, but to furnish to all the States of the Union copies of the standards which were in use by the Government, in the hope that the various States of the Union might follow its example and adopt these copies of the standards. This was done, and this was one of the first important functions of the Office of Weights and Measures, and nearly all the States of the Union adopted the standards distributed by the U. S. Government as their standard; that is, they adopted the copies distributed, and New York by and by gave up its standard, and thus they came to have an absolute uniformity.

I know of no subject to day on which ignorance is so prevalent as the subject of weights and measures; and it is a fact that there have been certain Territories and States which have very severe laws to punish anyone who uses false weights and measures, and yet there is no law whatever which prescribes what the weights and measures shall be. It all rests on tradition, there being no legislation. The United States Government has never prescribed a system of standard weights and measures, but in 1866 .the metric system was made permissive. Therefore, the Coast and Geodetic Survey, being engaged in doing this precise work and requiring a standard, it was easy to make the Superintendent of the Coast Survey the superintendent of the office of weights and measures, and that has continued from that time until to-day, and the Superintendent of the Coast Survey is to-day the superintendent of the office of weights and measures.

Now, the operations of that office are very varied and are of the utmost importance, and I wish to call your attention to a few of the operations which we perform in that office, after which I wish to refer to the relatively very small expense that the Government is subject to in the conduct of that office. These weights are obtained by the public from various sources, the Fairbanks Scale Company is one, the Howe Scale Company is another, and many other scale companies. Now, what guarantee have the people that the Fairbanks pound is a pound or that the Howe Scale Company's pound is a pound? There must be a standard of reference. Now, that standard is our office in the Coast and Geodetic Survey. The Fairbanks, the Howe, and all the scale companies invariably from time to time send their standards to us and we correct the standards for them and determine the error for them and thus they have necessarily kept in touch with us because our office is the only properly legalized representative of these weights.

Mr. GEISSENHAINER. May I ask you what is the average variation?

Prof. MENDENHALL. It will depend entirely upon the kind of weight you have. For instance, the weight which is ordinarily used for rough purposes in the market may vary as much as 10 per cent from the true weight, while the druggist's weight is much more accurate. It is to the credit of such great establishments as Fairbanks and Howe that they have taken the greatest pains and have gone to the greatest expense to have the most accurate and precise standards possible, and are doing that almost weekly. Such firms, for instance, as the Howe

Company will keep a pound a few years as a standard and then send it back and have it corrected.

Mr. GEISSENHAINER. How do you acquire your standards?

Prof. MENDENHALL. Our standard weights at present are fixed in a very curious and a very interesting way, and I am very glad to answer that question. The only general legislation which Congress has made in regard to weights and measures was in 1866, when they passed a law legalizing the use of the metric system, that will be known to many of you. So that, curiously enough, it happens that the meter and the kilogram are to-day the legal measures of weight and length of the whole United States, whereas the pound and yard have not been legalized by act of Congress. That is a curious condition of things, but, after all, many of us have considered it rather desirable; that is, we have not regretted that Congress has been slow in doing this because it enabled us more readily to put ourselves on the same plane with other great governments in adopting a true unit of measure and mass like the kilogram and meter. About twenty years ago an international organization was formed of a most interesting character for an examination of standard weights and measures, that is, for the construction and adoption of a standard meter and a standard kilogram, and about twenty-five nations are in this organization, which is known as the International Bureau of Weights and Measures. It does its work on a small plot of ground near Paris, which, as far as anything can be, is absolutely a neutral spot of ground.

This plot of ground was demanded by these twenty-five great nations as a neutral spot of ground and it is so. These nations have claimed it and the French have admitted it. During the last twenty years it has devoted itself to the construction of beautiful standard copies of the kilogram and meter. This work was carried on until about three years ago it was completed and these copies were distributed among the twenty-five nations, to England and all European nations and many of the South American nations. We received about three or four years ago two beautiful copies of this international meter, made of platinum iridium, and we also received two copies of the international kilogram, which is a weight of a little more than 2 pounds (22.10 pounds), also made of platinum iridium, and this standard in the absence of any legislation has been adopted as our standard. In view of the absence of any legislation determining our standard, and in view of the fact that our old Hassler yard, so-called, is a very rude and a crude standard, such as no civilized nation to-day would adopt, we have adopted the meter and kilogram in accordance with the international agreement as the standard of length and the standard of mass in this country, and the Secretary of the Treasury, in a bulletin issued a little more than a year ago, defined the yard as being a certain fraction of a meter and defined a pound as being a certain fraction of a kilogram, and so our pound and yard are derived from this international agreement and standard.

The CHAIRMAN. I would suggest, professor, that the hour has now arrived for the meeting of the House. How much more time do you desire to complete your remarks?

Prof. MENDENHALL. I should think I could get through in two more hours.

The CHAIRMAN. While your remarks are very interesting and instructive the point before the committee is whether you claim it is utterly impossible for the Navy Department and the Geological Survey to do the work which you are now doing, and the reason why?

Prof. MENDENHALL. It is just what I wish to present, but I would like to say now I do not claim of course the utter impossibility of their performing anything, but I claim this thing should not be done unless one or two things should be secured, greater efficiency or greater economy. Those are the points.

Thereupon the committee adjourned to meet on Friday, May 25, 1894.

COMMITTEE ON NAVAL AFFAIRS,
Friday, May 25, 1894.

The Committee on Naval Affairs this day met, Hon. Amos J. Cummings in the chair.

The CHAIRMAN. The committee will come to order, and if Prof. Mendenhall is ready to proceed with his remarks we will be obliged to him.

STATEMENT OF PROF. T. C. MENDENHALL—Continued.

Prof. Mendenhall then addressed the committee, he said:

Mr. CHAIRMAN AND GENTLEMEN OF THE COMMITTEE. I wish to refer very briefly again this morning to the operation of the office of weights and measures which I had just begun to consider at my last hearing before the committee. In addition to the standardizing of weights to which I then referred at some length, this office standardizes tapelines, yard measures, and all sorts of linear measures for engineers. In fact the whole engineering fraternity of the country depends upon the office of weights and measures for the accurate determination of their units of length. We have a long standard, 100 feet long, which is frequently in use for standardizing these tape measures for use as standards of precision for the engineers of the country. It is not necessary to mention farther the benefits which must result from this class of work.

In addition, referring to some perhaps rather more refined work and a work of great importance to the Government, the other work being of more importance to the people at large, I will refer to the standardizing of bars for the Ordnance Bureau. The very accurate and precise measurements which are necessary for the construction of ordnance are only possible, of course, through the acquisition and possession of very precise standards. These standards have been prepared at our office. The office also does a very extensive work for the Treasury Department which relates directly to the collection of internal revenue, not only for the standardization of the ordinary weights, etc., on which the whole collection of revenue depends, but a special standardization of alcoholometers and hydrometers which are used for the determination of the strength of liquors and various kinds of alcohols. These all come to the office of weights and measures and they are standardized and prepared for use. Also the very extensive collection of revenue from sugars throughout the last few years, and for many years in fact, has depended upon the standardization made by the office of weights and measures.

You are doubtless quite familiar with the methods of determining the various grades of sugar, and among others is what is known as the polariscope test. It may not be seen at first just what relation we have with a polariscopic test, but a slight reflection will show that it must be a close one. The principle of that test will be of interest to you doubtless, for I can illustrate it on a little arrangement I have here, so as to give you an idea of the work of that character. You are all aware of the fact that in ordinary eyeglasses there are two kinds of glasses which are commonly used, one of which is known as the pebble glass, the other the ordinary glass. The pebble glass is ground out of quartz, so that they are higher priced and usually possess some desirable qualifications, one being that the pebble glass is rather more transparent, but this difference is not apparent without a careful scrutiny.

If you go to a well-arranged optician's establishment and ask to buy pebble or ordinary glasses, he will show you at once the means of detecting one kind from the other, but they look very much alike and there is a great deception practiced all over the country in that respect. Many hundreds of thousands of glasses sold as pebble are not pebble glasses. The reliable optician will show you at once the manner of determining the true pebble, by means of a little instrument, which is the very instrument used in determining the standard of sugar. Because of its simplicity I thought it well to present it. Here is a device such as is used for the inspection of pebble glass made into spectacles. It consists simply of two plates of a peculiar crystal that is known as "tourmaline," one in front and the other in the rear and a space between for the introduction of the glass which is to be determined, or the sugar, if you are going to determine sugar.

This crystal has a very peculiar property of polarizing the light; that is to say, by looking through one of those crystals it is partially transparent, having a slight greenish shade, which is always a characteristic of this kind of a crystal, and if I look through the other it is equally transparent. If I put both together and look through them I will see clearly and distinctly. If I turn it a little, if I move it about in a certain line as I now turn it in this direction [exhibiting], in such a position, the light is absolutely cut off. In other words, it has a peculiar property that after the light has passed through one of these it can not go through the other unless the other is in a certain definite position. If I arrange it so [exhibiting] the light is cut off and then insert between those two glasses my own eyeglass and look through it, the light is still cut off. If, however, I insert a pebble glass, which is ground from crystal, instantly the field is clear, although the two glasses look precisely alike, and you are not able to detect the difference, yet one of them in the field renders' it instantly clear and transparent while the other does not. I have shown you this simply to make the point that a crystal possesses the property which it has been found is possessed by a solution of sugar that of twisting a ray of light after it has passed through one of these polarizing pieces and to turn it in such way that it can go on through the other, whereas if it is not twisted or turned in that way it can not go through the other.

The CHAIRMAN. How is it when the tourmaline crystals both carry the light: what effect does it have on the crystal itself?

Prof. MENDENHALL. None at all.

The CHAIRMAN. Is it dark?

Prof. MENDENHALL. No, sir; it is not dark. It does not change it sensibly, and if the quartz is a little different from the sugar the effect of the sugar would be as intimated, to twist this ray a little and reproduce the darkness, but unless the crystal is somewhat different from the solution of sugar it simply clears the field up in the manner I have indicated. It happens to some extent, if I insert here instead of this quartz crystal a solution of sugar, which is put in any kind of a tube about that long [illustrating], with the ends properly ground, and of clear glass; if we put that solution of sugar between these two polarizing pieces the result is that there is a certain rotation of the ray of light, the amount of which can be determined by this eyepiece in the manner I have indicated, and it is the amount of that turn, taken in connection with the length of the tube and the concentration of the solution of sugar, that determines the purity of the sugar. That is what is meant by sugar of so many degrees in your tariff laws. It is so many degrees of rotation of this eyepiece which clears up the field or appearance, or change of color, according to the system we may use.

Mr. GEISSENHAINER. What is meant by the word "fine?"

Prof. MENDENHALL. If it was 95° it would mean a rotation of 95° in order to produce a certain definite effect, and that effect varies; it may be used to produce the greatest degree of darkness, or probably to produce the maximum degree of light, or a certain color of light, and it is turned until that is produced. But in one way or another it is easily established that the amount of the grape sugar in this solution is determined with great precision by this method, and by a higher precision, of course, than any other simple method that has been devised. Thus you can in a moment determine—I mean in half an hour probably—the quality of the sugar, whereas a chemical analysis would be a long, laborious, and expensive affair.

Now, our part of this work, which has been of great importance to the Government, and which can not be done except, of course, where proper arrangements and proper men are to be found, consists in standardizing these quartz plates which are used here as an equivalent of the sugar solution. The quartz plates come from Europe, and they are ground to a certain definite degree of thickness and have a purely arbitrary numerical standard attached to them, and when they come, in order that they may be used, we prepare our own solution of sugar of so many degrees. We make various degrees of the solution of sugar. We put that sugar in these tubes. We then put these quartz plates in and work at it until we find what is the real meaning of the various workings of that polariscope in sugar strength. That is called standardizing the quartz plates, and we do that for all the custom-houses in the country. Three or four years ago there was a very great difference in the standards of sugar determination in the three great cities of Boston, New York, and Philadelphia, and the sugar dealers were constantly complaining that at one of these places, I have forgotten which, sugars of a very low grade were quoted as sugars of a high grade, or vice versa.

Mr. TALBOTT. It was stated against Baltimore in that way.

Prof. MENDENHALL. So as a result we were called upon to make a general investigation of the subject of the standardizing of these plates. I will say that the same subject was first referred several years ago to a committee of the National Academy of Sciences and they prepared one or two standard plates for use by the Government. But we found on taking up this question that even the National Academy had overlooked the consideration of one or two essential features which we were obliged to notice, namely, the effect of temperature on this quartz constant, and we spent, therefore, a good deal of time going over the work, with the final result that the sugar standard, when we finished that careful investigation, is to-day, I think, uniform throughout the United States at all points. Every now and then we get such quartz plates to be standardized.

More than that, we must standardize all the flasks which the sugar inspectors use. It would not do to let the standard of the flasks of the inspector at New York, or Washington, or Philadelphia, or Baltimore differ, because on this the uniformity of the work depends, so, we being separated entirely from the revenue collection, having nothing whatever to do with it, standardize all of these flasks, and then they are distributed. Thermometers are also standardized by us for the very same reason, and in the matter of the sugar standard alone I think it can be stated that the value of this bureau has exceeded many times its total cost to the Government in the last few years. It has saved in that time much expensive litigation.

I might tell you other things we do, while I am referring to the more important operations of the office of weights and measures. Another important thing is to come to us very soon, owing to the remarkable growth of a new industry in the last ten years. There has been a bill introduced into Congress (No. 6500) for the adoption of a system of units of electrical measure. We now have in the United States probably $200,000,000 or $300,000,000 invested in electricity, in electrical machinery, and instruments for the use of electricity, and all that enormous capital is doing a commercial business absolutely without measuring the product which it puts forth or consumes. It is very much as if we were to do our commercial business of the country without the means of determining what a yard or a pound was; everybody here realizes that commerce would be in a very confused condition in such a case.

That is true in regard to electricity at this time. You make contracts with electrical companies to do a certain thing to light your town or city, and they agree to put up so many candle-power lights aroundyour town or city, say 2,000 candle power, and they apparently comply with that agreement. You have no means whatever of determining if they do comply with that agreement and you have no legal process to make them comply with it. There is no legislation at all upon the subject. A 2,000-candle-power light is, for instance, almost unknown in the ordinary arc light. It is a tradition that the electric lights are 2,000 candle power. There are very few of them that have more than 1,000 candle power and they run from 600 or 800 up to, perhaps, 1,500 candle power for the very best, and yet contracts are made in terms of 2,000 candle-power lights. Now, both sides have suffered in the last few years from the lack of a standard.

The people have suffered, and have suffered with less complaint than those who furnished it, the contractors, but the latter occasionally have been made to suffer very materially by people refusing to fulfill the contracts which, after all, were being satisfactorily executed by the contractors, and thus there has grown, as I say without further detail, a very great demand for these electrical units. An international congress of electricity was held at Chicago last summer, the fourth held since 1881, for the purpose of determining electrical units. They were agreed upon unanimously, and a bill has been introduced in the House for a legal adoption of those units in this country. We feel, and have every reason to believe and hope the bill will become a law. There can not be any opposition to it, and it is requested by all the great electric companies in the country. Companies representing $100,000,000 have petitioned for the passage of that bill, and certainly the interest of the people demand it.

I give this to show that before long the furnishing of an electrical standard is a thing which must come to the office of weights and measures. There is no other place for it to go under the Government, and there can be no other place in the Government, and I think it will be readily seen that in order to conduct it properly it will require a class of men to supervise it and administer it who have given their attention and energies to this subject for many years. You can not put work of this kind, so obscure and difficult, in the hands of those who are not trained to it.

Now, a word in regard to the relation of this bureau and the Coast Survey. I said the other day, by reason of the relation of this bureau to the Coast and Geodetic Survey the maintenance of the bureau has been a great source of economy to the Government.

The cost of this bureau for the present year, with all of this very important work that I have detailed, has been the trifling sum of $4,690, and that is what it is proposed to appropriate for the coming year—only $4,690. In other words, we employ in that bureau only 4 persons—an adjuster, a mechanician, a messenger and a watchman—and the bureau costs nothing at all for rent of building. We have not even a clerk in that bureau. Now, this is possible, and only possible, by the fact that the superintendent of the Coast and Geodetic Survey is superintendent of this office of weights and measures, and he administers it, therefore, without additional compensation and without additional cost. The office has its home in the office of the Coast Survey, and it has its administration in its executive officer. In the officers of the Coast Survey there are several quite competent to do this work, and under the direction of the superintendent, who must be always one who has had more or less experience in this sort of thing, the work goes on in such a way that it has always been recognized as of high standing both at home and abroad

The relation we have determined between the meter and yard has a standing equal to, if not higher, than any European authorities, and if this bureau were to be taken away from the Coast and Geodetic Survey, under its present organization, its cost would immediately multiply itself many times. It must do that or else the Government must decide it will ignore an organization of this kind, which, of course, no Government can do. Its cost will not be less than $30,000, $40,000, or $50,000 a year, and most of the European governments spend as much as $100,000 on it, while in England they have a large building and a large corps of officers distinct from other bureaus for the execution of this work. This, I think, is one of the strong arguments for the continuation of the relations which exist between this bureau and the Coast and Geodetic Survey.

Now, gentlemen, having thus given in detail, which I trust has not been fatiguing, as I felt it necessary that you may have some idea of the work of the office, I will refer directly to the proposed change, the proposed modification of this bureau, and I will repeat what I said in the beginning, that any change of this kind ought to be made for some reason. I think all of you will agree with me, that unless there is some reason for this change it is uncalled for, and I fancy you will agree with me in the statement that that reason can only be one of two things—either to secure a greater efficiency in the execution of the work, or a greater economy in the execution of the work, or both—and I propose to speak as briefly and as rapidly as possible in regard to those two things.

As to the matter of efficiency I think I can justly say the efficiency can not well be better than it is now and may easily be less, but the fact that it can not be greater, I think I can show, if it is necessary, by the united testimony of those who are qualified to judge in this country and all over the world, as to the efficiency of this bureau. You may think it is too expensive, but I say as to the work, as to the output of the bureau, it has received the commendation of the civilized world; but I will refer a little more to this subject of efficiency, and particularly to the relation of the present system to the naval contingent of the Coast and Geodetic Survey. I want to speak first of the value of the present system to the naval officers and the value of the present system to the Coast and Geodetic Survey. To do that clearly I will invite your attention to what probably many of you know, and that is what the present system is.

We have now a detail from the Navy Department to the Coast and Geodetic Survey of 41 naval officers, the highest ranking officer being that of a lieutenant-commander (we have not had for many years a ranking officer higher than that) and running down to the rank of ensign, the larger number being lieutenants, and we have 250 men. That is our detail from the Navy Department at the present time. We are indebted, therefore, to the Navy Department, an indebtedness which we have never failed to recognize in every possible way, although I know the contrary has been stated, and which I wish to show is a misunderstanding before I get through. We are indebted, therefore, to the Navy Department for what I might say the loan of those men in the execution of the operations of the Coast and Geodetic Survey. The reason for that, of course, grows out of the original idea of the organization of the Bureau. As I said in the beginning, it is organized very much on the basis of the Light-House Establishment, which we know is precisely similar in this respect, except that the Navy Department loans officers of a very much higher rank than to us; it loans officers to the Fish Commission; it has been the same way in many bureaus, because the method had, as I firmly believe, many advantages on both sides.

I do not wish to fail to recognize the advantages of this organization, and I repeat, then, that we might say that the Navy Department has loaned those officers and men, and therefore the cost of the naval contribution to the Coast and Geodetic Survey is very easily and very accurately ascertained. It has been stated, I think either before the committee or elsewhere, that there were no means of telling what this Coast and Geodetic Survey was costing. A very curious statement certainly, and I remind you that there is no bureau of the Government, I think I may safely say that, which makes a more accurate and precise accounting to the Government of its works than the Coast and Geodetic Survey. Every year there is put before Congress, and every year there is put on your tables, I fancy, a letter written by the Superintendent of the Coast and Geodetic Survey to the Secretary of the Treasury, in which the expenditure of every dollar of the appropriation is shown and in which every man who receives a dollar of that appropriation is found. That is done annually and there need be no question or doubt in regard to what is done. We are therefore indebted, as I say, to the Navy for the expenses of these men, which amount to about $17,000 a month for both officers and men, or, in round numbers, almost exactly $200,000 per annum is what the Navy Department contributes at the present time. Now, it will be borne in mind that this is all they contribute. That is all, and I say that not wishing to lessen the value of the contribution, but the vessels all belong to the Coast and Geodetic Survey, all the maintenance of the vessels comes from the Coast and Geodetic Survey appropriation, and the pay of any extra subsistence which may be given to the officers or men, and the traveling expenses

of the men across the continent, back and forth, all comes from the Coast
and Geodetic Survey appropriation; in fact, every dollar of it, except
simply the salary of those men who are detailed. Now, these naval
officers and men at the present time are found upon eight vessels; that is
to say, we have eight vessels at this time in commission. These are not
large vessels; the largest of them, I think, is 600 or 700 tons burden
(the *Patterson*), which is a vessel engaged almost entirely in Alaska
work. They run from that down. We have seven steam vessels and
one schooner.

The CHAIRMAN. Are these vessels owned by the Navy or by the
Treasury Department?

Prof. MENDENHALL. They all belong to the Treasury Department.
We have nothing that comes from the Navy Department except the
men. The value of this connection to the Navy is one which has been
emphasized by very many people, and every naval officer that I know
of who has ever been engaged in this work at all has borne very earnest testimony to this fact. The value of that comes in several ways.
The young officers are here placed in positions of responsibility that
they would not reach until they became gray-headed in the naval service proper. They are here placed in command of vessels, in fact all
our vessels except one are under the command of officers ranking as
lieutenants. So an officer has a command in this way which he would
not get until he was gray-headed in the regular service of the Navy.
That additional responsibility carries with it also an additional amount
of freedom in the exercise of their work, which the officers appreciate
very highly.

Now, I could if I had the time, but my time is limited and I feel that
I must hasten along here, I could read the testimony of many officers
on this matter, and you will find, if you wish to look for it, in the report
of the joint commission of 1884 there is a great deal there, from officers
connected with the Survey, and there has not been an officer connected
with the Survey who has not testified to the value of the work, not only
the value of the work simply in itself, but the value of the work to the
naval officer on account of the existing organization of the Survey, and
they would say to you that the value of the work is greatly enhanced
by the fact that the naval officer, in making a detailed survey, is taken
out of the regular routine of naval discipline and brought in contact
with a class of men whose lives are entirely different, who have devoted
their time to a different kind of work, and whose standard of accuracy
is the very highest, and these naval officers come in contact with these
men and their work at the office in Washington, or elsewhere, and are
brought in contact with them directly.

I have combined civil and naval parties and . they have worked
admirably, and I can not point to a single instance in which there has
been any friction or any difficulty between the two branches of this
service, and my aim has been not to separate these two bodies but to
mold and fashion them together to a greater degree than before so
that I might get all the possible benefits of the amalgamation between
civilians and naval officers which might benefit all concerned. This is
what we have done in the last few years. They have, as I say, a certain degree of freedom in their work which is necessary; we allow it,
and I may say encourage it, for it is absolutely necessary for the proper
execution of work of this class, and that leads me to make this statement. In my judgment if this part of our work was to be transferred,
if it were possible to transfer the hydrographic part of the Coast and
Geodetic Survey to the Navy, there would be a decided loss of efficiency

growing out of the introduction of purely military methods and military control. Now this, perhaps, you have heard before and I think it is quite capable of proof, and after referring to one or two points, I will read some testimony of very eminent men in regard to it and give one or two reasons why I think it would be the case.

In the first place, on board Coast Survey vessels under the command of a naval officer, the man-of-war discipline is not maintained, and it is not the intention that it should be maintained, because man-of war discipline is not compatible with the highest degree of efficiency in this sort of work. I quote here the very words of a naval officer of the highest rank in the Coast and Geodetic Survey, where he says: "Man-of war methods of discipline will not work on the Survey vessels," and this was made not long ago in connection with the fact that on one of the vessels the work did not seem to be proceeding quite satisfactorily, and in the judgment of this Navy officer himself, not suggested by me or anybody else, it was due to a desire on the part of the commander of that vessel to institute purely military or naval discipline. It is not compatible with the greater degree of freedom which is necessary in this class of work. Another reason is the great amount of red tape—I use that word reluctantly, but perhaps there is no other phrase in the English language that quite covers it—the greater amount of red tape which is necessary in any military or naval control in doing work than in a civilian bureau.

I will say that I have served myself in a bureau under military control. I was two or three years in the War Department as a professor of electricity in the Signal Service; therefore I speak from personal knowledge of both civilian and military service, and I know the infinite difficulty of doing anything like scientific work under military control. If you had tried this you would fully appreciate my statement. The purchase of little things which are absolutely necessary to the carrying on of a piece of work under military control—it is quite difficult under civil control—is infinitely more difficult. I might give hundreds of examples, but I will simply mention two which came to my attention, one in connection with the furnishing of ice for the Mare Island navy-yard, which required 150 vouchers and 744 signatures to secure the payment of that simple item.

I do not say this to criticise the naval system of accounts, but I mention this to show the difficulty you have in administering anything like scientific work under a system of that kind. In my own office a naval officer told me within a few weeks, not in a conversation bearing upon this question, that he had known himself the purchase of a paper of tacks on board a ship to require 62 signatures. I do not say this, as I repeat, to criticise the system. It may be necessary in the Navy and it may be necessary in the Army, but it is not necessary in civil management of work, and it is not done in civil management of work. If a civil party or naval party, with the present organization, is doing work and they want a bit of muslin for a signal we go and purchase it, and if the necessities of the case do not allow advertisement, of course we do not advertise. These things are very trifling in cost and we assume the object of the Government is to have its work done and to have it done economically.

Now, this is one of the reasons why, if this part of the Coast and Geodetic Survey was thrown into the Navy, in my judgment, there would be a decided loss of efficiency. Now, there is another thing, and that is that subordination of rank must exist in any military establishment, without regard to ability or experience. And again, I wish to

say, I do not criticise the subordination of rank in a military establishment. I know it is absolutely necessary, and my own experience
has taught me that, but I do mean to say it is not only unnecessary,
but it injures any work of this kind. Let me illustrate what I mean
by giving a single instance in my own experience. Two or three years
ago I visited and inspected the work going on in Alaska, and I was on
board of one of our vessels. There were 8 or 10 naval officers, all
excellent men, very industrious and very faithful. I have never known
civilians to work more industriously or more enthusiastically than
those young ensigns on board that boat, and I was struck, I must say,
with this fact.

Just as we were about to start out—first I will say we sailed from
San Francisco, and when we got to Burrows Bay they started out for
the first bit of field work, and five of those ensigns went out and began
this work. I inquired of the captain of the vessel with regard to the
character of those young men and what experience they had. Now,
not much to my surprise, I learned this fact, that only one of that body
of five young men had done any work of that kind before, and he was
the junior of all, and therefore a man who could by no possible means
have control of that party. It would be utterly impossible for him to
take charge of it because of his junior rank. He had been on the vessel one or two years before, I think, and at that time learned the methods
going on and was familiar with them. I asked the captain whether he
would instruct the older officers in their duty in this matter, and with a
peculiar smile the executive officer to whom I happened to be talking
at the time said if he was asked to, which, I presume, was quite true,
and I presume they did ask him, and I think he did, because I think
those young fellows were all earnest in the execution of their work. I
mention this as one of the difficulties if a purely military control had
been maintained on that vessel. That young man, the only man who
knew the work, who had been in the field and knew anything about it,
was absolutely and entirely subordinate, and was only allowed to execute the orders of those above him.

Now, I may say in civilian service such a thing would not occur.
If a party of men goes into the field and one happens to be the older
in the service and if he is a suitable man to take charge of it we put
him in charge, and if he is not I have not hesitated more than once to
take a man who was younger because he knew the work and put him
in charge of the work. Subordination of rank, therefore, without regard
to experience and ability, does not exist in a civil organization. I need
not refer to the fact that a long training and experience is needed for a
proper execution of work of this kind. I am entirely willing and ready
to say an educated naval officer, a young man who has stood well in
his class, coming from the Naval Academy and going on one of our
vessels, where he comes in contact with those who know this work, I
am entirely ready and willing to say he can pick it up in a comparatively short time and he can take up in a comparatively short time
this hydrographic work to which I have referred, which, without this
previous training, he could not, and after a year we will say, some of -
them indeed after a few months, become quite expert in this work, and
I think it is very gratifying that this is the case, otherwise our work
would not be as well done as it is, and I believe it to be very well done;
but for the better parts of this work a civilian training and experience
is certainly very desirable, and certainly there ought to be combined
even if we admit the very great desirability of this naval contingent—
and I not only admit but claim it—there must be combined a knowledge

derived from traditions and practice that have been maintained by man after man and year after year.

Since I last appeared before this committee I had occasion to go to New York on business, and while there examined one of our vessels which was just undergoing repairs, the steamer *Bache*, and I entered into conversation with the commanding officer, and without thinking of developing his judgment on this question and without thinking of me, he immediately volunteered a statement of great importance, and that was that he wanted one or two more men and he wanted to get men who had previously been engaged in the service. He said it was impossible to send a man out in a boat who was new in this work, that they were like children and could not do anything at all, and he went on and enlarged better than I could upon the value of long experience in connection with the work. They get that experience under the present system, and yet the system of detail for only two or three years prevents the great experience and training which by tradition and experience makes a man a master in his profession. Now, the best hydrographer in the United States Navy to day (I do not hesitate to say this) is the present hydrographic inspector of the Coast and Geodetic Survey, a gentleman ranking as lieutenant-commander.

I think everybody will admit (I do not believe that there is any officer who will deny that fact) that he is the best hydrograper. By hydrographer I mean the best one to execute the kind of hydrography to which I am now referring. He has served in the Coast and Geodetic Survey I think about thirteen years altogether, and he is passionately fond of the work and has always gotten back to it from any other duty whenever he could. The result is he has come from the lowest place which he occupied at first and is now the ranking officer in our service. Of course he has the great advantage of years of training ——

The CHAIRMAN. What is his name?

Prof. MENDENHALL. His name is Capt. Moser. There are men who have served with us many years, not quite so long as Capt. Moser, but many who have served eight or ten years in the Coast and Geodetic Survey, and we value them highly. I will say I did not mention this before, that this service makes good navigators out of these men, and they realize it, and among the best navigators in the U. S. Navy are the men who served with us in this way, and I would like to repeat that I believe this is largely due to the fact that they are disconnected for the time being from the military or naval discipline to which they are subjected.

Now, something has been said to which I will refer only incidentally. Some assertions have been made in regard to the training of these officers to fit them for this kind of work. No one can go beyond me, I think, in recognizing the faithful service of these men in the work which they do and which they are competent to do, but I must say that for work which requires years and years of training it is clear that their education and training does not fit them. For instance, you are familiar with the course of study at the Naval Academy and know the length of time they spend in the study of navigation and seamanship, management of guns, maritime history, international law, physics, electricity, and that kind of things. Now, there is also some surveying in their course, and that is the reason why they learn how to use the sextant and why they pick it up so quickly when they come to us, but I submit that all those other things do not especially fit them for the work which the civilian branch of the Coast and Geodetic Survey must do in connection with naval work.

If it did fit them I should criticise the course of the Naval Academy as being a bad course, because it is not intended to fit them for that; it is intended to make them seamen and navigators, men who can fight ships and that kind of thing, and it is no disparagement of it to declare that it does not necessarily prepare men for work of this class. There is training which is just as essential and necessary to this work as the work of a physician is to that of a nurse, I will say, or even more than that. I may remark that these naval officers study chemistry, but they do not pretend to be chemists, and they study law, as we all know, but they do not pretend to be lawyers. Still, in case of emergency, they can do a little chemistry and they can do a little international law, and sometimes very well and happily, but after all it is not the kind of training which fits them for the work which they have before them.

Now, you will see I am leading to the supposition that the survey of the coast should not be put under the hands of naval officers. I will explain. It can not safely be placed there without injury to the work. It has been asserted that they have already done this work. You will remember that I showed you a survey of the coast, and that alone required triangulation, magnetic work, tidal work, and, if it is well done, also physical hydrography; generally it requires all of those things. I mean to explain, then, that there are certain of these, other than the mere hydrography which they now do very well, that the naval training does not fit them for, and under the system we have of details it would not be compatible, and therefore some scheme must be maintained for supporting that class of work.

Mr. ENLOE Who does that class of work when they make surveys elsewhere than on our own coast?

Prof. MENDENHALL. I am glad you mentioned that. They have made surveys elsewhere than on our own coast, where they have done that class of work, and this very work that they have done is the argument which I shall be pleased to submit to you as evidence of what I say. I do not mean to say that that work is not as good as could have been done under the circumstances, but it speaks for itself. It has been published and I will submit it to you, and I will be glad to have you consult anybody who ought to be considered as authority upon this in regard to the character of that work. It is better than none, and I may say in many respects it is very good, and some of the work is doubtless good. They have been doing that class of work in Alaska and much of it is very good. The trouble is, it does not hitch together; the parts are disjointed, whereas they ought to join. I do not mean by this to disparage our colleagues, and I would not have submitted that observation except that it was drawn from me. In other words, while we regard it as work useful and desirable, it is not the kind of work the Government wants and not the kind of work the Government should have, and is not satisfactory.

The CHAIRMAN. Right there let me ask you a question. How is the work on the Mexican coast; have you looked into that?

Prof. MENDENHALL. That is the very example I have in my mind.

The CHAIRMAN. How about the charts around Roncador Reef?

Prof. MENDENHALL. I do not know anything about that; I am glad to say we have no responsibility for Roncador Reef, as it is not in our bailiwick. I will say—you draw it from me unwillingly—its responsibility rests upon an office which published a chart more than 50 years old of that reef. That reef does not belong to this country, and we have nothing to do with it.

4561——7

The CHAIRMAN. I did not know but what you had been looking at the chart?

Prof. MENDENHALL. We are not interested in those charts, and we are not in the slightest degree responsible for them; but the point I was making is by combination——

Mr. ENLOE. Before going from that I would like to ask if the Navy Department is responsible?

Prof. MENDENHALL. No, sir, I think not; but I will say this, that I have heard naval officers say it was, but I do not say so myself.

The CHAIRMAN. I would like to ask another question right there. I believe it is a fact the Navy Department used British charts when they were navigating the *Kearsarge?*

Prof. MENDENHALL. British charts of Roncador Reef.

The CHAIRMAN. Were those charts drawn up under the management of the British naval department or the Coast Survey, the same as those of which you have been speaking?

Prof. MENDENHALL. Mr. Chairman, I have got that whole subject, and I am going to tell you before I get through just how that work is done in every country.

Mr. GEISSENHAINER. Do you mean to say the chart by which the *Kearsarge* was sailed was 50 years old?

Prof. MENDENHALL. So I am told by naval officers. I know that the subject has been much talked about, and I have understood those charts were 50 years old. That is my understanding, but I can not say it was true from my own knowledge; but still I think in regard to Roncador Reef there is a pretty strong belief the reef may be out of the way from the position on the chart, but I have not gone into that professionally in any way. I mean to maintain this, that when work has been done in which the naval officers have undertaken to combine with the hydrography the necessary triangulation, topography, and magnetics, and so on, which, as far as I am aware, they have never done except on the coast of Mexico, the result has been far below the standard accepted by the Coast and Geodetic Survey.

Triangulation and topography have been combined to a certain extent in Alaska and it has not been successful. It has been something, much better than nothing, and in Alaska we are glad to avail ourselves of the possibility of getting these charts out in that way, and I may say this was our plan, to ask naval officers to do this class of work, but we have always regarded it as a reconnoissance and preliminary survey which would furnish charts fairly accurate which would be better than no charts or inaccurate charts. This is my judgment in regard to that matter.

I wish to refer to some points about the present arrangement. I consider it a most admirable one. It resulted after a careful study of the whole question by a few civilians and a majority of naval and military officers, as I referred to in my first hearing, and it has gone on up to the present time with the result of producing charts the accuracy and precision of which have commanded the admiration of the world, and I do not see, therefore, why any change should be made; and I do believe that if the change is made, it would prove a very serious detriment to the accuracy and precision of those charts. I do not see why the present system can not continue—a system which I certainly believe it would be valuable to continue.

Now, I wish to refer for a moment to the other side of the bill which speaks of the proposed transfer of what might be left—whatever that might be, it is a little difficult to say what it would be—over to the

Geological Survey. The difficulty of determining what would be left I wish to refer to a little later on, but with reference to the Geological Survey it has been asserted once or twice that the same work has been duplicated by that Bureau and the Coast Survey, and that similar duplication has been often found to have been made by the Hydrographic Office and the Coast Survey.

I can not understand how such a statement can be made. There is no duplication of the work in the two offices, in my judgment. The Coast and Geodetic Survey itself is restricted by law to the survey of the coast of the United States for the purpose of preparing charts of that coast; the Hydrographic Office takes the charts of the Coast and Geodetic Survey, and also prepares charts of the rest of the world for the use of the Navy of the United States. In other words, the great commerce of the United States is supplied by the Coast and Geodetic Survey with charts of the coast of the United States, and the duty of the Hydrographic Office is to supply the Navy with charts of the rest of the world, which it compiles from English, French, Italian, and other surveys, and which it produces in sufficient number to make this distribution, which is a very proper function of that office; and I would like to say the Hydrographic Office has extended its functions beyond that in the introduction of the meteorological feature, which I consider admirable, and I consider the Hydrographic Office has done itself great honor in the extension of the pilot-chart feature and that sort of thing, but nevertheless I maintain that between the Hydrographic Office of the Navy and the Coast and Geodetic Survey, and they will concur in what I say, there is no duplication of work. If there has been any, it is merely accidental in a little area, and was not intentional at all.

It has been maintained that in the case of the Geological Survey and the Coast and Geodetic Survey there is also a duplication of work. That is not true. I say boldly that is not true, and the only instance of duplication of work that I know was purely accidental, and which came from a resurvey of a small part of the coast of Massachusetts, that is, a small area, 1 think 25 miles long and 8 miles wide. The Geological Survey had previously gone over that as a part of the map of Massachusetts, but as the officers of that Survey will tell you every bit of the work of the Coast and Geodetic Survey, every triangulation point, every base line, every bit of topography, is utilized and copied by the Geological Survey. They take this from our charts, and they will universally admit they are much more accurate and much more precise than their own work. I am not criticising my colleagues of the Geological Survey; our relations have been exceedingly pleasant, and we have cooperated wherever possible in every manner with each other, and they will not misunderstand me when I say that their work, as far as topography and triangulation and all mensuration work is concerned, resembles ours very imperfectly indeed, being of a very much less degree of precision.

The CHAIRMAN. Is that the case in the survey of the coast of Massachusetts?

Prof. MENDENHALL. Yes, sir; I can show you that, Mr. Chairman, if you would like to see it.

Mr. ENLOE. Is that due to the fact that you continue the survey to a degree of refinement which the Geological Survey does not?

Prof. MENDENHALL. Yes, sir; they have a very much lower standard than we have, though I am not quarreling with their standard. It is a question for the Geological Survey to determine what kind of a survey is good for geological purposes, and that is their object and not ours.

If they believe topography which costs $2, $4, $5, or $10 per square mile is sufficient for geological purposes, that is all right; I have no dispute with them; but when they say it is sufficient for purposes of navigation and defense, which they have never said, I say they are wrong, and it can be proved they are wrong. The transfer of this work to the Geological Survey, I say, would be entirely improper and not in accord and not fitted for the work of that Bureau, and I would like to say it is so regarded by the great majority of the geologists of the country, and I think the geologists of the country are men whose judgment ought to be consulted on this question. If there was appropriateness and fitness of this combination, the geologists might be expected to be rather favorably inclined and be prejudiced in favor of the transfer work to their own bureau than otherwise.

The CHAIRMAN. Prof. Mendenhall, the hour for the meeting of the House has arrived, and if you will excuse us we will adjourn now.

Mr. MONEY. Before you leave I would like to ask, do you understand the Hydrographic Office supplies charts and does not make hydrographic charts, but simply supplies them?

Prof. MENDENHALL. It does not make the United States charts at all. We furnish them to the Hydrographic Office and they supply them to the Navy. The foreign charts the Hydrographic Office copies, but it does not copy ours because we make them and furnish them.

Mr. MONEY. It copies the foreign charts and supplies those you make?

The CHAIRMAN. It copies the foreign and supplies those like the Mexican coast, for instance.

Prof. MENDENHALL. That is a single instance.

Mr. MONEY. Let me ask you a question which occurred early in your remarks; do I understand you to say that men of less efficiency by the transfer of the bureau would be substituted and——

Prof. MENDENHALL. That was one feature.

Mr. MONEY. I understood you to say that was the important feature.

Prof. MENDENHALL. I say it is one of importance. I say it is one of the great difficulties in the way. Now, we get all the benefits which come from the naval attachment. We get now, under the present system, all the benefits which come from the civilian attachment, and if you break up the present system you have lost it, and a very important feature.

Mr. ENLOE. I would like to ask something in regard to the cost of this work. I would like to know in that connection what is the cost of the coast and geodetic work in the interior when it is complete, per square mile.

Prof. MENDENHALL. Well, that is a very large question. You would first have to find out what is meant by coast survey work.

Mr. ENLOE. I mean the work you are doing.

Prof. MENDENHALL. We are not doing any topographical work in the interior—none at all. We have worked generally through State surveys; triangulation points are being furnished to State surveys, but we have no topographical work done under our direction.

Mr. ENLOE. This is confined to the shore line?

Prof. MENDENHALL. It is confined to the coast, and our interior work is triangulation, for the purpose of enabling every State to do topographical work.

Mr. ENLOE. What does that triangulation work cost per square mile when completed?

Prof. MENDENHALL. That is dependent entirely upon what you

make it. As I said the other day, the work which has been done is very small, and, in my judgment, very much more must be done in time, but I do not expect it to be done for a hundred years, consequently I do not expect to see it.

Mr. GEISSENHANER. The statement was made here the other day that it cost $600 per square mile.

Prof. MENDENHALL. That is absurd.

Mr. ENLOE. It was shown by a former investigation that it cost $100 per square mile.

Prof. MENDENHALL. Some does cost that much. This piece I spoke of along the coast of Massachusetts; I sent a young man, one of my most expert assistants, to do that, and it was done at a cost of $38 per square mile. The survey of the District here was made, not under an appropriation of the Coast and Geodetic Survey, but under the appropriation for the District Commissioners, and officers of the Coast and Geodetic Survey were detailed to make a survey of the District of Columbia and it was done, and it is the finest piece of work except the great ordnance survey of Great Britain, and it cost a large sum of money, but it was made for the use of the District engineers and they will tell you as to its accuracy. The contour lines are run for every 5 feet.

Mr. ENLOE. What was the cost of that work?

Prof. MENDENHALL. I have not calculated what the cost was per mile.

Mr. GEISSENHAINER. This was for the purpose of running water mains?

Prof. MENDENHALL. A topographical survey might cost $7,000 or $8,000 per square mile. I understand in the city of Baltimore they are making a topographical survey and $125,000 has been appropriated by the city.

Mr. GEISSENHAINER. An ordinary survey has no such relations as that?

Prof. MENDENHALL. No, sir.

Mr. ENLOE. Does the triangulation which you are doing where you carry it to the tertiary stage cost as much as $100 per square mile?

Prof. MENDENHALL. I really could not answer that, but I think much less than that.

Mr. ENLOE. Will you give us the information?

Prof. MENDENHALL. You know that is a difficult thing to answer, because our tertiary triangulation has thus far extended along the rim of the coast, and it is combined, therefore, with all the other operations in the Coast Survey, which are done by the same officers and done at the same time, and therefore it is impossible to separate that from the cost of the topographical survey.

Mr. ENLOE. Could you furnish the committee with the estimated cost of the tertiary triangulation separate and apart from any other?

Prof. MENDENHALL. We can approximate it, but we can not bring it down exactly.

Mr. GEISSENHAINER. If I understand you correctly the cost depends upon the minuteness of detail?

Prof. MENDENHALL. Absolutely. Topography is like a piece of furniture. You can get a table for $1.25 or you can pay $1,000 for it. It is usually worth what you pay for it, if topography is honestly done, and that is what we maintain about ours—it is worth what it costs.

Thereupon the committee adjourned, to meet on Tuesday, May 29, 1894.

COMMITTEE ON NAVAL AFFAIRS,
Tuesday, May 29, 1894.

The Committee on Naval Affairs this day met, Hon. Amos J. Cummings in the chair.

The CHAIRMAN. Prof. Mendenhall, if you will now proceed we are ready to hear you.

STATEMENT OF PROF. T. C. MENDENHALL—Continued.

Prof. Mendenhall then addressed the committee. He said:

Mr. CHAIRMAN AND GENTLEMEN OF THE COMMITTEE: At the last hearing I spoke of the objection to transferring a portion of the Coast Survey to the Navy Department based upon the difficulties of executing anything like scientific work or work of precision of this character under military régime. I refer to that this morning only that I may read a brief selection which I intended to read on that day but which I overlooked. This is a statement quoted from the minority report of the joint commission reporting on the organization of certain scientific bureaus in 1886, and the first quotation is from the report of the Secretary of War. He was speaking of the Weather Bureau in connection with the military affairs, and he says:

> It must depend upon the efforts of men who are engaged in technical study, and any officer who takes part in its work must be valuable for his studious and scientific labor rather than for his military ability and his soldierly qualities.

To that is added that of the chairman of the minority committee, that is the head of the minority, Mr. Herbert, I believe, who is now Secretary of the Navy:

> As a question of proper civil administration it seems clear to the commission, as appears in the general report, that it is not good government to put a branch of the service that has no necessary relations to military affairs under the regimen of a military establishment and under military organization and command.

This was agreed to, I will say, not only in the minority report, but by the majority, but it was put in the minority report. Also the following from the same report made by Mr. Herbert, now the honorable Secretary of the Navy:

> It is not consistent with the spirit of our Government that the military should dominate the civil power in any case where such a dangerous course of administration can be avoided. If we admit this principle as a necessity of the service in the quiet and uneventful conduct of the scientific studies of the weather, we shall be logically forced to the policy of enlisting all the active force of the other and like branches of the civil service we have alluded to, and could scarcely avoid the enlistment in the Army of all deputy marshals and whatever constabulary forces that may be needed for a faithful and efficient execution of the laws.

There is also a good deal more of that same character. I refer to this, and would like to remark, although it was specifically written and stated in reference to the Weather Bureau that it is equally applicable to the question now under consideration, for the reason that the Weather Bureau maintains, as you all know, establishments along the seacoast for the purpose of giving warning signals to mariners and that kind of thing. In other words, it is related also to commerce, and to the operations of the Navy, and to the same reasoning as in that case would seem to apply to the present question.

Then just at the close of my last hearing I was referring to the proposition to transfer a part of this Survey to the Geological Survey, and I was speaking of the fact that such a step was inappropriate, improper, and against the judgment of the geologists of the country. I could enlarge upon that to any extent. The geologists of the country, if a census was to be taken of their opinion to-day, would be found to be practically unanimous against such a proposition as this, for the reason that they believe, and have long believed, that the operations of the Geological Survey should be restricted to purely geological work to a very much greater degree than it is at the present time.

On the first day this question was discussed before the committee I was not present myself, but I learned afterwards, what I did not know before, that one of the leading geologists of the country appeared before the committee and spoke on this question. I allude to Prof. Williams, of Johns Hopkins University, one of the first authorities we have. I did not know that Prof. Williams knew anything of this matter until after he had made his address before this committee. I learned afterwards what he said, and I wish to remind you that he told you he had himself been for many years practically an employé of the Geological Survey—that is, he spent a good deal of his time in their service and received compensation from them, and in spite of that fact he recognizes and always has recognized the inappropriateness of transferring the survey work of the country to that bureau. While on that subject I will read, in addition, a letter which has come into my possession, or rather a copy which has come into my possession, which was addressed very recently to a member of Congress from one of the leading geologists of this country, the professor of geology in the Leland Stanford University, who was for a long time the State geologist of Arkansas, and who has a national reputation, having been employed in the international survey in Brazil. I refer to Prof. Branner. This is addressed to a Member of Congress, and a copy has been handed to me:

MY DEAR SIR: It has just come to my knowledge that an effort is being made in Congress to do away with the U. S. Coast and Geodetic Survey as it now exists (Enloe bill). Inasmuch as I was not long ago one of your constituents, I beg to express to you, and through you to the other Congressmen from Arkansas, an opinion in regard to the Coast Survey, based upon many years' knowledge of the work and results.

I should say at the outset that I am not, and never have been and never expect to be, connected with the Coast Survey in any capacity whatever, that I write to you entirely unsolicited, and that my views are simply those of an independent outsider who takes pride in all good scientific work done in our country, and who wishes to see only right and high standards of work maintained.

I don't need to call your attention to the great value of the work of the Coast Survey; indeed, I don't suppose that even those who want to have it abolished doubt that its work is essential to every civilized government. During the six years that I was State geologist of Arkansas I had occasion to use the geodetic work done by the Coast Survey along the Mississippi River and in the State of Arkansas. That work was not only indispensable to the best interests of that State, but I turned to it always with a degree of confidence that I never felt in that of any other bureau doing similar work.

The complaint has been made, and I presume will be made on this occasion, that the Coast Survey is slow. But I need not remind you that in mathematical work demanding the highest degree of accuracy, rapidity is dangerous, if it is not altogether out of the question.

It has been complained also that the topographical work done by the Coast Survey is unnecessarily expensive. I beg to tell you that for twelve years I have made topographic work a special study and that for two years I worked at it constantly. I am familiar with the methods used by the various Government bureaus in doing topographic work and with other methods that they do not use, and I can assure you in the most positive terms that with the degree of accuracy an I detail attained by the Coast Survey it is impossible to do the work more cheaply. That topographic work can be done at from $2 to $10 a square mile is quite true; indeed, I have done it myself at $1 a square mile, but good work—such as the Coast Survey does—can not be done in a country of average relief for any such price by any method in existence or likely ever to be in existence. If good work costs money, it is no more than other good things cost.

Another point worthy of attention is that the training of the assistants doing the Coast Survey work is such that there are comparatively few men in the country who are really qualified by experience to carry it on successfully. To change these men would involve the loss to the people of the very valuable experience of these trained men and would demoralize this important service temporarily if not permanently. The Coast Survey has been the Bureau, above all others, in which the scientific men of the country have all along felt that they could rely with confidence. Its work is the first pride of every American citizen, one that commands the attention and admiration of all civilized nations. To do away with it would be nothing less than a calamity.

This is the language, Mr. Chairman, of one of the leading geologists of the country, and reflects, I think, that of many other gentlemen belonging to the same profession, and I am not doing wrong when I say that within the last week there has come to my knowledge, and in fact I have at my office a copy, which came to me quite unexpectedly, as I was not aware of its existence before, a petition which is now being signed by many of the leading geologists of the country outside of the Government service urging and requesting that the Geological Survey in the future should be restricted to geological work, and the survey part of the work, which has occupied so much of its attention for many years, should not be continued in the way in which it is now carried on. I have no controversy with the Geological Survey over this matter. As I stated, the Coast Survey has never been grasping in its desires or tendencies and I simply mention this matter so as to give you the judgment of the geologists, and they are certainly entitled to an opinion in reference to the effect of such a transfer as this upon the work of the Geological Survey.

Mr. ENLOE. Will you allow me to ask you there, do they contemplate transferring the Survey to the Coast and Geodetic Survey later?

. Prof. MENDENHALL. I do not think that matter is covered by the petition. I will say in reference to that, about 15 years ago the question of the whole organization of the surveys of the country came up and was referred by the then Government authorities, the then Secretary of the Treasury and Secretary of the Navy, to the National Academy of Sciences, and the National Academy of Sciences appointed a committee consisting of the most able men of the country to discuss the question. In the first place, the chairman of this committee was the president of the National Academy of Sciences. I refer to Prof. Marsh, of Yale, who was himself employed by the Geological Survey; and they made a report in which they unanimously agreed that the whole question of the surveys of the United States should be combined under an organization which would have to be formed out of the Coast Survey, and the name which they proposed to give this organization was "The Coast and Interior Survey." They proposed also to combine the land surveys—that is, to have the land surveys done under the direction of this Bureau—and I think any one who has ever investigated that great plan will agree with what a geologist of the Geological Survey told me recently. He said the Academy plan is recognized as the ideal thing in the organization of the Survey of the United States; and I would like to call the attention of the gentlemen of the committee who wish to pursue this phase of the question to the report of the National Academy of Sciences, which is a public document and is easily accessible. Whether this question is touched upon in this recent movement I am sure I am not able to say.

Now, I want to refer to a few other difficulties which, in my judgment, would result in a less degree of efficiency in the survey if it was divided as proposed. One of the most important would be, still referring to the transfer of a part to the Geological Survey, I can not but feel, and I think everyone feels, that it would result in a very decided lowering of the standard of the work. That is, it could not and would not be kept up to that standard which has always been maintained, as I think we are all ready to concede, and which receives the praise of all of those who are competent to judge. Then a very serious difficulty to which I would like to refer would be in the matter of a division of the records of the Bureau. That is a question which is certainly a very important one. In our archives we have over at the Coast and Geodetic Survey—and you will pardon me, gentlemen, if I stop here to say that it would afford me great gratification, and I am sure it would our officers of the Coast and Geodetic Survey, to have the gentlemen of this committe, either collectively or individually, visit the office of the Coast Survey and examine the operations.

I have had little to say here about the operations of the Office, and I have purposely passed over that because they are to some extent similar to the ordinary office operations, but in many instances they are very different, and it would give us a great deal of pleasure for you individually or collectively to see the work going on in the Office of the Coast and Geodetic Survey, and I think if you can find leisure to take half an hour or an hour to examine the work before you decide to act upon the bill either one way or another, it would be certainly a very reasonable thing to expect and to ask. If you should do that you would find in a fireproof building there, one-third of what is known as the Butler Building, we have stored, and have had stored for many years, an enormous accumulation of material gathered by this Survey. We have there original sheets 50 or 60 years old, and record books 50 or 60 years old. All of the past history of the work is there.

Now, of course, that is almost invaluable and it would be difficult to express the value in dollars and cents any way, because we are constantly called upon to refer to these records in order to find out the changes which have taken place—for instance, the secular change in the magnetic forces—and we regard them as being invaluable. A division of those records in the way that is proposed would be almost practically impossible. I have thought of that a good deal. For instance, let us imagine for a moment the division which is proposed by this bill was made, and suppose the naval party was to be directed by the Superintendent, whoever he may be, or the chief hydrographer, whoever he might be, to go out and make a survey of the harbor. Now, the first step necessarily would be to have the naval officers obtain what is called the projection sheet, with triangulation points and all that kind of thing. Now, that is a necessary part of what might be called the interior work of the Coast Survey, the triangulation part of the Coast Survey. If you should transfer to the Navy all the records necessary to enable them to execute this work you would take away from the Geological Survey all that is necessary for their triangulation operations. In other words, the difficulty of separation is enormous.

Of course, if these two operations never had been combined as they have been, then this difficulty would not exist, but they have been combined and we have hundreds of thousands of dollars' worth of material there which might be duplicated, it is true, but at a very great expense and with a great risk of errors, etc. This I regard as one of the serious difficulties in connection with any such division a- proposed.

Now, incidentally, I will refer to some questions in regard to the efficiency of the service, and I will next take up the question of economy. You will remember I stated that if any change was made in this Bureau that it would be, I presume, for some reason, and I fancy the committee would not make a change of this kind, upsetting the traditions of nearly a century, without some good reason, and I said that reason could only be an increase of efficiency or an increase of economy. I will refer now as rapidly as I can to the question of economy. I say, therefore, that if this division is made it will not be again in the direction of economy, but it will be a loss in the direction of economy. The operations will cost more than they do now.

I could refer you to many facts that will support that, but I will say, in the first place, that the cost of maintaining and repairing vessels, if put under the control of the Navy Department, would be very decidedly greater than it is now under civil control. This is a question on which, I am sure, every naval officer who has ever served in the Coast Survey will agree with me very heartily. In the first place, referring to the cost of repair of vessels, which is, of course, quite a large item, we have our vessels repaired, and when we have them built by private contract, very much as the other portions of the civil branches of the Government do, and the result is, we have nothing to do with any entanglement with regard to navy-yard repairs and navy-yard matters. Only this last summer, and in fact every season, we have very extensive repairs; and one of the vessels, the *Bache*, of which I spoke the other day, was repaired last season at a cost of $15,000, and her commander assured me, and the hydrographic inspector assured me, that if it had been done in the navy-yard the cost would have been at least twice as much.

Occasionally we have small repairs made at a navy-yard, notably at Mare Island, San Francisco, and we have invariably found it was an expensive thing and have avoided it as far as possible. It is quite safe to say that 25 to 50 per cent of the cost of maintaining vessels is saved by our methods, the civil methods of doing it. In the first place we are not so particular about how these repairs are made. That is, we have them made substantially well, but we care less, perhaps, for the brass ornamentation and that sort of thing about the engines, as our vessels are for use and nothing else, and this is a very important item, as I think everybody can see.

Now, another increase would be in the maintenance of these vessels, and I think every naval officer will agree with me in my statement that this would be greatly increased if the vessels were to be transferred to the Navy. I infer this from the almost universal complaint which comes from naval officers, not made in a disagreeable way at all, but merely, I presume, a statement of the feeling to the effect that the Coast and Geodetic Survey is very poor.

That is always the cry when it comes to fitting up a vessel, that the Coast and Geodetic Survey is very poor, so that we can not have this and that, and so as a matter of fact we do not have the kind of vessels which in the Navy Department would undoubtedly exist. A very little examination will justify my belief that the expense would be very much greater if the vessels were transferred to the Navy than if they were left under civil control. We have a great deal of hard work done by our people that is done by naval officers and men really on board the vessels, and we save a great deal of money. Our appropriations have been very small, and we have been forced to economize in every way in this direction. If this was put under the control of the Navy, where a general repair fund furnishes this and that kind of thing, I think I could predict very safely that in a very few years the cost of maintenance would be double what it is now. Now, another increase to be included in the transfer and which is related to the work would probably result, because it would not necessarily follow, but which I think will naturally follow from the nature of things, is that an increased number of officers would be employed upon many of these vessels.

At the present time, since the service in the Survey is an irregular detail lasting two or three years, and since there is a good deal of hard work connected with it, we have had a great deal of difficulty in getting officers and have had for some time. The fact that we have officers to spare in the Navy, which has been used sometimes as an argument in favor of the transfer, that we have men there, plenty of them, does not prove to be a fact. In the last two or three years we have had to run our vessels sometimes short and have had to use every effort to induce the Navy Department to detail officers to us. Of course there was a time, ten, fifteen, or twenty years ago, when there were plenty of officers of the Navy, because there was a small number of ships, and of course you are aware of the tremendous increase in the number of vessels and the tremendous demand for naval officers to man them. This has continued until at present we have just about half the number of officers detailed on the work we had five years ago, and it is now difficult to get one.

Mr. GEISSENHAINER. What is the maximum number?

Prof. MENDENHALL. We had something like 70 or 80 some years ago, and we had some 41 a little while ago, but we have 30 to 35 now.

Now, I would like at this point, if I may be pardoned, to refer to a criticism which has been made several times, and I think by the honorable Secretary of the Navy, or at least the Assistant Secretary, a remark that has been made so many times, and, like many remarks of that kind, repeated until it comes to have weight. I have no question at all that those who made it thoroughly believed there was good argument in it, but I think there is none. I refer to one of the reasons given why this transfer should be made is to secure to the Secretary of the Navy a better administrative control over his own officers.

Now, I would like in the first place to invite attention to the fact that this same sort of detail is made to several other bureaus, as I stated the other day to the Light-House Establishment, where many officers go out of the immediate direction of the Secretary for years, and to the Fish Commission, and elsewhere, and I would also like to say, the Secretary of the Navy has, and always has had, a very close administrative control over all the officers who are in the Coast and Geodetic Survey. In fact, I might say in some respects he has had a much closer control than I would like. That is to say, he has never hesitated to call officers away to serve on court-martial or such other duty at any time. This has always been recognized, and officers have constantly been taken away from us; officers have received orders from the Secretary of the Navy to report for such and such a duty, positively without knowledge on the part of the Superintendent of the Coast Survey until they returned. So I say the facts of the case do not in anyway show that the Secretary of the Navy has not lost in the slightest degree, in my judgment, the control over his own officers on account of this detail. They are always under his direction and that fact has always been recognized by his own action.

Now, with reference to the economy of the transfer of this other part of the work to the Geological Survey, I will say that in my judgment, it would be very poor economy to do this, even supposing there was no other reason, because one of two things must be done: The work must be carried on essentially as it is now, which would certainly lead to increased expenditure under the direction of the Geological Survey, or else it must be carried on with a very much lower standard of accuracy. If it is carried on with a very much lower standard of accuracy, some time or other this work must be done over; in other words, it is not worth doing at all if not well done. My judgment is that this work can be done by the Coast and Geodetic Survey once for all, and the country will never have to do it over again, and that being the case it is certainly bad policy to take it from a bureau which has done it for many years and put it under one which has never done it.

Now, I wish to refer to a few other criticisms which have been made. It has been urged several times that the topography we were doing along the coast is of too refined a character. It has been said that we put in fences and houses, and that kind of thing, and it is too refined in character. Now, I contend that statement can not be maintained when we consider either of the two purposes for which we desire this work. You will remember that the two purposes for which the shore topography is designed are the purposes of defense and of commerce. For the purposes of commerce it is quite clear, in my judgment, that the topography is not more refined than it should be. The existence and presence of a small feature is sometimes the very thing that saves the vessel. The recognition of a very small thing, it may be a church spire, or a fence, or a peculiar topographical feature, is very often an intimation to the coaster of the position of his vessel and is of great importance in saving him. I have already referred to this on a previous occasion. Now, in regard to matters of defense, I wish to read here just a few words from what ought to be good authority. One of these gentlemen is major of engineers, brevet major-general, retired, Gen. W. F. Smith, an Army officer of high reputation, and is well known to many of you. He says in regard to the topographical work of the Coast and Geodetic Survey:

WILMINGTON, DEL., *June 30, 1886.*

A criticism has been made against the methods of the Coast and Geodetic Survey which I deem so unjust that I would feel disposed to reply to it if I knew exactly upon whom to direct my guns. I speak of the charge of extravagance in the topographical details in the published charts. I think it was as far back as 1843 when the plan for the work to be done by the Coast Survey was laid out and approved by the President. That plan looked forward to putting in so much of the topography in the published work of the Coast Survey as should be important "for the purposes of commerce or defense." Having held the position of engineer secretary of the Light-House Board, and been engaged in the field during the civil war, I feel authorized to express my opinion as to the amount of topographical detail necessary to cover both of the above points.

In the interests of navigation it is important that the topography on the coast charts should embrace all permanent, or reasonably permanent, objects, such as churches, houses, groves, hills, hedges, marshes, and embankments. These and their combinations always aid the navigator in determining his position when near shore, and yet unable from any cause to make observations; and all these could not well be determined and placed upon the chart without also determining other details.

For defensive purposes no minuteness of detail can be too great, and I know of instances in the late war where the character of a fence has determined the result of a battle.

No general is fitted for command who does not take into account all the topographical details of a position to be defended or assailed, and ignorance of the existence of a canal, as at Fredericksburg, may cost thousands of lives and millions of money. It was my good fortune during the war to have, through the liberal views of Prof. Bache, Coast Survey officers on duty with me during much of the war. There was no corps in the United States service capable of doing the work done by these officers. With the plane table they always made for me minute topographical maps of my positions when near the enemy. I knew all distances in my vicinity, and the artillery officers were never at fault if they had to open fire. I knew the depths of all groves, the height and extent of dykes and fences, altitudes of all hills, and consequently had all necessary information for offensive or defensive measures.

If there is any such thing as art in warfare, these details are indispensable to a general in forming his plans of battle and regulating his marches so that his columns can be at the key point of the battlefield at the right moment, or, if he is acting on the defensive, that he may take advantage of all the obstacles in repulsing an attack. To neglect these details is to show utter want of knowledge of fundamental rules of warfare.

I therefore assert that for navigation and defense the Coast and Geodetic Survey should embrace minute details of topography. To neglect them is to risk the honor of the nation, the safety of its ships, and the welfare of its people. As I do not know to whom to express my opinions on this subject, I give them to you for use if you can use them.

Yours, sincerely,

WM. F. SMITH,
Major Engineers, Brevet Major-General (Retired).

I am sure it is a fact which will be concurred in by many of you who have had that kind of experience.

Mr. ENLOE. What is the date of the letter?

Prof. MENDENHALL. This was written in 1886, a letter written at a time when a previous movement in this direction was made. It was printed at that time; at all events, we happen to have several printed copies. There is also a letter printed on the same sheet written at the same time by a former chief of engineers, Brig. and Bvt. Maj. Gen. H. G. Wright. He speaks in the most positive way, and says, in regard to the matter of defense:

1203 N STREET, NW.,
Washington, July 1, 1886.

DEAR SIR: I am in receipt of your letter asking my opinion in regard to the usefulness of the topography of the maps of the Coast Survey in relation to the purposes of coast defense, and have to say, in reply:

That as regards coast defense generally, and the operations of troops upon our South Atlantic coast, I have had considerable experience—enough to enable me to speak understandingly upon the subject—in the first connection as an officer of the Corps (of Engineers) charged with the defenses of the coast of the United States, and finally as its chief; and in the second, as closely connected with the so well known Port Royal expedition.

As regards the former, I can speak positively of the value and usefulness of the topography of the Coast Survey not only in its relations to questions of defense, but also in regard to river and harbor improvements, since we had occasion, during my term of active service, to make frequent calls upon the Coast Survey Office for maps showing not only the hydrographical features of various points on the coast but also the topography. The information, always readily supplied, was of much value as well as a great saving to the Government on the score of expense.

As to the latter, I may say that in the preparation of the so-called Port Royal expedition, the entire information regarding the coasts of South Carolina, Georgia, and Florida was obtained from the Coast Survey Office, and the project of the expedition was based thereon. In the matter of the detail into which the maps went it can be stated that instead of being unnecessarily minute they were often not sufficiently so, and that frequent calls had to be made upon the Coast Survey officials connected with the expedition for further details upon which to base ulterior operations. It would therefore appear that the topography supplied by the maps failed rather in want of minuteness than in its excess.

It may be further stated that, according to my experience in the late war, the Coast Survey supplied the only reliable data in regard to the topography of our immediate sea coast, and that it was of great value in the operations of our land forces.

Very respectfully, your obedient servant,

H. G. WRIGHT,
Brig. and Brvt. Maj. Gen'l (Retired), formerly Chief of Engineers.

I will not read all of this letter, but I might add to that a number of selections which I have made from letters written during the war and near the close of the war by those who were engaged in the operations where the Coast Survey officers were also employed. This is from Admiral Porter:

Great facilities would have been afforded the Army and Navy, for operations on the Mississippi River and its tributaries, had the Coast Survey or some institution like it preceded them. For the local surveys made for State or county purposes do not approach anything like perfection, and gives but little information adapted to military purposes.

*   *   *   *   *   *   *   *   *

When in front of Vicksburg I think I can say I had the most complete set of maps and sketches to be found anywhere in this vicinity, and the commanding general constantly came on board to consult them. I was mainly indebted to a small Coast Survey party which I had with me for these maps. The war can not be carried on without good maps. The general or admiral who has the best charts will be apt to gain great advantage over his antagonists. In a country like ours where States and counties are cut up into lakes, rivers, and bayous, known only to the inhabitants of the district, we must have good maps.

I think it is not necessary, as I have said, to read all these notices, and I have not time to read them, but recognition was given in a most generous way by all of these officers of the value of the accuracy of the work of the Coast Survey at that time, which accuracy has been maintained since then.

Now, as to the refinement of this work, I referred to that the other day, and I will not therefore speak of it at length again, but I will say we have also been criticised on account of the fact that we have carried this topographical survey too far from shore. I stated, and I would like now to repeat the statement, that I have made a careful examination of the practice of all the foreign countries in this respect, and I did that for my own benefit, and I found on the whole that we are rather conservative; that we have a somewhat narrower fringe of topography on our coast charts than other nations have. This is a fact.

Mr. ENLOE. I would like for you to state to the committee right here why it is this detail work has been carried to the extent it is along the Atlantic coast from the Chesapeake Bay around to the north, and so little done on the coast of the South, and what is the reason for this difference?

Prof. MENDENHALL. I no not know that there is any very great difference. Of course there would be topographical reasons for a difference. That is to say, when you go on a flat country, and most of the southern coast is flat, we have not the topographical features which the northern coast has, and there would be, naturally, not a demand for so much of a survey, the general practice being that the topographer must go back far enough. When we give topographers instructions we give them instructions to go back so far that all the objects which would be useful in navigation shall be taken in. For instance, if you are in a country where there are hills you have to go back to them. In Alaska we have on our charts mountains many miles distant from the coast, and they are of the greatest importance, because you can see these mountains from the sea, and for this reason they have to be accurately located.

Mr. ENLOE. In a flat country along the coast there is a great uniformity in the appearance of things?

Prof. MENDENHALL. That is true, and we go back in the interior far enough to cover everything that will be used, and you can easily see that in a flat country you might have material back, miles away, that can not be used by a vessel because it can not be seen from the sea. I know of no other reason than this. In fact, I would be very much surprised if there is a very great difference made between the northern and southern coast.

Mr. ENLOE. I think there is quite a difference in your work, which is generally around the cities along the Atlantic coast in the east from what you will find on the maps of the southern coast?

Prof. MENDENHALL. I should doubt that, Mr. Enloe. Now, something has been said about our fine map of New York City, and I am glad the matter has been brought up. I am sorry to say we did not make it; it is not our survey. We very rarely survey cities; we copy them, take them from the city engineers whenever we can get work which is reliable.

Now, about the map of New York City, of which a good deal has been said, we did make a survey of the shore line around New York City; that is our topographical survey, but the whole city itself is simply taken from the survey of the city engineers, and that is our uniform practice. It is the same way in regard to Boston. Just now I am having compiled the additions in the great growth of the city of Boston during the last forty years. Our chart of Boston Harbor is as old as that, and of course the city has changed wonderfully in that time. We are having this done as far as possible by compilation, and we make these compilations wherever we can get them, and they are reliable.

Mr. ENLOE. You accept these maps as absolutely accurate and rely upon them instead of your own surveys, then?

Prof. MENDENHALL. We do not make surveys of cities, because what we desire most in the city is to have the principal points in them, and those we locate ourselves. As I stated the other day, such objects as a large building, like the New York World building, whenever it is finished, we send a man and an instrument to the top of them to find the exact location, as we want that very definitely on our charts. We try to have them located with great accuracy.

Mr. GEISSENHAINER. How do you arrange when a building of that description is destroyed?

Prof. MENDENHALL. We have to keep correcting these charts constantly by hand. There is never a chart which goes out of the office, but which is not passed through a hand correction in which these changes are made. Now, referring to this question raised by Mr. Enloe, take the city of Charleston; I have only recently had the survey of that extended, and they are still compiling in that direction to make it as complete as possible. We compile it in the very best way, and certainly I should be surprised if there is any reasonable complaint in that respect.

Mr. ENLOE. I am not making any complaint of it; I only wanted to know, as it appeared to me on an examination of the maps it was a fact, and I wanted to know the reason.

Prof. MENDENHALL. I think there is no other reason than arises from topographical requirements. When the survey is extended back further you will find the topography of the country demands it, and certainly there is none other of which I know.

The next point to which I wish to refer, which comes in perhaps somewhat irregularly, but I think it is important, is with regard to the criticism that has been made upon the question of salaries of the officers who are employed in this office, and I want to say I think such criticism has no foundation whatever. It has often been urged that there was at one time a board organized for the express purpose of raising the salaries of those officers. I think I hardly need say to this committee that such a thing would be absolutely impossible, even if it were proposed, and I will therefore remark in regard to these salaries

(I am glad to have an opportunity to refer to this phase of the question), there is no bureau of the Government which has, as far as I have been able to ascertain, as long an average length of service as the Coast and Geodetic Survey. Making a list of all of the assistants as I did only recently, that is I made it up to the 1st of January, I find that these assistants, against whom this criticism is made, have served, on an average, the Government of the United States for thirty years. This is the average service. Many of them, of course, I need hardly say, have served much more than that. A number of them have served more than forty years and some of them, in fact I noticed one of them who just came in a moment ago, has served the U. S. Government as an officer of the Coast Survey for fifty-six years, that is, he will have done so on the 12th of July or somewhere about that time, and I want to say he is still pretty active and vigorous and does his work, as can be testified to by anybody who knows anything about it, quite as well as many younger men. Now, after this our next longest period is that, I think, of Prof. Davidson, of San Francisco, who has served the Government for about forty-nine years in the Coast and Geodetic Survey. Then we come to Mr. Rodgers, who has served forty-seven years, and Mr. Schott, the chief computer of the office, who has served forty-five years; another officer has served forty-five, and another thirty-five, and so we come down, and as I tell you, the average of all this is about thirty years. Now, if that be considered, such a corps is entitled to some consideration on account of the length of time they have devoted to the service of the Government, and when we look into the question——

Mr. ENLOE. I want to ask you on that point, do we understand this revision and rearrangement of salaries which took place in Fifty-first Congress was based entirely upon length of service?

Prof. MENDENHALL. No, sir; not entirely upon length of service.

Mr. ENLOE. Then upon what was it based?

Prof. MENDENHALL. It was based upon length of service and merit as far as that merit could be ascertained, and I would like to say I hold myself entirely responsible for that revision; I do not want to throw the responsibility on anybody else. I will say that it was made after I had been in the service about a year or more, and I would have been a very foolish man if I had not consulted the older men of the corps who knew all the men well and could give some idea of their relative abilities. The occasion for this revision was simply the fact that a large number of irregular salaries had been existing prior to that time. The Appropriations Committee requested me to make it, and as the arrangement was desired to be systematic the salaries were arranged to increase by $200 from grade to grade. A very few who were receiving the higher salaries were kept at the same rate without disturbing them. In fact certain changes were made, some salaries I think were reduced, and some increased, but I am frank to say none were increased as much as I wished they could have been.

The CHAIRMAN. What was the aggregate increase?

Prof. MENDENHALL. The total increase in the salaries, was, I think, only a few hundred dollars; but, pardon me, I will be glad to answer any questions you have to ask after stating——

Mr. ENLOE. Then, I will ask questions about that when you get through.

Prof. MENDENHALL. I would like to call your attention to this. I have here a very carefully prepared table of the compensation received by these gentlemen to-day and the compensation received by the same gentlemen ten years ago, in 1884. This is a table which was prepared from the official books and records of the disbursing officer, and the result is this. This table embraces 29 men. I have taken the older assistants, having left off a few of the younger men because they have entered the service since then, beginning at a salary of $700, but I have taken 29 out of about 42 or 43 officers altogether and this is the result, that of these 29 men 23 of them to-day are receiving less compensation than they did ten years ago in spite of the advance which has been talked about. Twenty-three are actually receiving less and only 6 are getting more, and that a very small sum.

I maintain, therefore, the criticism against the régime and arrangement which has nothing more in it than this is not very strong. I will explain. In 1884 the salaries of the Coast Survey officers were greatly reduced, considerably reduced by the action, which I have always maintained to be a proper action as my colleagues know, of my predecessor, Mr. Thorne, in cutting off the contingent subsistence allowed to officers in the field, but who, as a matter of fact, were allowed a certain amount of subsistence throughout the year. This had been maintained for years. It has never been maintained since, of course, but the fact is, this amounted to a very serious reduction in their compensation, and therefore when I had an opportunity in 1890 to advance some of these men I did it very cheerfully, and I regretted that I could not do more, because their salaries are still behind what they received in 1884.

Mr. MEYER. In what way was that subsistence given?

Prof. MENDENHALL. They were paid at the rate of so many dollars per day.

Mr. MEYER. Was it a ration?

Prof. MENDENHALL. No, sir; it was commuted. Let me explain our present plan. When we send an officer to the field he has to do one of two things. When he goes into the field where there are no houses or boarding houses he is obliged to live in camp, and the Government furnishes him with a tent and employs a cook and we only allow him $1 per day for subsistence in camp. Well, now, whenever he can live in a hotel or boarding house, which is cheaper for the Government than living in camp, we then allow him $2.50 per day. Formerly the allowance was $3 per day, and formerly it was allowed to certain persons continually throughout the year whether they were in the field or not, a practice which I say I believe to have been a dangerous one, but which existed many years and for which the officers receiving the allowance were not responsible—that is to say, it was their chiefs who were responsible. It was in regard to this manner of compensation which was considered when the increase of salary was made which took place n 1890.

Another complaint bearing, perhaps, on this same matter is that we have a number of field officers who are detailed to do work in the office. This criticism I am glad to have the opportunity to touch upon briefly. A most serious mistake would be made if this practice was to be abandoned, and I will say by degrees it came into existence during the time of my predecessor, Mr. Thorne, who, I think, was wise enough, and who, being a good business man, understood that the work of the office should be well done, thoroughly done, and that it should be done under the directi n of those who were thoroughly familiar with the character of the field operations. At the present time we have several officers who are detailed to work in the office, and I will enumerate the most important. I would be very glad to mention all of them. Mr. Schott, chief of the computing division, is one of those who has been in the office forty years, except probably on very rare occasions when he has been sent out into

4561——8

the field to do work, but not continuously, so I regard him as being permanently detailed in the office, and a detail which I regard as extremely necessary.

His services are extremely valuable to us in conducting the affairs of that very intricate and important division. Then we have the chief of the engraving division, but he is not necessarily all the time in office. Last year, for instance, he was in the field for more than six months in Alaska, rather to the detriment, I am afraid, of the work in his division, because I did not think it got on as well during his absence, but I like to send these men to the field occasionally for particular things, although I believe their presence in the office is of specially great importance. The engraving division is the largest division in the office and the chief has to be a practical expert in photolithography, photographing, engraving, and so on. The value of the charts depends largely, in my judgment, upon this division being controlled by one who is thoroughly familiar with field operations and especially with topographic work.

The CHAIRMAN. Has that division its headquarters here?

Prof. MENDENHALL. Yes, sir. The officer who has charge of it is the best topographer we have in the service, and last year he spent six months in Alaska, and this year I shall send him to the field again, but not for so long. Whenever a serious demand exists for sending these men to the field we send them in order to crowd a piece of work through. We do that in spite of the fact we believe it is wiser to have them in the office all the time. In the instrument division we also have a field officer in charge, and this has proved to be of the utmost value. It is of the utmost value because we must have there a man who can test an instrument before it is taken into the field. You can not have an instrument shop make satisfactory instruments if you have in charge an instrument-maker who is simply skilled in the mechanical construction of instruments; you must have one who understands the use of every instrument which goes to the field, and they must all be tested. Only a day or two ago we were about to send and instrument to the field when the chief of the instrument division applied a particular test to it and found it to be imperfect in that respect. I regard it of the utmost importance that we should have a field officer in charge of the instrument division. I ought to say, in justice to this man, that although he has been here three or four years continuously in charge of this division, during two of these years he also did field work. This man lives outside of Washington some miles, and there were some important investigations being conducted by the International Geodetic Association in regard to the variation of latitude, which we could not conduct here in Washington, or spend money for or spend valuable time on, so we put him alone at that work, and in spite of that fact he succeeded in making these observations, which have received high praise from the International Geodetic Association in Berlin.

We asked this man, who is in charge of the instrument division, to make these observations, and he left here, say, at 4 o'clock in the afternoon, and went to his home 16 miles away and spent the night until say, 1 o'clock in the morning, making these observations on every clear night, returning each morning to his duties in the office. The next division is the drawing division, and in that division all the drawings of the charts are made for the engraver and for the lithographer, and no one, except a man who is familiar with topographical work, would be fit for the kind of supervision required, so we have a field officer in charge. In the chart division also, which is the place from which the charts are issued, we have a field officer. He is a man especially familiar with hydrographic work. He was engaged for many years as a civilian in that work and is an expert hydrographer. He revises all the charts and reviews them, and I think it is of great value that this system should be pursued. In other words, the criticism that in the Coast Survey we have kept field officers detailed in the office is to me only of very little weight.

I should like also to refer to the cost of this topographic survey on which several comments and criticisms have been made. I referred to that the other day and spoke of the cost of one or two kinds. I will simply say that the cost of the topography depends entirely upon its character. It might cost anywhere from nothing up to $7,000 or $8,000 per square mile. Perhaps I had better say it might cost from $1 per square mile up to $7,000 or $8,000 per square mile, as I have known it to be all the way between these limits. The Coast Survey has made topography at a small cost, and is in the habit of doing it when it is necessary. We have a chart here that was made during the last year, and a very important and valuable chart it is. This is a chart made in connection with the boundary survey in Alaska, on which we are now engaged. This was made by one of our most competent topographers, who is at the same time one of our cheapest topographers. I have computed the cost of that survey. It cost about $1.80 per square mile.

The CHAIRMAN. For how many square miles?

Prof. MENDENHALL. For about 300 square miles, and I will say that it looks as well now as a map I might show you which might cost $1,000 or $2,000 a square mile. If I should make a map costing that much it would look no better. In other words, you can make a map costing $1 per square mile look as well as a map costing $1,000 per square mile, therefore the appearance of a map is only an evidence of good draftsmanship; it does not mean necessarily that it is a good survey. This survey was necessary for our work, and therefore it was made not cheaply, but as cheaply as possible.

The CHAIRMAN. Is it a part of the Alaska survey?

Prof. MENDENHALL. It is a part of the Alaska survey. This is the Stickine River you see here [exhibiting]. Our object in this survey, I will say, is to get an idea as to the shape of these mountains. It has been claimed and is now claimed on the part of the United States that there is no mountain range parallel to the coast in Alaska, and therefore our boundary line must run back a distance of 10 marine leagues, and my colleague representing the English Government is inclined to maintain that there is a mountain range running parallel to the coast. Now, the treaty says that if such a range exists the boundary line shall follow it, but my contention is, and it is justified by this map, that no such range of mountains exists, and, therefore, we have to fall back upon the second definition of the treaty, which carries the boundary line back 10 leagues. There is nothing whatever, I contend, to indicate a range of mountains running parallel to the coast.

The cost of triangulation was referred to here the other day, and therefore I have had a very careful computation made in regard to that, and I am very glad to be able to inform the committee on this subject. I have had computed the cost of primary triangulation, which is generally regarded as the most expensive kind. It is the kind most accurately done, but rather to our surprise the cost per square mile appears to be, on the whole, the least. This cost results from the very great area which is covered by this class of our triangulation. Some statements have been made, as you will remember, I think before the committee, that this interior triangulation costs at the rate of $100 per square mile, and even as high as $600 was mentioned on one occasion. The computation shows that the cost of primary triangulation, taking the systems out in the Rocky Mountains, west and east, instead of being $600 per square mile, or $100 per square mile, is actually about $1.40 per square mile.

This is the actual cost of that triangulation, and it includes, I will say, only the area covered by the triangulation. It does not include that area which the triangulation controls. If I may show you and explain this [illustrating on chart] chart I have also had drawn up, it will give you at a glance an idea as to what we have done in triangulation, and what we propose to do. This chart will tell the story better than anything else. The blue represents all we have done, and the red represents what we propose to do in the future in the way of primary triangulation. These marks where the blue is not solid means where we have had reconnoissances and it is only partly done, as, for instance, that part here [illustrating]. This is the great transcontinental chain to which I have referred so often. This is the place where we have computed the cost of this triangulation, and which turned out, as I have said, for the area covered, to be about $1.40 per square mile. There is a gap which we hope to complete this summer, and complete, therefore, this enormous line across here (illustrating), a greater chain of triangulation than ever before measured in the world. This red means exactly what we believe to be the necessary additions to this great system of primary triangulation. After the red is completed then there will come in certain other lines indicated here and some points run along the State boundary lines. I believe the best and most economical way to provide for State surveys will be to run these triangular lines upon which they can base their State work. So you will see this system of red and blue controls, therefore, the whole United States, and consequently if you want to compute the cost per square mile for the whole, here you will have to reduce the cost of $1.40, which is the cost of the area covered by the triangulation in the ratio of the area that the triangulation might control, which is about 4 to 1, and of course is relatively an exceedingly small sum.

Now, the cost of secondary and tertiary triangulations necessary for the projection of topography it is found difficult to compute, in very great measure, because it is so combined, as I said the other day, with hydrography and topography, the whole work being done in many instances by the same parties, but fortunately we have got an example of the work recently in the execution of work in the State of Massachusetts within the last few years where Massachusetts having been engaged in carrying on a State survey the triangulation was executed by the State of Massachusetts according to the methods of the Coast and Geodetic Survey and under the direction of that Survey. The chairman of the commission is an officer of the Coast and Geodetic Survey whose home happens to be in Massachusetts, and therefore the methods of the Coast Survey were carried out there, and we can get the percentage of cost of that which has been done independent of the topography.

This I have obtained through the presence of this officer, and it proves to be $2.44 per square mile. That is to say, the extension of all this triangulation down for topography was that amount. Now, I think you will admit that the cost of this work has been very grossly exaggerated. Statements have been made and so frequently made that many persons have come to believe the enormous cost mentioned as correct.

The assertion has been made also, I think before this committee and elsewhere, that the money appropriated for this Survey has not always been applied in a legitimate way—I think I can use these words with propriety—that it has been appropriated in lump sums, and it has not been possible to know exactly what has become of it. Now, I wish to show you how entirely untrue such a criticism is. In the first place, I referred the other day to the fact that annually we submit to Congress a detailed statement of the expenditure of every dollar that has been appropriated, and as far as those expenditures are concerned that is settled.

Now, as to the possibility of our doing what is intimated, that we have taken money appropriated in a lump sum and used it for any purpose when it was really intended by Congress to be used for another, I invite your attention to the last appropriation bill, or the appropriation bill of any of the last ten years, and ask you to compare the appropriations of the Coast and Geodetic Survey in the appropriation bill in which it appears with the appropriations for the Geological Survey, and you will find the appropriations for the Coast and Geodetic Survey are given in the utmost detail. We occupy a greater space in the sundry civil bill than I often think we ought to do or are entitled to, because we have gone to very great detail; but the largest item given in this bill is an item of $17,700, and that, as you will see, is detailed in itself to cover a large number of points to which the money is to be applied. Then they run from that down to $4,000 and $5,000, and there are 14 or 15 items.

The CHAIRMAN. Is this the sundry civil bill?

Prof. MENDENHALL. For the last Congress, or you may go back at any time in the last ten years, and you will find the same thing. Let me turn, for instance, to the Geological Survey, and there you will find for: "Topographical surveys in various portions of the United States, $200,000." One single item, not covered or protected by anything except "in various portions of the United States." Now, if you will compare that and other features of the bill with ours, I think you will see, as far as that criticism is concerned, there is very little in it. Compare it also with the Revenue Cutter Service. Here you have appropriated without specifying, except in a general way, the various kind of things to be accomplished (they are mentioned precisely as in our Survey), but the total sum of $925,000 is given in a lump. I do not criticise that mode of appropriation. It is perhaps often wise, but I ask your attention to the distinction between this and our own appropriation in the matter of detail.

Another statement to which I would like also to call your attention, gentlemen, is one which has been many times made, and often made, by those gentlemen in authority who ought to have known whether such a statement was correct or not, and that is the statement that all the hydrographic work is done by the Navy, and always has been done by the Navy.

Now, it is only necessary to appeal to the actual records to show how incorrect and how misleading that statement is. From the year 1861 to the year 1874, a period of fourteen years, inclusive, not any hydrographic work of the Coast and Geodetic Survey was done by the Navy; no naval officers were engaged in the work, but it was all done by civilians. That, of course, I think came from the fact that in 1861 all of the Navy and Army was called upon for other duties. It is a fact, I think, which is worthy of consideration here, that had the Coast and Geodetic Survey at that time existed in the way that it would neces-sarily exist if this bill should become a law, it would have been instantly broken up, its work would have been discontinued; but fortunately it had an organization which maintained itself, which enabled it throughout that whole period to perform such valuable services as have been testified to by every admiral and every naval officer and every Army officer throughout that whole unfortunate difficulty.

Now, therefore, I say from 1861 to 1874, inclusive, the hydrographic work was done by civilians. In 1874 Capt. Patterson, who was a retired naval officer, and who had for many years been the hydrographic inspector of the Coast Survey, that is to say he had occupied the place now occupied by a naval officer, became superintendent of the Coast Survey on the retirement of Prof. Benjamin Pierce, of Harvard University, and so he was naturally inclined in the direction of the Navy, and through recognition of the fact that it was a desirable thing to accomplish, because I believe it was at that time the Navy was brought again into the hydrographic work after an absence of very many years. It is instructive to consider what occurred at this time and what had occurred during this interim. In the first place, during this interim our Naval officers, I think, will admit very important improvements had taken place in the methods of doing hydrography.

The civilians of the Survey upon whom this entire work had fallen brought to that work a standard of efficiency, and an integrity of work which they had maintained throughout all their earlier work, and necessarily they at once improved, and in a very marked way, the character of the work which was done; but I also say if naval officers had been employed on this work in 1861, or at the close of the war, they would have naturally made the same advance, because just at that time we were ripe for improvements in these methods. It is also instructive to note when the Navy was brought back into the Survey to perform these hydographic duties the naval officers received instructions from the civilians. I mention this of course without any criticism on the naval officers, but as a simple statement of fact, and it is a fact that ought to be referred to, I think, in view of all these reputed statements about civilians having never done hydrography and that it has always been done by the Navy. Officers of the Navy were sent sometimes with civilian parties, and many of the officers in the Coast Survey to-day received these naval officers and instructed them in hydrographic work.

A gentleman to whom I referred a little while ago, the oldest officer in the Survey, who has had fifty-six years of continuous service, was called upon to go to Annapolis and give instructions to the naval officers there in the matter of topography, which he did, being detailed for that purpose. Thus it will be seen, in the matter of the execution of hydrography by civilians, it was done by them for a long time, and by them exclusively. Now, not only was that true, but at the present time very much of the hydrographic work is done by civilians. It is a mistake to say that the hydrographic work is now all done by naval parties. The hydrography I have constantly referred to here, the higher hydrography, the physical hydrography, is done by civilians, and must be so done. There is no question of this, and no naval officer will contend for a moment that to-day we have not the ablest hydrographers in the men in the civil corps of the Coast Survey. All physical hydrography, practically, including the study of currents and tides, and all work of that nature, has to be done by civil officers. Now, when this question was up ten years ago, a comparison was made as to the efficiency of the civil officers in this hydrographic work and naval officers in the hydrographic work, and I will just read to illustrate this comparison:

A comparison of the average work done each year for a period of years by civilians with the annual average done by naval officers for a similar period shows that a naval force 96 per cent greater than a civilian force produces only 1 per cent increase in the number of soundings; in the number of miles run in sounding only 47 per cent; number of records only 2 per cent, and hydrographic maps only 39 per cent.

This I believe to be a fair comparison, and was made as reported, as you can see, in this official document to which I have referred many times, which was certainly not prejudicial in favor of civilian hydrographers.

Mr. ENLOE. Who made that comparison?

Prof. MENDENHALL. I think it was made under the direction of the superintendent. It was made by a gentleman in the employ of the Geological Survey now, and has been for several years, Mr. Marcus Baker.

Mr. ENLOE. Was that made a part of the record of that investigation?

Prof. MENDENHALL. Yes, sir; you will find it in the report of the commission in 1884, in the testimony of Mr. Colonna.

Mr. ENLOE. Will you let me call your attention to some of Mr. Colonna's testimony on that point?

Prof. MENDENHALL. Yes, sir.

Mr. ENLOE. I quote from page 604 of the testimony, volume 4, Senate Mis. Doc., first session, Forty-ninth Congress. Mr. Colonna was asked the following questions by the chairman:

By the CHAIRMAN:

Q. Of this hydrographic work which is done under the Coast Survey $242,000 of the expense is performed by naval officers?—A. Yes, sir.

Q. And is paid out of the Navy appropriation?—A. Yes, sir.

Q. And $88,000 of that expenditure is performed by the Coast Survey, proper?—A. No, sir.

Q. By whom?—A. It is paid for by the Coast Survey and performed by naval officers.

Q. Out of the Coast Survey appropriation?—A. Yes, sir; and is expended by the naval officers.

Q. So that all expenditures for hydrographic work is made by the naval officers?—A. Yes, sir; practically so.

Q. And the work is performed by naval officers?—A. Yes, sir; at an expense of $330,000, all told.

Q. Is that work all performed under the immediate supervision of what you call the hydrographic inspector?—A. All except the physical hydrography. There is no law for such an officer as the hydrographic inspector that I can find, except the superintendent's will. The office of hydrographic inspector is mentioned in paragraph 57 of the regulations in connection with subsistence. I do not call to mind any other mention of it. He has been allowed to assume the function within the last few years of conducting the hydrographic work almost according to his own views.

Q. And the control of the superintendent of the Coast Survey is merely nominal?—A. That is what it has amounted to formerly.

Q. Are your opportunities of observation sufficient to tell us whether or not that work is being well performed; what is your opinion about that?—A. Yes, sir; I think the work is well performed in the main; in some instances with distinguished ability, for instance, the steamer *Blake's* past season's work, directed by Lieut. Pillsbury, is something that all may be proud of.

Q. I understood you to say a moment ago that the bone of contention was this Hydrographic Office?—A. The hydrographic work of the Coast Survey is what the Navy has been striving after for a long time—they virtually do all the work as it is.

That is Mr. Colonna's testimony.

Prof. MENDENHALL. A great deal of that is entirely correct, but I would like to take that up point by point if I had the time. The committee will bear me out in the statement that I have testified to the value of naval officers on the work. As to the intimation that the superintendence of this work being merely nominal, it is certainly not true in the last four or five years. The hydrographic inspector is constantly consulting the superintendent every day, and the superintendent has actual control over that as he has all other office work. I do not know of anything else in this statement to which it is important to refer; that is, any other essential feature. The work of the *Blake* was, of course, a very excellent piece of work, and has been commended very highly, and it deserves commendation. There is no contention with the hydrographic inspector in the office at the present time, and has not been for a long time. The most amicable relations exist, and the hydrographic inspector and myself are in entire harmony with regard to the operations of the Coast Survey, and also in regard to this question before us.

Now, if I am allowed, I will speak of one more fact in connection with this subject, which is an index of the character of work done in hydrography. All work which is original in its character and which is regarded as contribution to that science is published in the form of papers, appendices, or something of that sort, and out of 140 hydrographic papers that have been published, the civilians have contributed 129 and naval officers have contributed 11. Some of the contributions of those officers are very valuable contributions, and I would not like to be without them.

The whole question of tidal investigations, which is a very important thing in connection with hydrography, has been under the directions of civilians, and must always be there, in my judgment, if it is to be correctly carried on. All advances which have been made in tidal theories, to which I referred, I think, earlier in my testimony, have been advances made by civilians.

Mr. ENLOE. If you will allow me to ask you in regard to these papers in hydrography, you say 129 were furnished by civilians and 11 by naval officers. Is not that due to the fact it is the function of those civilians who do work of this character to furnish these papers, and naval officers are confined to the work in the field?

Prof. MENDENHALL. In some degree, yes. But, of course, naval officers, in connection with fieldwork, have found matters which they thought of sufficient importance to justify their being published; and this is also true with our own officers.

Mr. ENLOE. It was not incumbent upon the naval officers, but it was upon the others?

Prof. MENDENHALL. Not necessarily so; it was only incumbent upon the civilians in case anything was developed which was of sufficient importance, but I do not mention this fact at all as any reflection upon the services of naval officers in regard to hydrography. I am simply trying to put the civil officers engaged in hydrography on a proper basis. It has been represented that they have done none of it, that they never have done it, and I simply want to show the committee that there is no greater mistake than this assumption, and that the civilians are perfectly competent to do any kind of hydrography which is required, and have done it.

Another assertion which has been made, or criticism that has been made, in favor of this bill is that the execution of hydrography under a Treasury bureau is an anomaly, and it is strange that such a thing should be found in the Treasury Department. Well, the history of that, presented early in this hearing, I think, was sufficient to satisfy you in regard to this, that the experiment was tried twice of naval control and proved to be unsatisfactory in both cases, and I would like in addition to ask your attention to the fact that under the Treasury Department we have the Life-Saving Service, which is very directly related to commerce, and the Light-House Board, which is directly in the interest of commerce, almost entirely so; the Bureau ot Navigation is also directly in the interest of commerce, the Marine Hospital is another thing of which the same can be said, and the Revenue Marine, which not entirely in the interest of commerce, yet is more nearly a naval establishment than any of the others, and yet all of these bureaus that I have mentioned in addition to the Coast and Geodetic Survey have long been under the Treasury Department, and it seems to me very properly so.

The Light House Establishment, I may refer to that as being similar in very many respects to the organization of the Coast Survey. There naval officers are detailed for a period of years. There Army officers are detailed and civilians. I am myself a member of the Light-House Board and there is one other civilian member. The other members are three naval officers of high rank and three Army officers of high rank and the Secretary of the Treasury is chairman of that board. It is a civil board, distinctly so, although these Army and naval officers . are detailed to and serve on it and do so very efficiently, yet it would be a very great mistake to have it transferred to the Navy, as has been sometimes contended for by some few naval officers who are rather grasping in their desires. It seems to me the whole Light-House Establishment ought naturally to be where it is. The fact is you must discriminate between the Navy of the United States and the commerce of the United States. When you come to compare these two things you will find the ratio something enormous, and the commerce of the United States is enormously greater in importance and value than the cost of all the vessels of the Navy.

I made this comparison a few years ago. The Coast Survey is for the benefit of the commerce of the United States and not especially for the Navy. It is for commerce. Where there is one naval vessel enters a harbor there are thousands of merchant vessels. It is for the latter class that our work must be done.

This is true of other bureaus. The Life-Saving Service, the Light-House Board, the Bureau of Navigation, all belong to the same class.

Mr. ENLOE. I would like to ask you, do you think there is any more connection of all these commercial bureaus to the Treasury Department than they would be to the Agricultural Department?

Prof. MENDENHALL. I think so; yes, sir. Of course I will say this, I believe it would be very wise to collect all of these—and that has been attempted once or twice—to collect all of these bureaus to which reference has been made into a great department of public works which, in my judgment, is the ideal thing to look forward to; but, as we do not have a department of public works, we have the Treasury Department, which is a very large Department, and one or two bureaus additional do not materially interfere with its operations, and besides, there is a good deal in the relation which exists between these various bureaus. Now, the work of the Coast Survey and the Light-House Board is very closely related. We interchange our information that we get almost every hour, every day, and that relation is such as could only exist between two bureaus of the same department. Our relation with the Marine-Hospital Corps, the Bureau of Navigation, and Life-Saving Service is also very close, and we get a good deal of information from all these people and this close relationship is one which we consider to be desirable.

Mr. MONEY. Do you think all of these several bureaus you mention ought to be under one administrative head?

Prof. MENDENHALL. Yes, sir.

The CHAIRMAN. That has been done in France?

Prof. MENDENHALL. I think it was done under the ministry of public works.

Mr. GEISSENHAINER. You say this has been attempted?

Prof. MENDENHALL. I think such bills have been introduced into Congress.

Mr. GEISSENHAINER. There must have been some reasons for not doing it, then.

Prof. MENDENHALL. I do not know, I am sure; and I am not quite certain that bills have been introduced, but I do know this, that it has been considered because I have a pamphlet on my table published a few years ago sent to me recently in which a strong argument is made for combining all of these into one department.

Mr. MONEY. I suppose such an organization is more desirable than anything else, it matters not what you call it.

. Mr. ENLOE. Department of Commerce is a better title.

Prof. MENDENHALL. Now, I have been diverted to a point, which I think will come in properly, and that is a very brief statement of how this work is done abroad, and after that I will be pleased to answer any questions as fully as I can. In the first place I found it was somewhat difficult to collect this information, although aware of some of the facts, but not all of them, and I found particular difficulty in getting all of this information. I read a little detail of the plan as maintained in foreign surveys, and in each of the organizations of the surveys of these nations I have also given the number of the standing army in each country, because the division of public work of this character between the civilian and the military organizations in any country might be assumed to be based in some degree on the relative strength of these organizations.

ADMINISTRATION AND ORGANIZATION OF FOREIGN SURVEYS.

AUSTRO-HUNGARY.

Surveys are conducted by the Military Geographical Institute, under the war department. The personnel of the institute consists of staff officers, line officers, civilian assistants, noncommissioned officers, soldiers, and contract workmen. The head of the institute and the heads of the various divisions are staff officers. The staff has entire charge of the scientific part of the survey, but the line officers are detailed to aid in the work. The officers of the staff who belong to the institute are selected from private life by competitive examination, and receive their promotions in a special category of their own, independent of the other officers of the staff. This particular corps of officers, therefore, has a constitution only affiliated to the military organization.

Area, 240,942 square miles. Army, 316,942 (peace footing).

BELGIUM.

Geodetic and topographic surveys conducted under the war department, by staff officers of the army. Area, 11,373 square miles. Army, 47,225 (peace footing).

Surveys executed by the geographical and statistical bureau, under civil administration. Officers of the topographic brigade of the army and mining engineers may be detailed for duty under the bureau.

Surveys by the geographical service of the army, executed by the general staff. Astronomical determinations by astronomers of the Paris Observatory.

Area, 204,092 square miles. Army, 564,603 (peace footing).

Surveys by Geographic Institute under the war department.
Area, 110,623 square miles. Permanent army, 247,809.

Surveys under commissioners of works, Organization Royal Engineers, civilians. Corps, five-sixths civilian.

Department of home, revenue, and agriculture. Organization, royal engineers and civilians.

Surveys under the department of the interior, conducted by a geographic commission. Commission composed of several directors of departments of the Government. Organization mixed, civil, and military.

Geodetic commission. Civil administration and organization.

Geographic Institute. Civil administration. Organization mixed, civil, and military.

Prussian Royal Geodetic Institute. Civil administration. Topography by general staff of the army.

Military Cartographic Institute, conducted by general staff. Area, 8,644,100 square miles; army, 868,672, peace footing.

The CHAIRMAN. Did you mention England?

Prof. MENDENHALL. Yes, sir; I mentioned Great Britain and this statement is, as nearly true as it is possible for me to make.

Mr. GEISSENHAINER. I would suggest, Mr. Chairman, that if it be agreeable to the professor, for him to continue his remarks on Friday and that we adjourn now.

Thereupon the committee adjourned to meet on Friday, June 1, 1894.

COMMITTEE ON NAVAL AFFAIRS,
Friday, June 1, 1894.

The Committee on Naval Affairs this day met, Hon. Amos J. Cummings in the chair.

The CHAIRMAN. The committee will come to order and the statement of Prof. Mendenhall will be resumed.

STATEMENT OF PROF. T. C. MENDENHALL—Continued.

Prof. MENDENHALL then addressed the committee. He said:

Mr. Chairman and gentlemen of the committee, just at the close of the hearing the other day I was referring to another criticism which was passed upon the operations of this Bureau, in that it had been asserted that the cost of the work was steadily increasing, and this had been brought about, as was intimated, by means of a quiet extension of its work and the appropriations. I wish to positively state to the committee that this is absolutely contrary to the facts in the case.

An examination of the annual appropriations made for this Bureau in the last five years will show not an increase but on the contrary a continuous decrease of the cost of the Bureau. The appropriations and the estimates have been actually growing smaller. I have here a chart which I drew up some months ago illustrating this fact, which will give you a graphic picture of it very quickly. You will see this chart shows appropriations since 1871, the annual appropriations for the Coast and Geodetic Survey, including also the estimates. That is to say the red curves which are here show the estimates which have been made and the blue curves show the appropriations which have been made. This black line is the $500,000 line. When the red and blue curves pass above or below it, it indicates that the appropriations have been proportionately more or less than $500,000. The diagram is divided here simply for convenience into periods of a various number of years to distinguish the administrations of the several Superintendents. If you follow those two red and blue lines you will see what occurred in this matter of appropriations and estimates for the last five years.

Then again here you will see during these three years, that is from the beginning of the estimates and appropriations made under my own administration, they have been falling, less always than they have ever been before except a single year during the beginning of Mr. Thorn's administration, when for special reasons well known to most of you the Survey was decidedly reduced in its appropriations, but at the present time the appropriations are very much smaller even than that, and I call attention to the fact that this does not result by act of Congress, but it is by the act of the Superintendent that these reductions have been made. That is, during this year the appropriations and estimates are identical, and the Appropriation Committee appropriated the amount which was requested by the Superintendent. Last year there was a difference of perhaps some $30,000 or $40,000; I nave forgotten exactly what the difference is. Now, the estimates for the present year are much smaller in proportion than they have ever been made for the Survey. This diagram shows a considerable fluctuation in the cost of the Survey principally in the early days, in the seventies, along in 1874, 1875, and 1876. About that time the cost increased quite considerably, and then it diminished quite considerably; yet during the last five years it shows a steady diminution in cost as is shown both by the estimates of the Superintendent and the actual appropriations.

Mr. ENLOE. Let me ask you one question there before you put that map up, where did your administration begin on that map?

Prof. MENDENHALL. The first appropriation made under my administration was in 1891. I came in at the fall of 1889, and the estimates for the following year had then been made.

Mr. ENLOE. Were not your estimates submitted to the Fifty-first Congress greater than the appropriations made in the Fiftieth Congress.

Prof. MENDENHALL. The first estimates submitted under my administration were estimates prepared and made out previous to my coming into the office, and the result of first conference I had with the Appropriation Committee, or the chairman of the committee, was that they wanted me to revise and resubmit the estimates.

Mr. ENLOE. That was in the Fifty-first Congress?

Prof. MENDENHALL. Yes, sir; the first Congress under my administration, and then these estimates were accepted absolutely by the committee as I reported them, and they were for the succeeding year also.

Mr. ENLOE. The Committee on Appropriations sent them back to you for revision, I refer to the first estimates.

Prof. MENDENHALL. Not officially.

Mr. ENLOE. Well, the chairman of the committee did?

Prof. MENDENHALL. It was the result of a conversation with the chairman of the committee. I will say this, Mr. Chairman, that I discovered that the estimates had been made on the same basis many estimates were made, the practice being, as I was informed when I came into this work, and I think it is quite generally true of other bureaus, that estimates were made very largely in excess of what you really expected to get, with the expectation that the Committee on Appropriations would very largely reduce them.

Mr. MONEY. They realize that fact?

Prof. MENDENHALL. They do, and when I came into the office and found that all these first estimates were made out, at my own request I revised the estimates, announcing to the committee at that time my policy in the future would be to estimate for precisely what I thought the Bureau needed.

Mr. ENLOE. The estimates you recollect were made by your predecessor?

Prof. MENDENHALL. Yes, sir; they were made by my predecessor, Mr. Thorne, because he left the office before I came in.

Mr. ENLOE. And they were not made by you?

Prof. MENDENHALL. They were not made by me. When I came in, as I say, in the latter part of August the estimates were found prepared and I had little to do with them except to send them in. At that time I did not know very much about the necessities of the Bureau, but by the time the estimates came around to be actually considered by the committee I was then familiar with the work and knew something about the expenditures which would have to be made under them, and I was also told by my own officers that those estimates were really larger than the necessity of the work demanded, I think, because it was the expectation that the committee would revise them, and I then stated to the committee that I did not believe in that mode of making estimates, nor have I changed my attitude in that respect since, and the committee has for several years in succession given me precisely what I have asked for, and indeed in one case they gave me more than I asked for.

Mr. ENLOE. At that point I want to call your attention to the statement in Executive Document No. 180, which contains, I believe, a letter from you on this subject submitted to the Fifty-second Congress at its first session. You state there:

The original estimates for the expenditures of the Survey during the year, beginning at that date, were prepared within a few weeks after I assumed the duties of Superintendent and therefore necessarily before I had opportunities of learning much of the relative strength or weakness of the several branches of the service or for determining the wisest distribution of expenditures among these branches in order to secure an efficient and economical administration. They were substantially the same as those of previous years, with such additions and changes as naturally occur in such a service. The amount asked for was considerably greater than that finally appropriated, as has been the case, without exception, in all of the previous years of the history of the Survey.

On the occasion of their first consideration by the Appropriations Committee, early in 1890, I suggested certain changes, which a better knowledge, resulting from several months' experience, indicated as desirable. The committee then requested me to withdraw the estimates and revise them in accordance with maturer judgment, and to incorporate such changes in the organization as would, in my opinion, tend to increase its efficiency without increasing its cost. After a careful consideration of the whole subject, including consultations with the chiefs of divisions, the assistant in charge of the office, and most of all the older field officers, a new set of estimates were submitted, which were accepted by the Appropriations Committee and made part of the sundry civil bill, practically without modification.

The enactment of this as a law on August 30, 1890, necessitated and contemplated certain changes, which are exhibited in the accompanying lists, together with all others made during the year 1890.

Mr. ENLOE. Now, on that point I want to ask you who revised the salary list in the Coast Survey at the time; who were chiefs of divisions; who did that work?

Prof. MENDENHALL. Mr. Chairman, may I refer first to the question of revision, which is a question that has been several times touched upon? Mr. Enloe has suggested some new points, to which I will reply that I am willing to accept my letter written at that date as a more accurate statement, since what I stated just now was purely from memory. When I was appointed to the office, I came to Washington and took the oath of office and then told the President that it would be absolutely necessary for me to be absent several weeks to attend to some private matters. I then went away, and when I came back everything, of course, was unfamiliar. I knew nothing of the appropriations made, and these estimates were drawn up by my assistants, precisely as stated there in my letter, and I will accept that as the correct statement. Touching upon the matter of the revision of salaries, which is the point which Mr. Enloe raised, it is impossible for me at the present time to name with absolute accuracy the persons with whom I consulted, but I will say I consulted with the older people in the office. I particularly consulted Mr. Schott, who is the oldest officer we have in the Bureau, the next oldest to Prof. Davidson, and Mr. Whiting, who was here the other day, and I consulted Mr. Tittmann, whom I had known quite well, and Mr. Colonna, the assistant in charge of the office, who, in consequence of that position, which he had filled for several years, came in close contact with all these officers, and I presume I consulted others.

The CHAIRMAN. What was that revision of salaries?

Prof. MENDENHALL. It was a revision—that is the better word, as the history of the case shows there was not much change; there was but a small change in the total amount of the appropriations. There were some salaries increased, as I referred to the other day, and you will remember I also showed the other day that, even after that increased compensation had been made—some on account of promotion, that the great majority of these officers still to-day receive a lower compensation than they did ten years ago, in consequence of the fact that the subsistence had been abolished. The particular object of this provision was to remove a large number of irregular amounts that had been appropriated, such as $1,420 and $2,337, and such amounts as that, which grew up mostly in small additions from time to time, and it was felt to be desirable to take the whole salary list and arrange it by certain definite steps, and $200 a step was adopted and I will frankly say, as far as I could, I made the arrangement without a reduction in the salaries, because there was no salary I knew of that ought to be reduced, and there were a great many I think ought to be increased.

Mr. ENLOE. Let me ask you right there, is it not a fact that the salaries of the assistants, those who had their salaries increased, had an average increase of $110.29?

Prof. MENDENHALL. That may be so.

Mr. ENLOE. And that the plate printers got a decrease of from $100 to $330?

Prof. MENDENHALL. That may be true. I will say that the plate printers got a decrease, but I am not quite sure there was an average increase of the assistant.

Mr. ENLOE. Was it your impression that the plate printers received too much compensation?

Prof. MENDENHALL. That was my impression.

Mr. ENLOE. Was it not a fact that many of them resigned and went to places in the Bureau of Printing and Engraving?

Prof. MENDENHALL. Yes, sir; and it is a fact that these same men came back to us and asked to be reappointed, all except one, and they would have been very glad to be reappointed. In regard to that matter, I am sorry I have not with me the Congressional Record containing a copy of the debate on this question, as I would be glad to read the defense of my action.

The CHAIRMAN. Let me ask you some questions: The plate-printers, did they belong to any trades union or organization?

Prof. MENDENHALL. I do not know, sir. I did not inquire whether they did or not.

Mr. ENLOE. I can answer that question; they did.

Prof. MENDENHALL. I want to make a full statement in regard to that matter, and I am sorry I did not bring with me the Record containing the defense of my action by Mr. Herbert, now Secretary of the Navy.

Mr. MONEY. You can send a copy of it to us.

Prof. MENDENHALL. In which he takes the position, in defending my action in that regard, that as a rule those officers of the Government who do the higher quality of work receive a smaller compensation than that paid by great railroads and commercial organizations to the same quality of men; whereas, on the other hand——

The CHAIRMAN. Did they receive the same wages the plate-printers received at the Bureau of Engraving and Printing?

Prof. MENDENHALL. I will come to that in a moment and give you a full history—on the other hand, says Mr. Herbert, those who received a smaller compensation, those who do work which does not require an amount of skill and training and professional knowledge, receive in the Government service higher than they do outside. That you will find in Mr. Herbert's speech on that occasion. Now, to come to an actual statement of what occurred. The statement was made to me by several persons, I think first by the chief of the engraving division, that the work was costing more, that we were paying more than current rates to the plate-printers and also to some other people—I think we were also paying more to the people in the instrument division, such a statement was made to me—than was customary to be paid outside or was necessary, and that this was one direction in which judicious economy could be exercised.

Mr. MONEY. That is, they could get more pay with you than they could get outside?

Prof. MENDENHALL. Yes, sir; I investigated it, of course, before I took any action. I called before me the foreman of our plate printing establishment who was also a practical plate printer, and if I mistake not is also a member of the Plate-Printers' Union in good standing, and asked him what his judgment was about this matter. I said, "I am ignorant about this and I wish to do exactly what is right." And he said, "These men are now being paid more than they ought to receive."

Mr. ENLOE. What is his name?

Mr. MENDENHALL. His name is Moore. I have his written statement. I even took the precaution to ask him to put his statement in writing, that he could procure outside of our Bureau plenty of able men to do this work at a decidedly smaller salary. Now, of course, I felt it was incumbent upon me with that statement in hand to make that recommendation. I would have been false to my duty as a Government officer if I had not.

Mr. ENLOE. Do you remember Mr. Moore's initials?

Prof. MENDENHALL. I think it is F. W. Moore. He was our foreman then, and he is still foreman of the office.

The CHAIRMAN. And is still a member of the plate-printers' organization?

Prof. MENDENHALL. As far as I know.

Mr. MONEY. He would not likely be there if he was not.

Prof. MENDENHALL. But to go on with the history of these changes. After Mr. Moore told me that this was the case, I could not conscientiously avoid making the recommendation which I did. I did not want to discharge these men, so I told them they could go on with their work at this reduced salary. Now, Mr. Chairman, as to the comparison of the wages paid these men and plate-printers in the employ of the Bureau of Engraving and Printing, I know of no possible means to make a comparison. In that office they are paid by piecework, and in our office they are paid by the month and the work is entirely different. We print great copperplates, the largest printed in the country and possibly in the world. We used to use hand presses, but I relieved those men of that much to their gratification by the introduction of power presses, but at first we had to do that by hand power. It is impossible to make a comparison of wages paid by the two bureaus, and the only answer I can make to your question is this: that one or two of these men who refused to accept this reduction were very glad to get employment again in our office, and not long afterwards returned and sought reemployment in the Coast Survey. The fact is, our work is much easier there. In the Bureau of Engraving and Printing the men earn a large compensation provided they work very hard, as it is all piecework. With us they work by the month, which they usually prefer. We have not had the slightest difficulty and we have not had the slightest friction with the trades' union.

Mr. MONEY. What was the proportion of the reduction?

Prof. MENDENHALL. I have forgotten. Probably $1,000 or $1,300 all told, and perhaps Mr. Enloe has it in his mind. Whether the reduction was $30 or $130, or what, I can not tell, but I can furnish these facts if you wish them, but I can not tell now, as that was so long ago. I did that with the impression that it was the right thing for me to do.

Mr. ENLOE. If there is no objection, I want to say the Plate Printer's Union did disprove of this action of the Coast and Geodetic Survey, and I have a copy of some resolutions presented to me recently adopted by the local organization here approving my action in attempting to defend the rights of those people as they understood it in the Coast and Geodetic Survey.

Those resolutions are as follows:

WASHINGTON, D. C., *April 28, 1894.*

Hon. B. A. ENLOE:

DEAR SIR: At a regular stated meeting of the Plate Printers' Protective Union, 5041, American Federation of Labor, working under the auspices of the National Printers' Union of America, held on the above date, the following resolutions were unanimously adopted:

Resolved, That the thanks of this Union are hereby extended to the Hon. B. A. Enloe, of Tennessee, for the able manner in which he defended the workingman's cause in a speech delivered in the House of Representatives in May, 1892, and again on the 16th day of March, 1894, when he exposed the outrages perpetrated by the Coast Survey officials on the workingmen employed in that Bureau by having their salaries reduced in 1890 so that the officials might have theirs increased.

Therefore, be it further resolved, That we, the Plate Printers' Protective Union, recommend the Hon. B. A. Enloe, of Tennessee, to the workingmen of the country and the State of Tennessee for their kind consideration and support.

Given under our hand and seal of this Union this 28th day of April, 1894.

[L. S.]   EUGENE BETTES, *President.*
                 JOHN WOOD, *Secretary,*
                 ISAAC GIRRODETTE,
                 WM. JOHNSON,
                 JOHN T. CONNORS,
                 ARTHUR SMALL,
                 E. W. McRAE,
                         Committee.

Prof. MENDENHALL. I simply mean to say I myself know of no difficulty. We have never had any difficulty in filling the places as soon as they became vacant. It has been long since a vacancy has occurred.

The CHAIRMAN. You have not had any communication with the Union organization?

Prof. MENDENHALL. None at all.

Mr. ENLOE. If you will allow me, I would like to ask a question before getting from this subject any further in regard to the revision of the salary list and the increases. I find here the following assistants were increased at that time: A. T. Mosman, salary increased from $2,800 to $3,000; William H. Dennis, salary increased from $2,400 to $2,800; Cleveland Rockwell, salary increased from $2,400 to $2,600; J. W. Donn, salary increased from $2,400 to $2,600; William Eimbeck, salary increased from $2,300 to $2,400; Edward Goodfellow, salary increased from $2,300 to $2,400; H. L. Whiting, salary increased from $2,300 to $2,400; J. W. Parsons, salary increased from $1,800 to $2,200.

Prof. MENDENHALL. He is not an assistant in the Survey; he is in the office force?

Mr. ENLOE. H. G. Ogden, salary increased from $2,200 to $2,400; O. H. Tittmann, salary increased from $2,200 to $2,400; E. Smith, salary increased from $1,800 to $2,000; F. H. Parsons, salary increased from $1,400 to $1,800.

4561——9

Prof. MENDENHALL. Mr. Parsons resigned as an assistant and was made librarian.

Mr. ENLOE. But he was an assistant at the time?

Prof. MENDENHALL. He was subassistant I think at the time he resigned.

Mr. ENLOE. C. T. Jardella, salary increased from $1,500 to $1,600; W. Q. Vinal, salary increased from $1,500 to $1,600; J. W. Baglow, salary increased from $1,500 to $1,600; V. H. Vanorden, salary increased from $1,500 to $1,600.

Prof. MENDENHALL. I would like to call the attention of the committee to the fact that if the statement should be made as to the total increase of the cost of the corps before this revision and after it, it would be better for the purposes of comparison. I wish to remind you that this corps stands very largely in a line—that is to say, it is a matter of lineal priority—and the result is, when a single promotion is made, one single increase of salary makes a vacancy which may affect the salaries of 20 people, and a great deal of that which has been read is due to that fact. Just at that time there were vacancies existing. I have forgotten what they were; but I remember by the death of a single assistant, a man named Hergesheimer, which made a vacancy in a $2,800 place. You can see in order to promote one man to fill that vacancy a movement takes place along the whole line.

Mr. MONEY. Let me suggest to you to take this list Mr. Enloe has and mark opposite each man his place, and whether he has a scientific or clerical place, and also if he was promoted?

Prof. MENDENHALL. I can tell you now by looking at the list.

Mr. MONEY. I should prefer that it go on the record just exactly what position each one held, what his duties were, whether they were scientific or clerical?

Prof. MENDENHALL. I will do that, and I am ready to explain to you in regard to two of these men. Mr. John W. Parsons served for a long time, many years, as the accountant of the Survey. He was really the disbursing agent, but, as a matter of fact, he had not had that title. At the beginning of Mr. Thorne's administration in 1885, the disbursing agent of the Coast and Geodetic Survey was removed by the Treasury Department, much to the inconvenience of the business of the Coast Survey, and when I took charge that inconvenience was represented to me very strongly; I appreciated these reasons very fully then and I have been of the same mind ever since. I therefore requested the Secretary of the Treasury to make a disbursing agent for the Coast and Geodetic Survey, which he did, and he appointed Mr. John W. Parsons, he having served eighteen years at that time and now over twenty-three years in the Coast Survey. He was at the time the accounting clerk. He was made disbursing agent, and promoted, therefore, from $1,800, which he received as a fourth-class clerk. That explains his promotion.

The CHAIRMAN. There had not been a disbursing agent before that time?

Prof. MENDENHALL. There was one up to 1885, I think, but at that time the disbursement of the funds was taken to the Treasury Department, and it increased the labor vastly, as I showed at the time by letters to the Appropriations Committee and it, I think, was brought out on the floor of the House, also, that the making of Mr. Parsons disbursing agent resulted in actual economy in the disbursement of the money. As a matter of fact, it did, and it is very distinctly shown. In regard to Mr. F. H. Parsons, that was the case of a man who was promoted simply from a subassistant at $1,400 to $1,800. Mr. Parsons had been subassistant for a number of years, but he was peculiarly adapted to the duties of librarian. He had a physical weakness, being lame. This was found to interfere to some extent with his duties in the field, and, therefore, he was made librarian and given simply the salary which the librarian had always had; that was not a promotion, as a matter of fact, but simply a transfer of a man from one division to another. Mr. Parsons is still librarian, and has been so ever since his appointment. I will give you all this information in writing in regard to this matter.

Mr. MONEY. And I wish you would be careful to state whether their duties are scientific or clerical.

Prof. MENDENHALL. All are field officers with the exception of those two whom I have mentioned.

Mr. ENLOE. I would like to ask this question, please. You stated at the time you made this revision you were inexperienced in the Coast Survey and necessarily had to rely upon the advice of your leading assistants. Do you think it was very reliable advice upon which to make increases of salary when these men passed upon the increase of their own salaries?

Prof. MENDENHALL. They did not pass upon the increase of their own salaries.

Mr. ENLOE. Did they make suggestions?

Prof. MENDENHALL. There was no man who had the slightest suspicion the salaries would be increased. I think that is a suspicion that only needs to be made to be rejected.

Mr. ENLOE. The question arises how their salaries were increased; if you consulted them and got their advice in making this revision, how did their salaries happen to be increased, as you say you would not know in regard to this?

Prof. MENDENHALL. The older men in the service have reputations not only known in this country but all over the world. The younger men I did not know, and it was in regard to the younger men that the older men were consulted. More than that, as I have already stated, many promotions among the older men were simply those which took place on a vacancy, and I was naturally less liable to make a mistake by following the regular routine than in any other way, but I may say here that I am willing to have this committee, or any other properly authorized body, to take a census of opinion of all the assistants of the Coast and Geodetic Survey in regard to these promotions which took place at that time as to whether they were wise or proper. I think the universal judgment of the corps is that they were wise. As I say, certain of these men—Mr. Mosman, Mr. Whiting, Mr. Eimbeck, Mr. Tittmann, and that class of men were known everywhere, and I knew some of them personally before I came into the Coast Survey, some I knew by reputation, and I was guided by their opinion.

Mr. ENLOE. You went in office in 1889?

Prof. MENDENHALL. Yes, sir.

Mr. ENLOE. What time in 1889?

Prof. MENDENHALL. In the fall of 1889.

Mr. ENLOE. The salary list which you submitted here the other day showing a percentage between the salaries since 1884 I think you compared with 1893.

Prof. MENDENHALL. 1884 and 1885; I put the two years down, and then I took last year. The present year will make the same showing exactly, but the present year is incomplete, so I took 1893 because it was a complete year.

Mr. ENLOE. I have taken for the purpose the period between 1887 and 1893, which shows very large increase in the salaries since 1887. Is it your idea that these men were insufficiently compensated from 1884 to 1887 or 1888, when they began the system of increasing the salaries.

Prof. MENDENHALL. I should like to know on what basis that compensation is made that it shows a greater increase in 1893 over 1887.

Mr. ENLOE. These figures are taken from the official reports.

Prof. MENDENHALL. Have you included the subsistence these men received in both of those years?

Mr. ENLOE. It is the period between 1887 and 1893; I do not know that this statement shows it.

Prof. MENDENHALL. You can get it by application to the disbursing agent, but it is absolutely necessary in order to make this comparison. Now, I distinctly stated the other day that that was included in the statement I put before the committee. I showed that that was included. These gentlemen, ten years ago, received certain allowances for subsistence, and their total annual income from salary added to subsistence is, of course, the total amount they receive. They receive a certain total amount of money for their services. That is the practical outcome of it.

Mr. ENLOE. And subsistence is not given now in addition to the salary. There is no subsistence?

Prof. MENDENHALL. Subsistence is assumed to be administered on this basis, that it shall simply compensate the field officer for the additional expenses to which he is subject on account of the payment of his own board when he is in the field over what he would be subject to when he was in the office. For instance, when a field officer comes to Washington or is in Washington he receives no allowance for subsistence, nor receives any allowance for subsistence when he is at home, if his home be other than Washington. Take the case of Prof. Davidson, living in San Francisco, who receives no subsistence while residing in San Francisco, but the moment he goes to the field he receives subsistence, and we try to administer that subsistence so it will compensate for the increased amount of the expenses; but in the old days, in 1884 and before, subsistence was regarded by all authorities, and by the assistants themselves, as part of the compensation.

As I stated, officers remaining in Washington all the year round were allowed $2 or $3 a day for subsistence and the consequence was that salaries at that time were higher and men received more money for their work than they do at the present time. I think if you apply the same rule to 1887 you will find that it is still true. Now, answering your other question, I do believe that these men were not properly compensated after the removal of this subsistence, although I thought that method of compensation was wrong. I have always contended, from the moment I came into the office, that I believed the sudden removal of this subsistence, such a sharp and sudden reduction in the compensation of these men, which put them below what they had been receiving, was very hard on them and any small advances that I have been able to make them, and which have been very small, and which have come in the natural way by death, resignation, etc., I have been very glad to do.

Mr. ENLOE. There is a good part of the year a field officer is not engaged in actual work in the field?

Prof. MENDENHALL. Yes; sometimes half a year, and sometimes even more, and sometimes very much less. But these field officers are engaged nearly the year round in the field, dependent upon circumstances. Take Alaska, the length of the season there is restricted to about six months, and it is very largely restricted to that in the northern part of the United States, but we send people South in the winter, as many as we can, and they work there.

Mr. ENLOE. When they discontinue their work in the field they return to the office in Washington?

Prof. MENDENHALL. That depends entirely upon whether they are instructed to do so or not. Sometimes they do and sometimes not. They are allowed traveling expenses here. Those who are sent here by the instructions of the Superintendent to consult and advise with the Superintendent are allowed by act of Congress subsistence during the time they are here. However, that is not a common thing. It happens rarely that a man is brought here on that account. Usually they come from the field and their subsistence stops when they get here. But in fact there is a regulation which allows the Superintendent in his discretion to allow the subsistence to run for a certain limited number of days after the assistant reaches home in order to allow him to select a proper boarding place, etc.

Mr. ENLOE. I understand you have here such a thing in connection with the Geodetic Survey during the winter months as a geodetic convention composed of these assistants?

Prof. MENDENHALL. We did have this last winter; yes, sir. I brought to this office five or six assistants, and those assistants brought here were allowed subsistence according to the regulations. That that convention was of the very utmost importance I need hardly say. Let me go back and say this is the second conference we have had, the first, as you are doubtless aware, being that of the topographers. I found here a corps of about 50 men, many of whom had served for thirty or forty years in the Government, who did not, in some cases, know each other personally; and I found them engaged in the same line of work scattered in different parts of the country, dependent entirely upon traditions and through correspondence, and that kind of thing, for a knowledge of methods and operations and therefore I think if in my administration of the Coast Survey there is one thing of which I am proud it is the organization of these two conferences. I called these topographers together, and they spent several weeks here in studying methods of topography and various other work which I need scarcely discuss at great length, for their report is published in volume, which has received the highest praise everywhere, and is referred to as a standard authority on those questions. That was two years ago. This past season, for the same purpose, I arranged to have a conference of the geodesists, those specially engaged in doing triangulation and astronomical work, and they also labored assiduously and profitably, and I think no just criticism can be made against a policy of that kind, as the cost was so small and the results were so valuable.

Now, if you will allow me, I would like to go back to the question which was raised in regard to the dismissal of these people. I mentioned the matter of instrument-makers, and I will conclude what I started to say about that. I, at the same time, reduced the compensation of the instrument-makers and dismissed several from the service, and I did that knowing fully and entirely what I was doing. It so happens that my life has been such that I know something about instrument-making, although I do not know anything about plate-printing, as I have never had anything to do with it. I have worked in the shop myself and I know what it is, and I know what fine instruments are, having used them for a quarter of a century. The result was I found the instrument division of the Coast Survey in what I considered a very bad condition. Men were paid salaries there far beyond anything they could get outside. More than that, they had become indolent and lazy, and some declared that they could never be dismissed from the service, because their influence was such that it was impossible.

That is the condition I found in that bureau. Those in charge of that division will tell you these men were reported as being inefficient. I dismissed several of those men, and then when I had an opportunity to revise the appropriation I reduced their compensation, and I reduced it only so far as to still make it easy for me to secure, whenever I want, the finest instrument-makers in the country. There are not very many of them, but we have no trouble in getting them. The highest compensation we pay an instrument-maker is $1,200, but when there is taken into consideration the permanency of the work, the short number of hours of work, and the number of holidays which they have, all of which I think is perfectly legitimate for them to consider, it is easily seen why I am able to procure the best instrument-makers in the country for this amount. Before I undertook this I examined into the matter by correspondence with fine instrument-makers in the country, with Brashear, of Allegheny, the Queen Company, of Philadelphia, and others. I visited these establishments, and I know precisely what the men are paid.

Mr. MONEY. Do you have any trouble about getting competent instrument-makers?

Prof. MENDENHALL. I have had to hunt a little to get the highest type of them. For instance, a vacancy occurred just a year ago. A man resigned, who is now back at work again. He left here at the time, but he came back. After the original discharge of those two or three men from the service, I tried to put myself into communication with the best talent in that direction in the whole country, and I did that by means of correspondence with those men of whom I spoke, and also by advertising. I advertised in the newspapers in the West and East for instrument-makers. The result of that was that I came into a correspondence with perhaps two or three dozen of the finest instrument makers in the country. I could only appoint two or three, but I wrote them all, and told them to keep me informed constantly in regard to their location, so that when there is any vacancy I could appoint one of them. They have done so, and in that way I got the last one, who is one of the finest workmen I have ever seen. I followed him up by letters. ·

Mr. MONEY. Is the present force satisfactory to you?

Prof. MENDENHALL. Entirely so. I found this man in St. Louis, where he last was, and I got him from there. Now, that is what I have to say in regard to that act, and I do not believe it needs any defense.

Now, Mr. Chairman, I will have to proceed very hurriedly in the remainder of this because I do not wish to trespass upon the patience of the committee further, but there are some important points that I must press upon you, and if you will pardon me I will do so. Allow me to submit here a letter from the Secretary transmitting a letter from me containing all of the detailed expenditures of the Coast Survey, of which I have spoken several times, which has been forwarded to Congress ever since the year 1885, therefore Congress has always had in its possession the most perfect detailed account of the expenditures of this Bureau, and there can be no reason for criticism in that direction.

Now, I want to refer very briefly to a newspaper clipping which I have here, purporting to contain selections from a letter of the Acting Secretary of the Navy, or Assistant Secretary McAdoo, and I trust I am not going beyond the proper limits of the discussion of a question of this kind when I do this, because there are several points here which I think should have attention. Most of the points Mr. McAdo raises here, advocating the transfer of a portion of this Bureau to the Navy Department, have already been touched upon; and, therefore, I will not take that up in connection with this argument, but I will call your attention to this clause:

Congress would then have an itemized estimate for the entire work before it each year, and a complete and accurate statement of expenditures could be easily prepared at any time, so that Congress and the people could always know just what the work of the Coast Survey was costing.

It is hardly necessary to say that has always been done, and that complete and itemized estimates were always before Congress. The particular thing I want to reply to is the intimation in this paper that the Coast and Geodetic Survey authorities have attempted to deny and overlook or ignore the relations of the Navy and their services in connection with this work. This is the statement in the paragraph which I now read, where he says:

As an evidence of the deliberate attempt to cover up the connection of the naval establishment with the present work, your attention is called to the statement in the annexed letters, wherein it is shown that the names of naval officers participating in the work of the survey, and which by long custom were usually affixed to the charts, have been recently taken therefrom. On the other hand the Coast Survey office has constantly on dress parade a long list of its employés, in the full dress of their official distinctions and learned titles.

Now, Mr. Chairman, I would imagine before writing a paragraph like that one would take the trouble to look and see whether there was any foundation for such a thing, and I am sorry to say I fear that was not done.

The CHAIRMAN. Is that correct?

Prof. MENDENHALL. I am going on to state whether it is correct or not, as I wish to explain this. In the first place, referring to the general proposition, there has never been any disposition on the part of the Coast Survey to conceal or in any way ignore the value of the services of the U. S. Navy. On the contrary, we have taken the same care to give due credit to naval officers as we have to represent the value of the work of our civil assistants. If you will consult any of our reports you will find there has never been a naval officer connected with the Survey whose name is not there, and whose name is not attached to every bit of work he has done. There is no naval officer who has prepared an appendix for which he has not had full credit for that work. There is positively and absolutely no distinction between the treatment of a naval officer and a civil officer in connection with our publications, except one, and that is in favor of the naval officer and not the civilian. That is to say, the statement as made here that the Coast Survey has always on dress parade a long list of its employés in full dress of their official distinctions and learned titles is without foundation. Mr. Chairman, to satisfy myself since seeing this, had several persons busily searching the charts prepared by the Coast Survey, as I was sure one has never appeared with the professional title on it, and I have not found a single case in which a civilian has appeared on that chart with any other than his plain name and the word assistant.

Mr. MONEY. Why should it not be so?

Prof. MENDENHALL. It is right and proper it should be so. As to the Navy, we have always given the full naval rank in every case, and that is right. I have added afterwards the title which we have given the officer as an assistant of the Coast Survey, which many of them, I am pleased to say, are glad to have added. Now, that is a fact. If you will look at the thousands and hundreds of thousands of charts we have printed you will see that is the case right straight through, and we have never deviated from that. Examine our charts and you will see we have there given the naval officers their full rank. I have had all other publications also examined and I found two or three cases in which men have had the title of "professor" applied to them, but in hunting these cases down I have found invariably they were papers which were prepared by those men before they were attached to the Coast Survey. Take, for instance, Prof. Bache. He was known by the title of professor by everybody, and was for a long time a professor before coming to the Coast Survey, and had published a valuable work on magnetics, and, after coming to the Coast Survey, the Coast Survey published that paper, which is a very valuable contribution. That is one instance. We found in one case a professor had written a paper on tides, to which the title of professor had been applied. In modern times there is only a single case, a single exception. Mr. Wainwright remembered and called to my attention that in the report of the topographical conference to which I referred there was a translation made from the French by one of the assistants, Mr. Hodgkins, to whose name were attached the letters "C. E.," civil engineer, which was his degree. This being so, I maintain that this criticism is not justified. The Coast Survey people have never been on dress parade with their titles, and have been entirely just and fair to the Navy.

Mr. MONEY. To what extent in foreign charts do they print the titles to the engineers?

Prof. MENDENHALL. I am coming to that, because the next criticism is here:

As an evidence of the deliberate attempt to cover up the connection of the naval establishment with the present work, your attention is called to the statements in the annexed letters wherein it is shown that the names of naval officers participating in the work of the survey, and which by long custom were usually affixed to the charts, have been recently taken therefrom.

I would like to call the careful attention of the committee to the history of that matter. What are called authorities on the charts you will understand when I show you this chart [exhibiting same]. This will give you a good idea as to the conditions of things up to a certain period in regard to the charts. I have drawn with a red pencil lines around this space, where you find printed that the triangulation was done by J. Ferguson and E. Blount, assistant; topography done by H. L. Whiting, S. A. Gilbert, A. M. Harrison, etc., assistants; hydrography done by Lieut. Commander R. Wainwright, T. A. Craven, H. Mitchell, F. H. Gerdes; and P. F. Ness, assistants. On that chart you see that much. That is what we call the list of authorities, giving the names of all who have been engaged in this work. Now, on this sheet [exhibiting] those engaged in the triangulation are all given here. The triangulation is by F. W. Hassler, the first Superintendent of the Coast Survey. This work was done long ago, but is still used for the construction of this chart recently published in 1889 during my administration; also the names appear of Ferguson, Blount, Edwards, etc., all of whom are now dead; Marindin, J. W. Donn, E. T. Dickins, E.

Bradford, and A. T. Mosman, assistants, were all engaged in this triangulation at a later date.

Next comes those who were engaged in topography, who were: H. L. Whiting, S. A. Gilbert, A. M. Harrison, F. H. Gerdes, E. Boschke, F. W. Dorr, etc. Next come those engaged in hydrography, Lieuts. W. Maynard, W. I. Moore, H. B. Mansfield, etc. It shows astronomical observations were made by S. P. Walker, etc. Magnetic observations were made by J. Renwick, etc. The names of all men engaged appear upon it. There are nearly fifty names on that chart, and it has been noted for many years that there has been a steady growth of this matter of authorities on charts. That is, these lists occupied a large space on the charts, and it became a difficult question to decide, although it was one continually arising.

The question of the selection of these names was determined by the chart board. If a man had been sent to a place and done an hour's work or a day's work, oftentimes he felt his name should go on the chart. We were continually receiving letters of complaint of naval officers, and of our own civil officers as well, that their names had been omitted, that they had done a little work, and would like to see their names on the chart, and this finally gave rise to a discussion which began before I came into the office.

A year and a half after I came in the question was brought to a focus by the action of this chart board to which I have referred. The chart board is a board I organized after I came into the office, consisting of the hydrographic inspector, the assistant in charge of the office, the executive officer, the chief of the chart division, the chief of the engraving division, and the chief of the drawing division, who would meet regularly in consideration of all questions in regard to the charts, changes of charts, issuing charts, etc. They would submit the result of their meeting to the Superintendent, who would approve or disapprove of their recommendation as he saw fit. Now, I want to read a note of the proceedings of June 16, 1891, when the following resolution was passed by this chart board:

Resolved, The Superintendent is requested to have the names of all persons, except the Superintendent, removed from the charts, and in the future allow the name of no person except the Superintendent to appear on any chart issued from the office.

The reason for doing that was the difficulty of determining among such an enormous number whose name should go on. At any rate, that proposition came to me. Now, I at first was very much opposed to that action; that is, I was loath to take that action. My instinct has always been, as the work of the Coast Survey shows, to give the fullest credit to every man in the service for the work he does. I think I can justly turn to the publications of the Coast Survey to prove that fact. Whereas before you had to hunt a good deal to find the names of authors of papers, now you will find the name of the author on the title page in the plainest type, as I wish to see every author given due credit.

Mr. ENLOE. Who constitutes that board of which you spoke?

Prof. MENDENHALL. The assistant in charge of the office, Mr. Colonna; the hydrographic inspector was Lieut. Ackley; executive officer, Braid; chief of chart division, Bradford; chief of drawing division, Dennis; chief of engraving division, Ogden. This is dated June 16, 1891. I had that under consideration for more than a year, and was reluctant all the time to approve of that recommendation. In the meantime I listened to arguments on the question, and I want to say the strongest argument brought to me in favor of this was brought by the representative of the U. S. Navy, Lieut. Commander Ackley, the man who had started this movement in the chart board. Instead of originating as a desire on the part of the civil authorities to cut down recognition of the Navy, it originated absolutely with the representative of the Navy, and Lieut. Commander Ackley will tell you so, and he presented his reasons for this change.

Then about a year after this time, the following winter, came the organization of this topographical board to which I have referred. I was still unwilling to consent to the recommendation, although I realized the difficulty of selection and that we were filling spaces on the charts that ought to be filled by magnetic or other notes. You will observe on these charts we have a good many notes of the tides, etc. Now; here is the space occupied by authorities on this chart and it was justly argued this space could properly be filled with information which mariners would like to have, while they would not care for the list of authorities. I brought the question therefore before the topographical board, and before that board it happened Lieut. Commander Ackley appeared in order to present his views, and I quote from the minutes of the conference which gives a summary of the views which he expressed on that occasion, so you may see the origin of this movement.

The hydrographic inspector maintained that it was his experience that nobody, unless connected with the Survey in some way, would consult or even read the authorities shown on the charts. He regarded the practice of publishing such lists as an advertisement of but little value for the names given, and the engraving of such lists on the plates retarded the publication of the charts and they were of no practical benefit to anybody.

Then there were some remarks from somebody else, and he added:

The hydrographic inspector upheld his former opinion and added that the charts being issued by the Government, no reference to the different governmental sources from which the published data had been received need be made, and the rule of expunging all authorities could well be carried out. Printed charts could not be regarded as records, and many important authorities were omitted even now from the published lists.

Now those are the views of the hydrographic inspector who started this movement and was the main representative of the U. S. Navy in the Coast Survey.

Now after this I authorized or rather directed two or three of my assistants, I think Mr. Wainwright was one, to make an examination of the system of foreign governments with regard to it, as I wanted to know what their custom was, and found this to be a varied custom, as I explained in letters to the Secretary of the Treasury, which perhaps have been submitted to this committee. You will find my full statement of that matter in those letters. I found in some countries that there were no names whatever published on the chart; that the stamp of the Government bureau was considered sufficient authority. In other countries the chief or one or two of the subordinates only appeared on the charts, but there was no country that approximated to the fullness of the publication of authorities the United States gave up to this time on its charts. That was found to be a fact in the publication of foreign government charts.

I would like to say here now, that just about the time this question was under consideration I had a consultation with the chief hydrographer of the Navy, and he said, " I understand you are considering the matter of removal of authorities from the charts," and I said I was.

Mr. ENLOE. Who was that?

Prof. MENDENHALL. Lieut. Commander Clover, and he said to

me this, " I think it is a very wise move." It also seemed to be the opinion of the geographical board of which he was a member, so I was reinforced here on all sides and I had to take this action, although I would confess I was reluctant to do it. I would be entirely willing to see the thing go back as it was. I wanted you to understand fully the causes which led me to this. After waiting, therefore, until October 14, 1892, here is the record I made: "Approved October 14, 1892." Nearly a year and a half after the original action of the board, and that was only because of those arguments which were brought to bear upon me.

The CHAIRMAN. Was it under that action that the name of Lieut. Maury was removed from the charts?

Prof. MENDENHALL. I do not know the name of Lieut. Maury had been removed.

The CHAIRMAN. I received a letter the other day stating his name had been taken off the Coast Survey charts because he had been in the rebellion.

Prof. MENDENHALL. I would like to explain that the man who has more to do with what goes on the chart and what goes off was himself in the rebellion the whole four years, and it is hardly likely he would do it on that account. I did not know Mr. Maury's name was ever taken off.

Mr. ENLOE. But the Secretary of the Treasury made an order requiring the full names to be restored?

Prof. MENDENHALL. The Secretary wrote me a letter, not exactly an order, requesting the former policy to be reestablished.

Thereupon the committee adjourned to meet on Tuesday, June 5, 1894.

<hr>

COMMITTEE ON NAVAL AFFAIRS,
Tuesday, June 5, 1894.

The Committee on Naval Affairs this day met, Hon. AMOS J. CUMMINGS in the chair.

STATEMENT OF PROF. T. C. MENDENHALL—Continued.

The CHAIRMAN. The committee will come to order, and the hearing of Prof. Mendenhall will be resumed.

Prof. MENDENHALL then addressed the committee. He said:

MR. CHAIRMAN AND GENTLEMEN OF THE COMMITTEE: I wish, first, to submit a statement in response to the request which was made at the last hearing with regard to the changes which were made in respect to the force of employés of the Survey during the year 1890. I answered on that occasion practically the questions which were asked in regard to who those people were, but for fuller information I submit a copy of the letter which was sent by me to the Secretary, explaining in detail all of those changes; that is, every promotion, and every decrease or increase of salary, and every resignation or death during the whole year of 1890, which will be found in this letter. I summarized it the other day by saying, that while there were many of this force who had their compensation increased, there were also some, a much smaller number, who had their compensation diminished, but that there was what is usually called an equalization of salaries, an adjustment, and in the field force I explained that nearly all of the promotions that appear on that list, which is not a large number compared with the total number of the field force, nearly all are to be attributed to the changes which occurred during the year. That is, there were two deaths and three resignations which occurred during that year, and the promotions to fill the vacancies thus produced, of course, make quite a large showing. I would repeat, which is found stated definitely in this letter, that the appropriations for field operations that year after that change had been made, compared with the appropriation before the change was made, was just $100; that is, $100 greater in the sum of over $119,000.

When I last appeared before the committee it desired certain information in regard to the changes made in the force of employés of the Coast and Geodetic Survey during the year 1890.

My letter of March 23, 1892, addressed to the honorable Secretary of the Treasury, contained in H. R., Fifty-second Congress, first session, Ex. Doc. No. 180, a copy of which I herewith furnish to the committee, gives very full information on that subject.

I desire to add, moreover, that of the 22 names read by Mr. Enloe all are field officers, except F. H. Parsons, who resigned his position in the field force to accept the position of librarian in the office, and J. W. Parsons, who was promoted from the position of accountant in the office to that of disbursing agent.

Of the 29 officers of the field force advanced in pay during the calendar year of 1890 the larger number owed their promotion to the two deaths and three resignations of assistants which occurred in that year, since the field officers stand in a lineal relation to one another, so that if a vacancy occurs well up in the list a number of advances becomes at once possible.

The total amount of the salary list for the field force was increased over that of the year before only $100.

[H. R., Fifty-second Congress, first session, Ex. Doc. No. 180.]

LETTER FROM THE ACTING SECRETARY OF THE TREASURY, TRANSMITTING, IN RESPONSE TO RESOLUTION OF THE 21ST INSTANT. INFORMATION RELATIVE TO THE CHANGES MADE IN THE FORCE OF EMPLOYÉS IN THE COAST AND GEODETIC SURVEY DURING THE YEAR 1890.

TREASURY DEPARTMENT, OFFICE OF THE SECRETARY,
Washington, D. C., March 28, 1892.

SIR: In response to the resolution of the House of Representatives of the 21st instant, calling for information in regard to the changes made in the force of employés in the Coast and Geodetic Survey during the year 1890, I have the honor to transmit herewith a detailed statement of the Superintendent of the U. S. Coast and Geodetic Survey, showing all changes made in his office during the calendar year of 1890.

Respectfully, yours,

O. L. SPAULDING,
Acting Secretary.

The SPEAKER OF THE HOUSE OF REPRESENTATIVES.

U. S. COAST AND GEODETIC SURVEY,
OFFICE OF THE SUPERINTENDENT,
Washington, D. C., March 23, 1892.

SIR: I have the honor to send herewith information concerning appointments, dismissals, and changes in the compensation of employés of the Coast and Geodetic Survey during the year 1890, as requested by resolution of the House of Representatives, received on the 22d instant, and in so doing I beg to submit a few remarks explanatory thereof. It will be observed that the greater part of these changes occurred on or soon after the 30th of August, which was the day of the approval of the sundry civil bill making appropriations for the fiscal year beginning on July 1. The original estimates for the expenditures of the Survey during the year, beginning at that date, were prepared within a few weeks after I assumed the duties of Superintendent, and therefore necessarily before I had opportunities for learning much of the relative strength or weakness of the several branches of the service, or for determining the wisest distribution of expenditures among these branches in order to secure an efficient and economical administration. They were substantially the same as those of previous years, with such additions and changes as naturally occur in such a service. The amount asked for was considerably greater than that finally appropriated, as had been the case without exception in all of the previous years of the history of the Survey.

On the occasion of their first consideration by the appropriations committee, early in 1890, I suggested certain changes, which a better knowledge resulting from several months experence indicated as desirable. The committee then requested me to withdraw the estimates and revise them in accordance with maturer judgment, and to incorporate such changes in the organization as would, in my opinion, tend to increase its efficiency without increasing its cost. After a careful consideration of the whole subject, including consultation with the chiefs of divisions, the assistant in charge of the office, and most of the older field officers, a new set of estimates was submitted which were accepted by the Appropriations Committee and made a part of the sundry civil bill, practically without modification. The enactment of this as a law on August 30, 1890, necessitated and contemplated certain changes which are exhibited in the accompanying lists, together with all others made during the year 1890.

In the first statement will be found the changes which occurred in the pay of field officers, arranged in chronological order. The field officers of the Survey in a large degree stand in a linear relation to each other, so that if a vacancy occurs well up in the list a number of advances become at once possible. This is well illustrated by the large number of promotions in May, as shown in the list, all growing out of two or three vacancies created by death and resignation. Several of the changes under date of July 1 are due to a similar cause, a vacancy having been created in June by the death of one of the oldest officers of the Survey. Other changes of that date grew out of the revision of the list which became a law on August 30, as stated above, but with a provision inserted by the committee making the new act effective from the beginning of the fiscal year.

The principal change wrought by this act consisted in the elimination of salaries of uneven and irregular sums, and the arrangement of a regular series of graded salaries, with uniform increase from grade to grade. Not more than a third of the officers were affected by the application of this principle, which was suggested by the committee, some of the changes shown in the list originating in existing vacancies. Two of the older officers who had long been inactive, having been placed on furlough without pay on October 1, 1886, were stricken from the list by the passage of the sundry civil bill, and another resigned to become chief of the division of library and archives. A distinguished expert of long experience and high reputation, whose services were much desired in the Bureau, was transferred from another department and appointed at an annual salary of $3,000.

All of these changes, by which it is generally admitted the efficiency of the corps was increased, were made with practically no change in the total cost, there being an increase of less than 1 per cent. The amounts appropriated for salaries for the fiscal years 1890 and 1891 were, respectively, $119,500 and $119,600.

Referring to the changes in the office force, it became evident, before the question of a revision of the estimates arose, that some changes in the personnel of two or three of the divisions would be necessary before that degree of efficiency which the public had a right to demand could be secured. The assistant in charge of the office and all of the chiefs of divisions were called upon to consider and to recommend such changes as in their judgment would materially contribute to the efficiency of the service without materially increasing its cost, and recommend such reductions as in their opinion in the good of the service demanded. The result was the revised estimates for the office force as submitted to and accepted by the Appropriations Committee.

The most important changes in the office force were confined to the instrument division, the engraving division, and the accounting division. Before submitting estimates for the instrument division, in which there was some reduction in salaries, I made inquiry at the principal instrument shops in the country as to wages paid skilled workmen, particularly investigating those widely known for the high character and skill of their employés. This inquiry clearly proved that the best men available could be obtained for the sums proposed in the revised estimates from that division, which were accordingly adopted. The cost of the instrument division in salaries, including the clerk, before this change was made, was $12,900. Several persons employed in the division were discharged and a careful search made for the best men to take their places. The places were filled and the cost in salaries after the change was $12,100, a saving of $800. As to the increase in efficiency of the division, it may be said that separate estimates made by four officers who are in a position to know very thoroughly what was done and what is now being done, and including both quantity and quality of work, place it at over 100 per cent.

In the engraving division the principal reductions were in the salaries of plate printers. In this case, as in that just mentioned, precaution was taken to ascertain that plate printers possessing the necessary experience and skill could be obtained for the sums named in the revised estimates, and positive evidence of this was required before adopting the estimates

Soon after the reductions took effect, those who had been employed resigned and others were appointed to fill their places. The cost in salaries before the change was for 4 plate printers and 2 helpers, $7,010, and after the change it was for the same number of printers and the same number of helpers, $6,000, the salaries of the helpers undergoing no change. There was thus a saving of $1,010.

As to efficiency, the chief of the division reports a decided increase, and in order that it may not be necessary to base this claim of increased efficiency on personal opinion only, an examination of the records has been made, covering seven months under the old conditions and the corresponding months under the new, the only period during which it is possible to make a comparison of the two, and it is found that during that period immediately following the change 4,431 more charts were printed than in the corresponding period before the change was made, or an increase of efficiency of nearly 25 per cent. It will be seen, therefore, that this reduction is in no way responsible for the appropriation of 1891, for two additional plate-printers and three helpers. On the contrary had it not been made, the cost of this additional force would have been much enhanced.

The addition of these men, together with new presses and power for running them, appropriated for in 1891, had long been demanded, and Congress had before been asked to grant it. It grew out of the difficulty and often impossibility of meeting the demand for the charts issued by the Survey, back orders for which sometimes amounted to as many as 3,000. The completion of these arrangements in the near future will make it possible to supply all calls with only a slight increase in the cost of the producing plant.

In what was previously known as the accounting division some changes were made, resulting in the diminution of the cost of that division by $1,200, and a decided increase in efficiency, as all who have had dealings with it will agree, the improvement being of such a nature as to result in a saving to the Government in many directions.

In other divisions of the office some changes were made, some salaries were increased by small amounts and some decreased by small amounts, always on the recommendation of the chief of the division and the assistant in charge of the office, their opportunities for accurate and just discrimination being greater than those of all others.

To the cost of office force, as apparently shown by the act for the fiscal year 1890, must be added $3,760, appropriated for salaries under the head of office expenses, which in the revised estimates were thrown into the regular salary list. Thus the cost before the change in 1890 was $136,465, and after that change $136,630, there being an increase of only $165.

I have gone carefully and at some length into these explanations in order that members of the House of Representatives, in receiving these lists of changes effected in 1890, may understand the circumstances under which they were made, and to furnish some reasons for believing that the desire of the Fifty-first Congress that the efficiency of the service might be increased without increase of cost had been realized. For further proofs of this and for evidence that in all changes that have been made the good of the public service has alone been considered, the Coast and Geodetic Survey will cheerfully welcome the most thorough and exhaustive scrutiny of its operations.

Respectfully, yours,

T. C. MENDENHALL,
Superintendent.

The SECRETARY OF THE TREASURY,
Washington, D. C.

[Extract from sundry civil act of August 30, 1890.]

* * * *Provided*, That in case where, by reason of change in grade or otherwise of the employés of the Coast and Geodetic Survey, by the provision of this act a new appointment or designation becomes necessary, no additional oath of office shall be required, and compensation at the new rate shall begin with the date of approval of this act (amount appropriated, $256,061.65). (Joint resolutions of June 30, 1890, and subsequent dates, and sundry civil act, August 30, 1890.)

Statement showing changes in grade and salary in the list of field officers of the U. S. Coast and Geodetic Survey during the calendar year 1890.

Date.	Name.	Change, etc.
Mar. 31	Ellicott, Eugene	Assistant at $1,500, resigned.
Apr. 10	Bache, C. M	Assistant at $2,300, died.
May 5	Whiting, Henry L	Assistant at $2,000, to assistant at $2,300.
May 5	Marindin, Henry L	Assistant at $2,000, to assistant at $2,200.
May 5	Perkins, F. Walley	Assistant at $1,800, to assistant at $2,000.
May 5	Granger, F. D	Do.
May 5	Hodgins, W. C	Assistant at $1,500, to assistant at $1,800.
May 5	Preston, E. D.	Do.
May 6	Parsons, Francis H	Subassistant at 1,400, to assistant at $1,500.
May 6	Winston, Isaac	Subassistant at $1,300, to subassistant at $1,400.
May 6	Morse, Tremont	Subassistant at $1,100, to subassistant at $1,300.
May 13	Marr, R. A	Subassistant at $1,400, to assistant at $1,500.
May 13	Welker, P. A	Subassistant at $1,100 to subassistant at $1,400.
May 27	Nelson, John	Aid at $900, to subassistant at $1,100.
June 22	Boutelle, C. O	Assistant at $2,000, died.
July 1	Mosman, A. T	Assistant at $2,800, to assistant at $3,000.
July 1	Dennis, William H	Assistant at $2,400, to assistant at $2,800.
July 1	Rockwell, Cleveland	Assistant at $2,400, to assistant at $2,600.
July 1	Donn, John W	Do.
July 1	Eimbeck, Wm	Assistant at $2,300, to assistant at $2,400.
July 1	Goodfellow, Edward	Do.
July 1	Whiting, Henry L.	Do.
July 1	Ogden, Herbert G	Assistant at $2,200, to assistant at 2,400.
July 1	Titman, Otto H	Do.
July 1	Smith, Edwin	Assistant at $1,800, to assistant at $2,000.
July 1	Iardella, C. T	Assistant at $1,500, to assistant at $1,600.
July 1	Vinal, W. Irving	Do.
July 1	Baylor, James B	Do.
July 1	Marr, R. A	Do.
July 1	Van Orden, C. H	Do.
July 1	Turner, J. Henry	Subassistant at $1,300, to subassistant at $1,400.
July 1	Morse, Fremont	Do.
July 1	Flemer, J. A	Subassistant at $1,100 to subassistant at $1,400.
July 1	Nelson, John	Subassistant at $1,100, to subassistant at $1,200.
July 2	Woodward, R. S	Appointed assistant at $3,000.
Aug. 29	Parsons, Francis H	Resigned.
Aug. 29	Longfellow, A. W	Assistant at $1,500 (placed on furlough, without pay, from Oct. 1, 1890). Connection with the Survey ceases from and after date of approval of sundry civil appropriation act for year 1891, no provision having been made for his compensation as assistant.
Aug. 29	Dean, George W	Assistant at $1,500 (placed on furlough, without pay, from Oct. 1, 1890). Dropped from the list of field officers of the Survey, no appropriation having been made for his salary as assistant.
Aug. 30	McGrath, J. E	Subassistant at $1,400, to assistant at $1,600.
Aug. 30	Fairfield, W. B	Appointed subassistant at $1,200.
Sept. 9	Young, F. A	Appointed aid at $900.
Dec. 31	Marr, R. A	Resigned.

CHANGES THAT TOOK PLACE IN THE OFFICE FORCE OF THE COAST AND GEODETIC SURVEY DURING THE CALENDAR YEAR 1890.

Parsons, John W.—Disbursing agent for Coast and Geodetic Survey in sundry civil bill, approved March 30, 1890, at a salary of $2,200 per annum, dropping the office of accountant at a salary of $1,800 per annum.

Parsons, F. H.—Chief of division of library and archives, August 30, 1890. Was transferred to this position from assistant at $1,600 per annum. Salary as chief of library and archives, $1,800.

Hensel, Martin.—Clerk to the superintendent. Position made by act of August 30, 1890 (new). Oath September 27, 1890, at a salary of $1,200 per annum.

Simons, A. B.—Clerk to assistant in charge of office. Salary, $1,000 per annum. Oath October 3, 1890. Salary first appropriated for August 30, 1890. He was promoted from watchman, weights and measures division, at a salary of $720 per annum.

Smith, J. L.—Clerk at $1,200 per annum. Was discharged March 21, 1890.

Duesberry, J. M.—Clerk at $1,000 per annum. Was discharged August 28, 1890.

Chilton, W. B.—Clerk at $1,500 per annum. Made clerk at $1,650 per annum. Act approved August 30, 1890.

Martin, A.—Librarian at $1,800 per annum, was reduced to clerk at $1,400 per annum August 30, 1890.

Green, F. R.—Clerk at $1,175, was increased to clerk at $1,200 per annum on August 30, 1890.

Maupin, W. C.—Clerk at $1,350 made clerk at $1,400 per annum by act of August 30, 1890.

Wills, Eugene B.—Accountant at a salary of $1,800 per annum. Reduced to clerk at $1,200 per annum. Act of August 30, 1890.

Cook, Frank A.—Clerk at $1,200 per annum. Oath November 15, 1890. Appointed from civil service in place of R. C. Glasock, discharged.

Edmunds, F.—Clerk at $900 per annum, was increased to clerk at $1,000 per annum by act August 30, 1890.

Glasock, R. C.—Accountant at $1,400 per annum, was reduced to clerk at $1,200 per annum by act August 30, 1890. He was discharged November 13, 1890, and his place supplied on call from civil service by Frank A. Cook, on November 15, 1890.

Hein, Miss S.—Typewriter and copyist, was promoted from $600 to $720 per annum after departmental examination. Oath May 6, 1890.

Turnbull, Miss C.—Copyist, resigned May 23, 1890; salary, $720 per annum.

Barker, J. H.—Was, under the reorganization necessitated by the act approved August 30, 1890, designated as a chart-corrector to correspond to his occupation, and his pay fixed at the rate of $1,200 per annum instead of $1,330 per annum, heretofore paid him as draftsman.

Wyrill, E. H.—Designation changed from draftsman, at $1,200 per annum, to chart-corrector at $1,200 per annum; act August 30, 1890.

Whitaker, J. W.—Computer at $1,250 per annum, was transferred to chart division as chart-corrector, with salary at the rate of $1,200 per annum, by act of August 30, 1890. Mr. Hayford filled the vacancy of computer, at $1,250 per annum, made vacant by the transfer of Mr. Whitaker.

Nesbit, Mrs. M. E.—Writer at $800, was reduced from $840 per annum, by act of August 30, 1890. She was transferred to the office of Commissioner of Internal Revenue, Treasury Department, and promoted to $900 per annum July 14, 1891.

Carlisle, Miss A. F.—Writer at $720 per annum. Oath, October 30, 1890. Miss Carlisle is one of the writers who was on the extra labor roll when the Coast and Geodetic Survey Office was placed under the civil service; she therefore came under civil service with the Bureau, and was transferred to this regular position as above and without change of salary.

Bailey, Miss F. B.—Stenographer and typewriter at a salary of $900 per annum. Resigned November 1, 1890. The vacancy was filled by the promotion of Miss L. A. Mapes.

Mapes, Miss L. A.—Writer at $900 per annum; promoted from $720. Oath, November 4, 1890.

Harrison, Mrs. V.—Copyist at $720 per annum; was promoted to $900 per annum. Oath, December 12, 1890. Took departmental examination before promotion.

Benton, W. H.—Draftsman, at a salary of $1,200 per annum. Resigned after the 26th March, 1890. David M. Hildrith was promoted from a salary of $1,100 per annum to the vacancy caused by Benton's resignation.

Peck, Miss I. M.—Writer, from civil service; was promoted from $600 to $720 per annum. Oath, December 12, 1890.

Jackson, M. P.—Was promoted November 2, 1889, from $940 per annum to $1,100 per annum, in the place of Hildrith, promoted. Jackson resigned in June, 1890.

Lindenkohl, A.—Draftsman. Salary fixed at $2,400 per annum by act approved August 30, 1890, being an increase from $2,350 per annum.

Lindenkohl, H.—Draftsman. Salary fixed at $2,200 by act approved August 30, 1890, from salary at $2,100 per annum.

Hildrith, D. M.—Draftsman; was rated at $1,400 per annum, in place of E. Molkow, in accordance with act of August 30, 1890. He first stood departmental examination; civil service. His previous pay was $1,200 per annum; in place of W. H. Benton, resigned.

Dietz, C. H.—From civil service. Oath, March 11, 1889. In the reorganization under act of August 30, 1890, his pay was fixed at $1,200 per annum.

Pohlers, G. F.—Was certified from civil service to Indian Office at $1,200 per annum, but accepted transfer here at $900 per annum, and took oath of office March 27, 1890. He was rated at $1,200 on reorganizing, in accordance with act of August 30, 1890.

Errichsen, P.—Draftsman. Salary fixed at $1,000 by act approved August 30, 1890, from salary of $1,400 per annum.

Mahon, C.—Draftsman. Under act approved August 30, 1890, was rated at $1,000 per annum, instead of $1,260 per annum as before.

Molkow, E.—Dropped from the roll at $1,400 per annum on August 28, 1890. He was reinstated by the Secretary of the Treasury September 1, 1890, granted thirty days leave of absence with pay at the rate of $900 per annum, and was again dropped September 30, 1890.

Pond, E. J.—Appointed on certification by civil service and took the oath October 15, 1890, at $900 per annum.

Mitchell, Everett S.—Draftsman at $900 per annum; appointed on certification by the civil service; took oath November 24, 1890.

Courtenay, E. H.—Computer. His pay was increased from $1,850 to $2,000, per annum on the reorganization of the office force under act of August 30, 1890.

Doolittle, M. H.—Computer. His pay was increased from $1,850 to $2,000 per annum on the reorganization of the office force under act of August 30, 1890.

Shidy, L. P.—Computer, was promoted from a salary of $1,500 per annum to one of $1,600 per annum by act of August 30, 1890.

Farquhar, H.—Computer. Pay reduced from $1,420 to $1,400 per annum, in accordance with act of August 30, 1890.

Bauer, L. A.—Computer. Pay increased from $1,300 to $1,400 per annum, in accordance with act of August 30, 1890.

Kummel, C. H.—Computer. Pay decreased from $1,260 to $1,200 per annum, in accordance with act of August 30, 1890.

Little, F. M.—Computer. Pay increased from $1,100 to $1,200 per annum, in accordance with act of August 30, 1890.

Knight, H. M.—Engraver at $2,060 per annum, was, under act of August 30, 1890, reduced to $2,000 per annum.

Thompson, J. G.—Engraver at $1,960 per annum, was raised, under act of August 30, 1890, to $2,000.

Sipe, E. H.—Engraver. Pay raised from $1,565 to $1,600 per annum by act of August 30, 1890.

Davis, W. H.—Engraver. Pay raised from $1,500 to $1,600 per annum by act of August 30, 1890.

Thompson, H. L.—Engraver. Was promoted from $900 to $1,000 per annum under act of August 30, 1890. •

Wurdeman, F. G.—Engraver, by contract, at $35 per month. Began work September 22, 1890.

Smith, Edward H.—Engraver at $120 per annum. Resigned after November 15, 1890.

Moore, F.—Plate-printer. Pay decreased from $1,700 to $1,600 per annum under act of August 30, 1890.

Hoover, D. N.—Plate-printer. Pay decreased from $1,330 to $1,000 per annum, under act of August 30, 1890. He resigned September 27, 1890.

Harlow, C. J.—Plate-printer at $1,000 per annum. In place of Hoover from October 2, 1890.

Beck, J.—Plate-printer. Pay decreased from $1,330 to $1,000 per annum, by act of August 30, 1890. Resigned October 7, 1890.

Sullivan, T. A.—Plate-printer at $1,000 per annum from October 20, 1890. He takes the place made vacant by the resignation of James Beck.

Craufurd, C. B.—Plate-printer. Pay decreased from $1,250 to $1,000 per annum under act of August 30, 1890. Resigned October 30, 1890.

Bright, R. S.—Plate-printer at $1,000 per annum, in the place made vacant by the resignation of Craufurd. Mr. Bright took oath of office December 6, 1890.

Clark, Dr. J. J.—Adjuster of weights and measures. (See legislative, executive, and judicial bill.) Resigned January 1, 1890. Salary, $1,500 per annum. He was succeeded by L. A. Fischer, who had been in the instrument division as mechanician, at a salary of $1,330 per annum.

Fischer, L. A.—Mechanician. Salary, $1,330 per annum. Discharged February 18, 1890, and appointed adjuster of weights and measures, at $1,500 per annum, in place Dr. J. J. Clark.

Eschleman, E.—Mechanician. Pay, $1,565 per annum. Discharged April 13, 1890.

Vierbuchen, P.—Mechanican, at a salary of $1,250 per annum. Resigned May 1, 1890.

Gerhards, T.—Mechanician, weights and measures. His salary was at the rate of $1,250 per annum, in Bureau of Weights and Measures. (See Legislative, executive, and judicial bill.) His resignation took effect July 1, 1890. He was succeeded by W. H. Bullock, who was selected from a number of applicants who responded to the advertisements of the Survey. Oath administered August 1, 1890.

Regennas, E. C.—Instrument-maker. Oath January 23, 1890. He succeeded Vierbuchen, and the pay was fixed at $1,000 per annum by act of August 30, 1890. He was selected from applicants who responded to advertisements.

4561——10

Kearney, S. A.—Instrument-maker. His salary was reduced from $1,175 to $1,000 per annum by act of August 30, 1890.

Whitman, W. R.—Instrument-maker. Pay increased from $900 to $1,000 per annum, by act of August 30, 1890. Selected from skilled men in Washington navy-yard.

Lanxman, M. J.—Instrument-maker. Pay raised from $545 to $700 per annum, under act of August 30, 1890.

French, H. O.—Carpenter. Pay increased under act of August 30, 1890, from $1,565 to $1,600 per annum.

Clarroe, G. W.—Carpenter. Pay increased under act of August 30, 1890, from $800 per annum to $900 per annum.

Darnall, C. N.—Carpenter. Pay increased from $500 to $700 per annum under act of August 30, 1890.

Bassett, R. T.—Map-mounter. Pay was decreased from $1,020 per annum to $1,000 per annum, act of August 30, 1890.

Keyser, L. P.—Assistant electrotyper. Pay increased from $500 to $900 per annum, under act of August 30, 1890.

Butler, W. H.—Head messenger. Increased from $875 to $880 per annum, by act of August 30, 1890.

Denis, Vicente.—Messenger. Reduced from $840 to $820 per annum, act of August 30, 1890.

McLane, W. R.—Driver of office wagon. Increased from $730 to $820, by act of August 30, 1890.

Dyer, Horace.—$570 to $630 as fireman, by act of August 30, 1890.

Flynn, Mrs. F. E.—Charwoman. Raised from $315 per annum to $365 per annum, by act of August 30, 1890.

Grinage, J. F.—Messenger. Pay at $550 per annum. Oath November 1, 1890.

Bowen, S. J.—Watchman Bureau of Weights and Measures at $720. Oath December 10, 1890. He came in Simons's place.

Now, Mr. Chairman and gentlemen, I feel you have accorded me a very great courtesy and consideration in listening to me so long and I am going to content myself with reading from the opinions of others whose judgment I think you will admit should be considered in any adjustment of this question. And the first paper to which I refer is a letter from Rear-Admiral Jenkins, of the U. S. Navy. I will say that this letter was originally prepared in 1857; that in 1880, however, when this question was again before Congress on a division of this Bureau and disposition which is now proposed by this bill, Admiral Jenkins, having written this letter in 1857, was asked whether he was still of the same opinion, and I will read you just a few words of his reply on that particular point. He says:

WASHINGTON CITY, *June 5, 1884.*

The following remarks (made by me about 1857) having been shown to me, and the question asked if I had changed my views, I unhesitatingly say I have not changed one opinion in regard to the present organization of the Coast and Geodetic Survey, and of the proper department under which it should be. If I could do so, I would put all the scientific bureaus of the Government under a separate and distinct Cabinet officer, to be created. Neither the Treasury, Navy, nor Interior Departments, as at present organized, can properly and intelligently supervise these great operations; but in the absence of such a new department as I have indicated, in my opinion any other change would result disadvantageously, if not disastrously, to the Coast and Geodetic Survey and the operations now authorized by law.

THORNTON A. JENKINS,
Retired Rear-Admiral, U. S. Navy.

The letter itself is quite lengthy, and it is a very able presentation, in my judgment, of the argument against such a change as proposed here, and has great weight, and should have, coming from an old Navy officer of long experience, and one who had been connected with the Survey. I may read two or three paragraphs only. He says:

It is not a work appropriate to the Navy. The Navy performs all the duty properly belonging to it—that of hydrography—and it receives full credit individually and collectively for all it does. It is, therefore, unjust to the officers of the Army and to the civilians to claim it exclusively; and no officer of the Navy who is actuated by purely disinterested motives, and is at the same time competent to judge fairly on the subject, can feel or affect to feel that it is any reflection upon the service to admit that it is not the duty of the Navy. There is no fear of misapprehension in the public mind of incapacity.

The Coast Survey has proved a most advantageous and admirable school to a few officers of the Navy, who availed themselves (against great odds) of the opportunities of that service.

Perhaps I may read this:

> The Navy Department has the same control over the hydrographic parties that it has over the rest of the naval forces. The manner in which applications are made for provisions and men is the same as it would be if the Survey were under the Navy Department.

The following is applied to that point which was made the other day that the Secretary had less administrative control over his officers in detailing them to the Bureau than he should have. Admiral Jenkins also speaks of the difficulties of selecting these hydrographers in accordance with the methods which would naturally prevail in a bureau of the Navy Department, that is, by means of seniority alone, and thus speaks against it:

> To select chiefs of hydrographic parties from the Navy Register without reference to fitness and making seniority the only guide would render it necessary for the Department to detail some other lieutenant or passed midshipman of known ability to perform the duties, while the commander would, from incapacity, do nothing, and, receiving all the credit for the work of his junior, inflict an irreparable wrong upon him and upon the service.

I will say as to the selection of naval officers for service in the Coast and Geodetic Survey, while of course no officer can serve in the Survey without being detailed by the Secretary and nothing of that kind would be possible, as Admiral Jenkins says here, yet it is customary to select those who have a taste for this work—who have some inclination toward it. Almost invariably we succeed in finding some men of that class. The hydrographic inspector, to whom I have referred several times, who is the principal officer detailed to the Coast and Geodetic Survey, and has his office with us in Washington here, is constantly looking out for men who like and who are fond of this kind of work, and requests their detail. Of course if their services are required elsewhere we do not get them. That gives us the means of selection which Admiral Jenkins distinctly says would not exist if the ordinary method of detail was used.

Now, I have a few remarks which were made on this subject also in 1884, which I will read first, and I may say I read these, although they were given ten years ago, for this reason—for two reasons perhaps. In the first place, many of those gentlemen have given recent assurances that their opinions were even stronger upon this subject than they were at that time. Perhaps a greater reason than any other is that these letters which I will read, being dated 1884, were called forth by a letter, or a series of letters, sent to those gentlemen by a member of Congress, and not by anyone in the Coast Survey or anyone connected in anyway with the Coast Survey. The inquiries were made by a member of the joint commission which had to consider this question of these several gentlemen, and in response they wrote these letters, which I will read and which have never been published. It was found that they were not really needed as the commission had made up their minds—at all events, they were never printed or published. These are the views of gentlemen who had opportunity for knowing the character of the work of the Survey. I will read a selection from a letter of Andrew D. White, long time president of Cornell University, well known to everybody, in which he says:

PRESIDENT'S ROOM, CORNELL UNIVERSITY,
Ithaca, N. Y., June 30, 1884.

* * * I can only say that considering the high position which the Coast Survey holds in the estimation of thinking men throughout the country, especially at every college and higher institution of education in every State of the Union, very clear and cogent reasons ought to be presented if a change is made.
I remain,

AND. D. WHITE.

The next is from President James B. Angell, president of the University of Michigan, in which he says:

UNIVERSITY OF MICHIGAN,
Ann Arbor, June 17, 1884.

* * * I say that it would be a serious disaster to the Coast and Geodetic Survey to place it under the direction of the Navy Department.
The history of the organization under which so brilliant results have been accomplished should deter one from making so radical a change as is proposed in the newspaper paragraph you have sent to me.
Yours, very respectfully,

JAMES B. ANGELL,
President.

I believe a newspaper paragraph was the means of getting the opinions of these gentlemen. Another extract is from the letter of a distinguished member of the National Academy of Sciences, Mr. Fairman Rogers, secretary of the National Academy of Sciences; he says:

NEWPORT, R. I., *June 20, 1884.*

DEAR SIR:

*   *   *   *   *   *   *

I consider that the transfer of the hydrographic work to the Navy would seriously damage the scientific interests of the country and would impair the value of the work itself.
You know how the military rules and customs of the Navy tend to cramp everything that is done by it, and the scientific work intrusted to it would no doubt be kept strictly within the usual routine and the outside scientific aid and sympathy of the country would be immediately lost to it. * * * The charts of the Coast Survey are now so far superior to those of English harbors made by the English navy that hardly any comparison is possible between them. I am certain that geodetic work would suffer almost unto death by being placed under the Geological Survey. * * * The U. S. Coast and Geodetic Survey as at present organized has done its practical work in the best way, nothing better has been done in the world, and its collateral scientific influence upon the country has been incalculable.

FAIRMAN ROGERS,
Formerly Secretary National Academy of Sciences.

I may say this gentleman speaks with good authority, because he is a yachtsman of high reputation and has traveled around the coast of the United States and abroad extensively, and consequently he has used the charts of the United States, as well as those of foreign countries, and I would like to invite your attention to the fact that he makes a comparison of our work with that of the English.

Prof. H. A. Newton, of Yale College, the eminent astronomer, says:

YALE COLLEGE, *June 17, 1884.*

* * * I should regret the breaking up of the Coast and Geodetic Survey organization, and the distribution of its functions to the Interior and Navy Departments as disastrous in the extreme.

H. A. NEWTON.

Mr. Charles W. Elliott, president of Harvard University, says:

HARVARD UNIVERSITY, *June 17, 1884.*

In reply to your inquiry of June 14, I beg to say that every presumption seems to me to be against breaking up an organization which has done such efficient and honorable work as the Coast and Geodetic Survey.

CHARLES W. ELLIOTT,
President.

Dr. Gillman, president of Johns Hopkins University, says:

PRESIDENT'S OFFICE, JOHNS HOPKINS UNIVERSITY,
Baltimore, June 16, 1884.

I should deplore any hasty or unconsidered legislation which would tend to impair the efficiency of one of the most honorable and important branches of the public service—the U. S. Coast and Geodetic Survey.

D. C. GILMAN.

Prof. W. P. Trowbridge, for a long time professor of engineering in the School of Mines, Columbia College, says:

SCHOOL OF MINES, COLUMBIA COLLEGE,
New York, June 17, 1884.

I can not imagine a greater national disgrace in connection with our public surveys and improvements at this time than the dismemberment of the Coast Survey.

W. P. TROWBRIDGE,
· *Professor of Engineering.*

Prof. C. A. Young, professor of astronomy at Princeton College writes as follows:

PRINCETON, N. J., *June 16, 1884.*

* * * I am sure that I express the judgment of nine-tenths of the scientific men of the country in saying that the abolition of the Coast and Geodetic Survey and the transfer of its duties to other organizations would be considered nothing less than a calamity.

C. A. YOUNG.

Prof. George H. Cook, of the Geological Survey of New Jersey, so well known to all of you, says:

GEOLOGICAL SURVEY OF NEW JERSEY,
New Brunswick, June 16, 1884.

* * * The Coast Survey is thoroughly organized * * * and is doing work that is of the nicest and at the same time most useful character, in the most creditable manner and with a rigid economy of money.

The Coast Survey supplies us with information on accurate points of latitude and longitude, on magnetism and the variations of the compass in parts of our country, on tides, and on those abstruse but necessary questions which have to do with the figure of the earth.

GEORGE H. COOK.

Mr. GEISSENHAINER. He is recently deceased?
Prof. MENDENHALL. He is recently deceased. · I have here several more expressions of opinion of the same character. Now, I come to those of more recent date. Perhaps I may read, however, bearing upon the matter of our work, a letter written about the same time and written by Mr. W. C. Kerr, of North Carolina, who also made a geological map of the State. He said:

JUNE 23, 1884.

For example, in my own experience, after making a triangulation of the State of North Carolina, in connection with the Geological Survey and for the purpose of constructing an accurate geological map of the State, I was only able to utilize this work of half a dozen years, as well as the previous labors of Prof. Guyot, after the Coast and Geodetic Survey gave us a chain of triangulation through the eastern piedmont of the Appalachians.

Now we come to some comments which have been made within the last few months. The first one I happen to have is a selection from the Engineering News, a leading engineering journal, as you all know, of date of March 29, 1894. It says:

ABOLISHING THE COAST AND GEODETIC SURVEY.

* * * No other government has carried forward so thorough and accurate a system of surveys over so large a portion of the world's surface as has the United States.

It further says:

Of late years the Bureau has been giving very valuable aid to State surveys along the Atlantic coast, utilizing for this purpose the primary triangulation of the Coast Survey; and as a result of this cooperation of the national and State governments we have the extremely complete and satisfactory maps of New Jersey; and similar maps of New York, Connecticut, and Massachusetts are either already being published or are well advanced. * * * It is only when this system is extended to all the States of the Union that the United States Government will possess an accurate and complete map of its wide domain, and such maps are now much needed by every department of the Government for the proper transaction of department business.

Now, some college institutions have expressed themselves about this matter, and this is from the chancellor of the Washington University, St. Louis, Mo., in which he says:

WASHINGTON UNIVERSITY,
St. Louis, Mo., March 30, 1894.

I am heartily opposed to the action, as a man interested in scientific work, it is my duty to make as vigorous a protest against this action as possible. I do not see that the new plan promises to do the work of the Survey at a smaller expense or with greater regard to the public need, and as for the standard of work, I believe it would be seriously threatened by such transfer as proposed. * * * I feel impelled to take much more vigorous action than would seem becoming were the subject one which could be more readily understood by the people at large.

W. S. CHAPLIN.

Also, an expression from the professors, and especially the professor of geology, who is one of the leading geologists of the country, in the Ohio State University. They say:

COLUMBUS, OHIO, March 30, 1894.

That the dismemberment of the U S. Coast and Geodetic Survey would inevitably result in the lowering of the character of the work done and would thus prove detrimental to the public interest * * *. In short, we find insuperable objections to the objects of the Enloe bill and we fail to see a single advantage which it is justly entitled to claim.

Signed by the professors in charge of department of science of the Ohio State University.

Mr. ENLOE. Will you allow me to ask you a question right on that point?

Prof. MENDENHALL. Yes, sir.

Mr. ENLOE. Has there been any communication sent from the Coast and Geological Survey to these various colleges to get this expression of opinion?

Prof. MENDENHALL. I am glad to answer this question.

Mr. CHAIRMAN. When this bill was introduced, and in fact when the action was taken before the introduction of the bill, that is, the attempt made to accomplish this by amendments to the sundry civil bill, which you will all remember, the attention of a number of people in the country was at once called to this action, and the office of the Coast and Geodetic Survey began to receive personal letters from people all over the country. The first communication I had in fact was from the farthest point, that is California, and I had two or three letters just as soon as the mail could carry them; and before we had fully appreciated ourselves this bill had been proposed we had a communication from the University of California which I will read further along.

Mr. ENLOE. What I want to know is if any communication had been sent out by the Coast and Geodetic Survey.

Prof. MENDENHALL. I will come to that and explain that in a moment. Then we were called upon in the next forty-eight hours by a number of newspaper reporters who wished to know what the feeling of the Survey was about the matter, and naturally we were reticent in expressing our views, except to say naturally enough we believed it was an objectionable movement. Letters written in the newspapers originated in that way. The reporters came from several New York papers to talk with me about the matter. Then the next step was the coming to this city of one or two college professors—you will remember this—one gentleman appeared here from Johns Hopkins University, a distinguished geologist, opposing quite vigorously the passage of this bill. I knew nothing of the attitude of Johns Hopkins University until he came to see me afterwards.

Mr. TALBOTT. He wrote me a communication about that before you knew anything about it at all.

Prof. MENDENHALL. Yes, sir; also the Columbia College people were interested—I do not know how they learned of it—and two or three of their faculty volunteered to come here and express their views. Now, those gentlemen came here to see me, and in conversation with them I stated I believe there was no harm in calling the attention of my friends and a number of the friends of the Survey in the country to this bill which had been proposed, and I am free to say, Mr. Chairman, I did it. I wrote to perhaps 10 or maybe 15 people, but not so many, probably, as that, around the country and sent them copies of the bill stating that I would be glad to have an expression of their opinion.

Mr. GEISSENHAINER. Asking for something in the direction of an opinion?

Prof. MENDENHALL. Yes, sir. They responded, and I will say also——

Mr. GEISSENHAINER. Without any prejudice?

Prof. MENDENHALL. Yes, sir. I will say Cornell University also wrote officially a long letter, I think it was written to this committee without my knowledge, and I think I can justly say the movement was entirely spontaneous.

The CHAIRMAN. Let me ask you a question right there. Are any of the faculties of any of these colleges employed in any way by the Coast and Geodetic Survey?

Prof. MENDENHALL. We have 3 men at the present time who are employed during a portion of the year by the Coast Survey.

The CHAIRMAN. Who are they?

Prof. MENDENHALL. That is in accordance with a system which I am very glad to explain. Under the appropriation which we have to furnish points to State surveys it has long been the practice, in fact, I think, for fifteen or twenty years, ever since that appropriation was made, to employ during the summer months a college professor to take the field, if we can find one who is fitted for it. Then we term him acting assistant in the Coast Survey. We have at present one in the State of Minnesota, one in the State of Tennessee, as perhaps is well known to Mr. Enloe, Prof. Buchanan, and we have also one in the State of New Jersey.

The CHAIRMAN. You have three altogether?

Prof. MENDENHALL. I think that is all; and those men have for many years been in our Survey in that capacity.

The CHAIRMAN. They were in the Survey when you came in?

Prof. MENDENHALL. They have been there for many years, Mr. Chairman, and I did not have anything to do with the selection or appointment of any of them.

Mr. ENLOE. What is the object of employing a college professor?

Prof. MENDENHALL. The object is, we can get the work done, I think on the whole, at a less cost than by putting our own men in the field.

Our own corps is small and oftentimes during the summer we have not a sufficient number of men to do this, so these men were selected. As I say, it was the policy which was adopted twenty years ago as far as I know, and in my judgment it is a wise policy. These men are civil engineers. They are generally professors of civil engineering in these colleges and they naturally like to do this kind of work. We pay them $4 a day for their services and they naturally like to do it, because it gives them opportunity to do high-class work, and they in turn can teach their pupils how it is done, and altogether the work is excellent, proving an excellent arrangement for those States. Take your own State——

Mr. MONEY. A good way of spending a vacation and getting healthy, too.

Prof. MENDENHALL. In your own State, Mr. Enloe, the officer there is regarded by the office and has been, as I learned when I came to the office, one of the most efficient men of the whole corps. The other 2 men are efficient men also, and they all need no praise from me as far as the efficiency of their work is concerned.

Mr. ENLOE. Will you furnish the committee with a list of the persons connected with colleges who have been employed by the Coast and Geodetic Survey during your administration?

Prof. MENDENHALL. I think I have already furnished it, sir. There have been no other men employed. In fact, when I came in, I dropped off 2 or 3 who had been employed before.

Mr. ENLOE. There are now only 3.

Prof. MENDENHALL. I think there have been no more since I have been here, except those 3. I dropped off 2 or 3 because I happened personally to know that they were not the most competent men to do the work, so I dropped them off and there remained only those 3 men.

Mr. GEISSENHAINER. How long had that full corps of 6 men been working?

Prof. MENDENHALL. Of 6?

Mr. GEISSENHAINER. If you dropped off 3, there must have been 6.

Prof. MENDENHALL. I do not know now how many I dropped. I remember now of dropping 1 in a Western State, and I did not continue the work in that State. The work had been going on in the States of Ohio and Indiana, and I discontinued the work in both of those States, because on investigation I thought the men were not the best men who could be selected, and, secondly, I did not like exactly the scheme which had been started for the triangulation there, so it was stopped. Now, this system has been in operation—how long, Mr. Wainwright, fifteen years?

Mr. WAINWRIGHT. I think so; as far back, I should say, as 1871.

Prof. MENDENHALL. At one time I think as many as 6 were employed. I doubt whether there were ever more men than that employed at one time.

Mr. GEISSENHAINER. Those you might designate as outsiders?

Prof. MENDENHALL. Yes, sir; acting assistants. I will say we have only 2 men at the present time having that title besides Prof. Alexander Agassiz, who is an acting assistant of the Coast and Geodetic Survey. He was appointed a year or two ago, but without compensation whatever, and never received a dollar from the Survey; but when he goes to Cuba, for instance, to pursue his geological investigation, he has an official title, so they receive him in a little better way, and with the permission of the Secretary of the Treasury, two years ago I gave him that title. He costs the Coast and Geodetic Survey nothing and turns in any results as to soundings and that kind of thing.

Mr. ENLOE. Is your regular force then insufficient to do this work? Prof. MENDENHALL. The regular force could have done this work in the States if it was thought to be desired.

Mr. MONEY. But they are doing something else.

Prof. MENDENHALL. Yes, sir; but I must say I consider it desirable. We have a few men in the States who are employed in that way, and they do their work fairly well. We send men frequently to inspect this work. We do not allow it to go out without it is first-class. I can give you every evidence of that.

Mr. ENLOE. Did you have Mr. Charles S. Pierce here at one time unemployed?

Prof. MENDENHALL. No, sir; if the committee wants to hear the story of Mr. Charles S. Peirce I will tell it.

Mr. ENLOE. I would like to hear it, very much.

Prof. MENDENHALL. It is perhaps interesting. He is the son of Prof. Benjamin Pierce, for a long time professor of mathematics at Harvard University, and for about six or eight years Superintendent of the Coast and Geodetic Survey, succeeding Prof. Bache as Superintendent. Charles S. Pierce was one of his sons, and the other is now professor of mathematics at Harvard. Prof. Benj. Pierce was a man of great ability, and was one of the leading astronomers, ranking with Bowditch and others of high standing, and his son was a man of great ability, thought by many to possess higher mathematical attainments than his father. Charles S. Pierce came to the Coast Survey perhaps during his father's administration, perhaps before. At any rate, in 1873 there was assigned to him the work of carrying on gravity determinations in the United States, and when I came into the Survey I found him in the Survey employed in that capacity; that is, as an assistant. He had been so employed for many years, and he had been so employed during the time of my predecessor, Mr. Thorne.

I discovered that he had been put on office work by my predecessor, that is to say, having made a number of observations extending through several years he had not reduced those observations, had not gotten out of them all that ought to have been gotten out of them and all that should have been gotten out of them, and Mr. Thorn had sent him to his home in Pennsylvania, with instructions to reduce those observations, and I think that Prof. Peirce was there at least two or three years before I came into the Survey, engaged solely in trying to complete that work. He had an immense mass of material which he tried to get out and he never succeeded in doing it. Nevertheless he worked on that at that time to try to do it. I came in five years ago and found that condition of things. I very soon began to ask Mr. Peirce for the results of his work, but he began to make one excuse after another for not having finished these results and I then had him by and by send on the material which he had and I made a careful examination of that, and I was not quite satisfied to let the matter depend upon my own personal judgment, so I submitted it to two or three of the most competent experts, Prof. Newcomb, of the Nautical Almanac, and Prof. Newton, of Yale College, whose name I mentioned just now. I sent a number of papers and documents to those gentlemen in order to be sure that they might agree with me or say I was wrong in my judgment with regard to the character of the work.

Now, in justice to Prof. Peirce I will say much of his work was of the highest character, and it has received praise from the European geodetists and others, physicists, etc., but it lacked that practical quality which I believed to be essential. That is, while I absolutely believe in the duty of a Government Bureau like this, which needs so much and gets so much from science and scientific men, while I believe it to be the duty of such a Bureau to make some return in kind when it can do so incidentally, yet at the same time I believe, and I have tried to keep to that idea, the final outcome should be practical results. I discovered after a careful examination that Prof. Peirce was not getting practical results. In the meantime I took up the subject in which he was engaged actively myself, as I had been long interested in it, at least ten or fifteen years altogether, and began to do some work on it, and began to devise such instruments and methods which would greatly reduce the cost of labor connected with those very valuable determinations, and before many months I became convinced that Prof. Peirce's services to the Survey were no longer necessary and that they should not be longer retained; that I could not in justice to my obligations to the Government retain Prof. Peirce any longer. I therefore called his attention to his attitude in the whole question, and his not furnishing practical results, and the fact that we had new methods and devices which were going to inevitably outstrip him in getting those practical results. I have been carrying on some of those operations in the last few months, and I found in determining the force of gravity at several stations, that the cost per station has been greatly reduced; something like $100 per station, whereas it cost under the old methods perhaps not less than from $1,000 to $1,500. something like that, which represents something like the reduction which has been made.

I will say that after representing this matter to Prof. Peirce he tendered his resignation and that was accepted and his connection with the Coast and Geodetic Survey ended. That is, I think, a full history of the matter. I will be glad to answer any further questions any gentleman may wish to ask about it. I ought perhaps to add, the judgment of those experts to whom I submitted those results was in entire accordance with mine that the material was not valuable. Perhaps I ought also to add, as this question has been raised, that there was nothing whatever personal in connection with my action in regard to Prof. Peirce, as there has not been anything personal in connection with anyone connected with the Coast Survey. He was one of my oldest friends in the Coast Survey; I corresponded with him ten, twelve, fourteen years ago on a subject in which we were greatly interested, and it so happened that he was the first man to send me a telegram of congratulation after my receiving the appointment as Superintendent of the Coast Survey. So I will say I was guided in this matter purely by motives of what I believed to be public policy.

Now, Mr. Chairman, if I may go on, this is a letter which I desire to read from the State geologist of the State of Missouri. This is addressed to a member of the Senate, but a copy of it has been put in my hands since I was here the other day, and as he gives the opinion of a geologist on this question, I take pleasure in reading it. He says:

[Extract from letter of Arthur W. Winslow to Hon. Francis M. Cockrell, U. S. Senate, dated Jefferson City, May 28, 1894.]

*   *   *   *   *   *   *

I sincerely hope that this bill will not become a law. I feel that it would practically effect the disorganization of an important public work which has heretofore been conducted in a highly efficient manner and with great credit to the Government.

I will not attempt to argue the case within the space of a letter, but will content myself with an expression of my views. You know that I am entirely friendly to the Geological Survey, and what I say is prompted by no disregard of its interests; but I do not feel that that Bureau has either the corps or the equipment to conduct the refined geodetic work of the Coast and Geodetic Survey. A transfer would, I think, tend to the subordination and ultimate deterioration of the geodetic work proper. I think the interests of the national as well as of State geological surveys better subserved by a strengthening and rapid extending of the work of the Coast and Geodetic Survey. Upon its triangulation and precise leveling the topographic and other maps of the Geological Survey should be based. I know that the past work and recent assistance of this survey were of direct and material aid to the Missouri geological survey while under my charge. " * *

The transfer of the coast and marine work to the Navy Department is, on the face, plausible, but I see no advantage in it that will in any way offset the demoralizing effects of disorganization. That naval officers can conduct this technical and highly scientific work without the aid of civilians is out of the question. I speak with some knowledge of the case, being of a naval family myself, my father, several cousins, and two brothers having been in the service, the last for several years on coast survey work.

     *   *   ●   *   *   *   *

Prof. E. A. Bowser, of Rutgers College, says:

MARCH 22, 1894.

It requires mathematicians of a high order and several years of special training. There is no survey in Europe superior to it. It is a work in which every American may take pride.

E. A. BOWSER,
Rutgers College, New Jersey.

Prof. Francis H. Smith, of the University of Virginia, says:

UNIVERSITY OF VIRGINIA, March 30, 1894.

I am shocked to learn of the movement hostile to the Coast Survey.

It is incredible that men acquainted with its history and its services should seek its destruction, for division means that.

FRANCIS H. SMITH.

I may say with reference to Prof. Smith that he was one of the committee of 10 or 12 persons appointed, I think, about twenty-five years ago, by the American Association for the Advancement of Science, to investigate the work of the Coast Survey and to report what in their judgment was its character, and such modifications as they thought ought to be made. That report is found in the report of the American Association, I think, for the year 1859-'60, so that it is more than twenty-five years ago; but it is an exceedingly lengthy and valuable report of the operations of the Survey.

Prof. John C. Waite, a member of the American Society of Civil Engineers and Professor of Engineering of Harvard University, says:

NEW YORK, March 30, 1894.

We are advised that there is an effort to be made to abolish the Coast Survey Department or to break it into two parts, giving a portion of the work to the Navy and the rest to the Geological Department. This I personally should very much regret.

    *   *   *   *   *   *

JOHN C. WAIT,
Member American Society of Civil Engineers
and Professor of Engineering, Harvard University.

I may say this letter was written to me personally, and how he was advised of this matter I do not know; but it seems he did learn.

Prof. Alfred E. Burton, of the Massachusetts Institute of Technology, writes as follows:

BOSTON, March 31, 1894.

In regard to the proposed bill for the transfer of the Coast and Geodetic Survey, I assure you that I feel most sincerely that such a change would be disastrous to the execution of the best work and would cause a distinct loss to the scientific world generally. * * *

ALFRED E. BURTON,
Massachusetts Institute of Technology.

I spoke a moment ago in regard to the first communication being a letter from California, and this is a letter written by the professor of structural engineering of Leland Stanford University, addressed to a Representative in Congress, from whom I have obtained a copy of it— that is, he has furnished me with a copy of it. It is as follows:

[Leland Stanford Junior University, Palo Alto, Santa Clara County, Cal.]

The record of the Coast Survey is one of quiet, steady, accurate work. No attempt has ever been made to do work in order to make a showing or for political ends. With a broad, comprehensive plan covering years of continuous, uninterrupted work for its completion, they have gone ahead with the means at their disposal, accomplishing a little each year until they have nearly completed a network of monuments extending from the Atlantic to the Pacific. Monuments that can absolutely be relied upon for accuracy and durability and which should form the basis of a vast system of accurate topographical surveys similar in character to those possessed by the civilized nations of Europe and that have proved of vast economical value in the developing the internal ways of communication for which those countries are noted. This method that has just been outlined is in direct contrast to the methods employed by the topographical surveys of the Geological Department, who have mapped large territories with imperfect methods and with nothing more definite or more durable than a fence post to begin with. Such maps 'are absolutely unreliable and of no use whatever from an economical or engineering standpoint. Like the time-table folders of the railroads, they represent only the interests of the publishers and serve well enough for something to show, but practically are far from satisfactory in regard to truthfulness.

Any interference or change in the management of the Coast Survey must impair its usefulness. Its history will show the effect of management by the Navy Department.

The right men in the right place are doing the right kind of work, and are doing it without desire for show or other reward than the appreciation of the value and reliability of their work by those in a position to know and judge of its usefulness.

I therefore, unsolicited, deem it my duty to call your attention to the universal verdict of the engineers and astronomers of the country as to the character of the work being done by the U. S. Coast and Geodetic Survey, and to protest against the contemplated change in its organization.

CHAS. B. WING,
Professor of Structural Engineering.

I do not entirely indorse all that this letter says about those maps of the Geological Survey, but I simply read what he says.

Now, I have a number of protests from other institutions of learning, but as they are nearly all of the same character I may save time by referring to them, and then insert them in my remarks.

UNIVERSITY OF MISSOURI.

Protests on the ground that the plan proposed does not guarantee work of the same high character as is now done by the Survey under its present organization and leadership.

OHIO STATE UNIVERSITY.

The Survey would necessarily be held subordinate to the demands of their (Navy) profession and its work would be at all times liable to serious and costly interruptions.

WESTERN UNIVERSITY OF PENNSYLVANIA.

Dismemberment would destroy coordination of its work, which is now efficiently performed, of great practical usefulness, and its results are such that every American citizen should be proud of it.

UNIVERSITY OF MINNESOTA.

Would result disadvantageously for the surveys of Minnesota.
The transfer to the Navy has been tried and found unsatisfactory.
The high order of work demanded on each of the several lines in which the Survey is engaged—triangulation, astronomy, leveling, gravity, topography, hydrography, and magnetics—is such as can not be successfully prosecuted, except by the most trained experts, and must suffer if placed in other hands.

COLUMBIA COLLEGE.

[By its president, Seth Low, and many members of its faculty.]

The passage of the bill will (1) interfere seriously with the efficiency of the important work now carried on. (2) Would ultimately largely increase the cost of the work unless the standard should be most undesirably lowered. (3) Would place the control of the geodetic work in the U. S. Geological Survey under the charge of a geologist and anthropologist.

UNIVERSITY OF WISCONSIN.

The value of the services rendered by the Coast and Geodetic Survey is attested by the bill (Enloe) itself, which provides for a continuation of those services by the dismembered parts of the Bureau. * * * The work of the Bureau is a unit and can not be divided among distinct organizations without serious detriment.

UNIVERSITY OF VIRGINIA.

Regards "this measure as a step backward in National progress."
Its labors, the triangulation from our coasts to the whole interior of our vast domain, which undertaking will settle our much confused geography and unify and harmonize the work of our State surveys, all of priceless value to the country.
The subjects it covers are foreign to naval and geological fields, both of which include more in their special lines than can well be accomplished with existing forces.
If economy be the object sought we respectfully suggest that the dividing out of this great Bureau will be likely to secure less efficiency at greater cost.

LEHIGH UNIVERSITY.

Express high appreciation of the scientific and practical results of the Survey and confidence in its methods of administration and believe that the transfer would be detrimental to the best public interests.

INDIANA ACADEMY OF SCIENCES.

The bill will vitally affect all commercial, economic, educational, and scientific interests of the country.
The disruption of the work will lead practically to its destruction.
The unity of plan of its operations and processes of measurement would be destroyed. Under different management the methods would be different.
The Superintendent is custodian of national standards of weights and measures. These must be in charge of men trained in physical measurements and research. This department of the service should be extended and made to include all standards that may enter into the arts and professions, such as electrical and others.
By law these standards belong under the control of the Secretary of the Treasury. If a special department of weights and measures is to be created, to make it efficient would cost a considerable sum of money; there would be no scientific bureau under the Treasury to which its work could be attached if the Coast and Geodetic Survey were removed.

TECHNICAL SOCIETY OF THE PACIFIC COAST.

The contemplated step would lead to nothing less than an utter annihilation of a meritorious and deserving department whose work lies before the nation as an open book, demanding the admiration of every citizen who will give this matter a moment's serious attention.
It can not be said that the work of the Coast and Geodetic Survey has been confined to abstruse mathematical and scientific problems. On the contrary. if there has ever been a proof of the practical use of exact science that proof has been amply furnished by this department in its long career of usefulness and conscientious labor.

THE GOVERNOR AND OTHER OFFICERS OF THE STATE OF WASHINGTON.

It is believed that a change so vitally affecting the nation in a most important direction, its commerce, should not be made without a most thorough and unbiased consideration, and that by a commission composed of men so eminently practical

.

and free from bias that the decision they reach would commend itself to all who have the interests of the country at heart. Such men can be found in the great transportation companies, the marine insurance companies, the National Academy of Sciences, and the great educational institutions of our country.

CUMBERLAND UNIVERSITY, LEBANON, TENN.

The bill will, in our opinion, deprive the Government of the source of many of its greatest, most illustrious, and useful scientific results.

Expediency, economy, prudence, and the experience of sixty years combine to forbid the dismemberment of the Coast and Geodetic Survey. Six reasons:

(1) Transfer made twice and found detrimental.
(2) Scientific men have always opposed it.
(3) Commercial and marine organizations have never asked for it.
(4) Leading naval and army officers have opposed it.
(5) Character of work interferes with naval training, and in case of war would have to be abandoned.
(6) Long course of theoretical and practical training necessary.

Prof. Lewis M. Haupt, late professor of civil engineering of the University of Pennsylvania, and a learned engineer on topographical matters, says:

* * * The strongest reasons for declining to dissever the Coast Survey arises from the frequent changes in the stations and duties of the officers engaged in the bureaus to which it is proposed to transfer it, thus destroying, to a large extent, all sense of personal responsibility for results or their effects, and making it necessary to obtain records from two bureaus which are now supplied by one.

Mr. GEISSENHAINER. He is the one who laid the pipe lines?

Prof. MENDENHALL. Yes, sir. Prof. Fuertes I think has written a letter to the committee, but he says:

Neither the education nor the objects in life of the sailor and the geologist contribute to the proper administration of problems which on account of special experience the Coast Survey is the best organization to solve.

The geodetic engineer must be a specialist, and must dedicate his entire life not only to a certain amount of routine work but to the investigation of the most difficult portions of several mathematical and physical sciences.

The results that it (Coast and Geodetic Survey) can turn out and has turned out have made the scientific reputation of this country second to that of no other, and it can not be kept up by the fortuitous detail of inexperienced men to perform certain work simply because their turn for it has arrived, whether or not they are competent or incompetent. * * *

The Chamber of Commerce of Tacoma passed a resolution against the transfer, which is as follows:

Resolved, That the services rendered to commerce during the past seventy-five years by the U. S. Coast and Geodetic Survey have been both efficient and satisfactory.

That the interests of our country will be best subserved by continuing the work of the U. S. Coast and Geodetic Survey as it is at present organized.

The Chamber of Commerce also, of San Francisco, passed a series of resolutions which I think have been sent to the House of Representatives:

To the honorable the Senate and House of Representatives in Congress assembled:

Your memorialist, the Chamber of Commerce of the city of San Francisco, hereby desires to express its great regret that a bill has been introduced in Congress (H. R. 6338) proposing to disturb the present efficient organization of the U. S. Coast and Geodetic Survey.

The work of this Bureau of our Government in the past has been eminently satisfactory; it has gained the entire confidence of our country and the acknowledged admiration of foreign governments conducting similar surveys.

Congress has assigned to this Bureau the execution of work demanding experience of the highest class. That which it has done commends itself so strongly to the maritime and other interests represented by this Chamber that it is to be earnestly hoped the just claims of the public service will not now be ignored by the passage of the above-named bill.

The Chamber of Commerce of San Diego also passed the following resolutions:

On March 19 a bill was introduced in the House of Representatives by Mr. Enloe, of Tennessee, "To abolish the Bureau in the Treasury Department known as the Coast and Geodetic Survey, and transfer the work of said Bureau to the Hydrographic Office in the Navy Department, and the Geological Survey in the Department of the Interior."

As representatives of the commercial interests of the port of San Diego, Cal., we earnestly protest against this attempt to abolish a Bureau which has done so much in the last forty-five years by its accurate surveys of the harbors of the Pacific coast, and its accurate maps, to lessen the dangers of navigation and to develop coastwise commerce.

We have every confidence in the present management of the Bureau and are convinced that the disruption of the present organization and the division of its present work between the Navy and Interior Departments would be detrimental to the best interests of the Government.

I will say in regard to these chambers of commerce I do not know how the resolutions originated. Here is one which came also a day or two ago from the Philadelphia Maritime Exchange. It says:

To the honorable the Senate and House of Representatives of the United States in Congress assembled:

This memorial of the Philadelphia Maritime Exchange respectfully represents:

That a bill has been introduced in the House of Representatives of the United States (H. R. 6338) having for its object the abolishment of the Bureau in the Treasury Department known as the Coast and Geodetic Survey, and the transfer of the work of said Bureau to the Hydrographic Office in the Navy Department, and to the Geological Survey in the Department of the Interior.

That in the judgment of your memorialist the efficient and highly important work done by the said Bureau in the many years of its existence, and the continued need for its services, warrant its continuance as a separate Bureau, especially equipped as this is, to carry on the delicate and technical operations coming within its province, the thorough and intelligent performance of which in the past by this Bureau has been of the greatest value to the country; therefore,

Your memorialist, The Philadelphia Maritime Exchange, earnestly petitions your honorable bodies that no action be taken to dismember the Bureau known as the Coast and Geodetic Survey, or to remove it to the care of other departments; but that it be retained in the Treasury Department, as at present.

GEO. E. EARNSHAW,
President.

Attest:
[SEAL.]

E. R. SHARWOOD,
Secretary.

PHILADELPHIA, *May 26, 1894.*

Now, I will pass to some of these longer communications. I would like to read a letter written by Prof. E. A. Fuertes, who is director of the College of Engineering at Cornell University, and a very distinguished man in his line, who has only recently completed extensive works in Brazil for the Government, and whose judgment is worthy of consideration, particularly on account of his long acquaintance with the work of the Bureau. His letter is as follows:

To the Committee on Naval Affairs:

GENTLEMEN: I have read with great alarm the tenor of the bill which intends to suppress the work of the Coast and Geodetic Survey, breaking it into two parts to be assigned, respectively, to the Hydrographic Office and the Geological Survey. I feel it my duty, as a student of science and as a professional man intimately acquainted with the aims and results to be accomplished by the Coast Survey, to make as strong a protest as may be possible against the enactment of a law that will do incalculable harm to the best interests of scientific progress, and also to the Hydrographic Office and the Geological Survey. Neither the education nor the objects in life of the sailor and the geologist contribute to the proper administration of the problems which, on account of special experience, the Coast Survey is the best organization to solve. It may be, and doubtless is, a popular notion, having some apparent justification, to believe that a sailor educated at a naval academy can survey our coasts; but such is not the case. It may also be supposed that the geologist need only to employ surveyors to reproduce the features of a given topography; but such is not the case also. The geodetic engineer must be a specialist and must dedicate his entire life not only to a certain amount of routine work, but to the investigation of the most difficult portions of several mathematical and physical sciences. The Coast Survey prepares the groundwork of a very large number of problems from which an enlightened nation will derive incalculable benefits. Its aim is not to reproduce in a small scale the features of land and water, the heights of mountains and depth of oceans; this is indeed only an incidental feature of the much deeper meaning of its work.

It is perfectly proper for a nation like ours to dedicate considerable sums of money for the preparation of work of so advanced a nature that its importance may not be understood by a vast majority of its inhabitants; in fact, one of the most persistent phases of human nature is the resistance to improvement by the very persons most likely to be benefited by the advanced work of its leaders; and even the short history of this, the most enlightened nation, is not lacking in typical examples of this peculiarity, as witnessed by the slavery question, the Pacific Railroad, the Erie Canal, the canalization of the American Isthmus, etc. Such a work as the Coast Survey is called upon to produce requires absolutely the employment of experienced experts. Nothing is more likely to produce perfunctory and inefficient work in undertakings of this nature than the proposed transfer of the Coast Survey to a military organization. A recent example of this fact can be seen in our naval observatory, which in times past was a great credit to the intelligence and power for scientific thought of this great country; but since it became subject to the rules of military discipline, it has been, as to original investigation, as silent as the grave, and the American import of national astronomy has dwindled down to insignificant proportions.

The astronomical work of the Navy is to-day eclipsed by that of a score or more of private observatories; the knowledge of our earth as affecting problems of the utmost moment to the human race will be utterly demoralized and rendered fruitless by such a transfer. The Coast Survey has now the opportunity of picking the best scientists from this or any other country, who, by their special training and personal aptitude and genius, have been born for its work. The results that it can turn out and has turned out has made the scientific reputation of this country second to that of no other, and it can not be kept up by the fortuitous detail of inexperienced men to perform certain work simply because they have their turn for it has arrived, whether they are competent or incompetent. Of course it can be said that only competent men will be detailed; but the horizon from which to choose these men is not only exceedingly limited; but, furthermore, physicists can not be improvised to order any more than a general or a poet.

Further, such a step is retrogressive and unworthy of the scientific status of the country. This change is opposed to the policy which made the transfer of the Weather Bureau from a military organization to a civil bureau, where specialists can be trained, and will in the end become experts, to the great benefit of the commercial, industrial, and agricultural interests of the country. The same reasons that obtained for that transfer exist with momentous consequences against the contradictory transfer proposed. I am prepared to prove also before any committe of Congress that the Navy Department does not give in any portion of the career of its members the training that is necessary for the purpose, neither in the requirements for admission to the Naval Academy, nor in the curriculum of the studies prosecuted there, nor in the subsequent employment of its members. The mere work of its scientific training is inferior to that of hundreds of private schools. It must not be understood that I desire to belittle our naval establishment; but the Naval Academy as well as the Military Academy at West Point are very much behind the times, not on account of lack of enthusiasm or dutifulness or manliness or probity on the part of the officers charged with their educational policies; the fault is altogether on the side of Congress, that fails to make suitable appropriations for the very expensive teaching demanded nowadays by the advanced condition of our methods of scientific instruction.

Much can be said against breaking into two separate provinces a work in which such a separation of administration is an inherent impossibility due to the nature and correlations of the work itself. It would be as impossible to obtain suitable results from such a disjointed arrangement as it would be to make a chronometer by putting together wheels of any size in a haphazard fashion.

It is true that in monarchical countries much of the work of the coast survey is done under military organizations, but the results thus obtained, with a dominant military purpose in view (for which we have no need), do not compare in direct usefulness, transcendental value, economy, and swiftness of execution, with what our Coast Survey has done, and has made it conspicuously the first scientific organization of the country, respected and praised by all the academies of science and national scientific institutions of every civilized government; and while opinions differ as to the scientific value of our Geological Survey, there is absolute unanimity among the scientists of the world as to the useful work of the Coast Survey. Upon expert investigation it will also be found that in Europe the degree of military interference in those surveys is not equally intense in every country, or even in the various colonies in the same country; and it will be found, without exception, that those countries like England, for example, which are freer and less under the stress of militarism, the scientific merit of their surveys are in the inverse ratio of their military control. This is especially conspicuous in the Indian survey. I am sure that the rank of supremacy now held by us in this branch of the national service will assume a position of mediocrity, if not worse, by the abolition of the best means of prosecuting the ground work carried on so admirably by our Coast Survey.

Taking for granted that the Geological Survey may do such violence to its natural instincts that its future work in geodesy may become independent of the natural geological bias that will tend to subordinate geodesy to geology; taking for granted, also, that as a civil organization that Survey may eventually employ proper scientific experts; what advantages will result by such a change that are not now better served by the present Coast Survey? Many of the purposes of geology can be effectively served by simple approximate delineations of the earth's crust; in fact, approximate sketches will be sufficient for geological purposes in a vast majority of its topographical needs. Is it then to be expected that a geologist will spend the money necessary for geodetic accuracy, which is not indispensable for his purpose, to the prejudice of the geological hobbies which give enthusiasm to his life work?

Again, there are now stored in the Coast Survey Office tons of notebooks and interwoven data, some of them not yet worked up, the value of which is equally important to the geodetic and hydrographic work. Upon what system of division can the share of this valuable and expensive data be distributed between the Geological Survey and the Hydrographic Office? My experience in cases of this kind indicates that these notebooks will be mixed up or thrown away, thus rendering them useless even with a great expense and risk of mistakes in recopying, thus losing all the advantages for which the expense of collecting them was incurred.

In my judgment, based upon no little experience in matters of this nature, as well as with men and with affairs, I am led to believe that such a transfer as is now proposed will deprive the Government of perhaps its most brilliant and prolific scientific activity without benefiting the Navy or the Geological Survey. It seems also an injustice to deprive the Coast Survey from reaping the benefits of its scientific labors. The nature of the case made its progress necessarily slow in the beginning; and it has been constantly harassed both by prejudice and jealousies and by the exactions of persons who could not understand that the active work and hardships of triangulation from mountain peaks was indispensable as the basis and foundation of all subsequent work; and since the time of the great Hassler, the Presidents and Congressmen have not adequately appreciated the heroic work done by the Coast Survey in triangulating the vast extent of our territory. It seems to have been expected that instead of preparing a solid foundation for the truthful topography of our country, and the actual shape of the earth, pretty maps filled with inaccuracies, of no possible value, should have taken the place of the early empty sheets with chains of triangles looking like the spider web made by a crazy spider. Yet such work is absolutely indispensable to make useful the delineation of the features of our continent, and for scientific purposes the difficult work is of an importance that can not be exaggerated. It is indeed a strange fact that, with very few exceptions, we have to-day a more accurate knowledge of the service of the moon than of any county in any State of the Union; and I believe that the proposed transfer will make confusion worse confounded, and will postpone for an indefinite number of years the fruits of the labors which the Coast Survey is about to reap with a degree of credit of which any nation might well be proud; and which, if lost, could not be recovered without heavy expenses.

There are at present a large number of physical discoveries which have been brought to a standstill, for lack of sufficient knowledge in some directions, like electricity, the force of gravity, the fate of the earth upon its course about the sun, etc. The settlement of these open questions are of immense economical and utilitarian value to the denizens of the earth; and many of these questions can not be developed much further until some of the work which the Coast Survey has under way may throw light upon the very dark corners of our present knowledge of physical science.

It may be said that this method of thinking lacks the horse sense of practical life, and are the dreams of college professors and long-haired enthusiasts; yet similar lines of argument were made to Columbus, Luther, Galileo, and Wendell Phillips; and the inquisition has filled thousands of graves and destroyed epochs of progress,

because the popular sentiment is usually unable to appreciate benefits to be obtained
by activities they do not understand. It may also be argued that both the Navy
Department and the Geological Survey can also work in the proper channels that
will develop the scientific progress so urgently demanded, as well as the Coast Survey; but this would be an idle assumption. Our present age demands specializa-
tion in everything. While it is difficult to understand the logic that would justify
the throwing out of their sphere the Navy officers, who should have plenty to occupy
their time and activity in naval matters, it is still more difficult to perceive any
good reasons for switching them into investigations upon subjects foreign to their
calling and about which they have no adequate conception, and absolutely no
training at all. We might, with better reason, put the Weather Service in charge
of the sailors, because the Navy of the nation and its commerce are so much affected
by the laws of storms; or we might also put the Navy Department under the Geological Survey, because the forms of our coasts and the bottoms of our oceans are a
legitimate field of study for the geologist. I invoke the exercise of conscience and
justice in government. The true meaning of the assault upon the Coast Survey is
neither patriotic nor disinterested. It is the illegitimate outcome of a long struggle
that has made the success of the Coast Survey the object of envy for many years
past, and ignoble jealousies, not worthy of serious consideration, for they are born
of class prejudices and unwarrantable ambition, which now threaten to consign to
obscurity one of the best scientific bureaus of our country. A gain in efficiency
by the proposed change is as impossible as a gain in economy of administration, for
it can not be supposed that there is not plenty of work to be done by our naval officers
in their own field, and the Geological Survey certainly should not have sinecurists
waiting for additional business to give them employment. If geodetic work is to be
done, it must be paid for, no matter who does it. The question to consider would
be, who has more experience, who is better trained, and what organization possesses
the technical requirements to do the technical work demanded?

I believe that I have no prejudices, as I have no interests of any nature whatever
in reference to the subject, beyond a desire to see our scientific work respected
among other nations by its solidity, truthfulness, and ever increasing usefulness.
I believe I have had sufficient knowledge and have had sufficient contact with the
three interests involved, viz, the Geological Survey, the Navy, and the Coast Survey, by critical study, personal experience, and scientific training, to believe that I
am competent to judge that the proposed change is unwise and needless. I can also
say that if I were mistaken or utterly incompetent to pass judgment on the matter
upon my own deductions, I can not certainly be mistaken in the statement of the
fact that I do not know one person capable of judging upon the true import of the
Coast Survey whose opinion does not coincide with mine. I further believe that it
would be exceedingly easy, and the duty of Congress, before such an important change
is made, to obtain the expert opinion of the scientific bodies in this country or, at
least, of the Academy of Sciences; or to summon before them such disinterested
experts, as I have no doubt could be obtained by the hundreds, whose names and
judgment would be a guaranty of their fitness to testify upon the merits of this
question, and who, I venture to say, will oppose such a change.

In many Government undertakings, the choice of evils is a necessary expedient
even though it must necessarily lead to waste of resources. I think, however, that
it would be more beneficial to the country to lose the benefits that might be derived
from a minute geological survey, if such should be the case, rather than injure the
preexisting rights and prerequisite labor of the Coast Survey; but I am very certain that no such loss is necessary or in the least probable if the Coast Survey is let
alone.

The geological survey is a question of vast importance; but its interests can not
suffer for the lack of an accurate triangulation. In fact, its director told me a few
months ago, before several witnesses, that the "plane table" (which is rather a
coarse surveying instrument employed by engineers for filling in topographical
details) was the most accurate instrument he had found for his purposes. It certainly
answers all the requirements for details of restricted, or not large areas; and if the
geological features of so large a surface as a State have to be delineated, the necessary smallness of the scale will obliterate such details; and only approximate
features and conventional signs admit of being recorded in such maps. Eventually
all geological detail must be studied from the large scale sheet, on which the triangulation is of no moment whatever.

I can see no objections, in the case of the Geological Survey, that it should make
such plan-etable surveys as it needs, resting on such triangulation as it may need,
and if such work can be utilized by the Coast Survey in filling in details so surveyed, so much the better. But I can see also a decided advantage in retaining in
the control of the Coast Survey the triangulation, gravimetric, magnetic, metrolog-
ical, tidal, hydrographic, and other scientific work that can not and will not be
properly cared for by the Navy or by the geologists, unless their organizations

reproduce in duplicate what the Coast Survey now does much more economically and of the superior grade demonstrated by experience.

I have also a few selections made from the public press. Here is an article from the Sun of Wednesday, April 18, 1894:

THE SURVEYS OF NEW YORK HARBOR.

If we were to search the records of the Coast and Geodetic Survey at Washington we should find that a very large fraction of them are the surveys, the discussions, and the recommendations forming the documentary evidence of the part that Survey has taken, within the past sixty years, in promoting the prosperity of New York City.

*   *   *   *   *   *   *

It has also provided the State of New York with a series of charts of her entire coast line that are unexcelled by those of any nation on earth. Work like that which has stimulated our prosperity has been done for every harbor in the country in proportion to its importance. The charts of the Coast and Geodetic Survey are accepted in the courts as accurate. Land questions have repeatedly been settled by reference to them. For several years an average of 20,000 persons a year were questioned as to the accuracy of these charts, and the result has shown that they are practically perfect, though some of them now need revision.

APRIL 9, 1894.

*   *   *   *   *   *   *

The surveys and cartographic products of this Bureau have never been surpassed in any part of the world. There is much work still before it. Considerations of expediency and economy are opposed to the dismemberment of the Coast and Geodetic Survey.

Here is an article from the Boston Evening Transcript of Thursday, April 5, 1894, which is as follows:

THE ATTACK ON THE COAST SURVEY.

That restless spirit of change which from time to time takes one or another of our governmental institutions for its target has again broken loose in Washington, and is this time bending its energies against the Coast and Geodetic Survey. This is to be regretted, for the Survey has been for more than half a century a department of which we might with reason be proud, and an injury to it of the nature of the present attack can not be otherwise than a serious matter.   *   *   *
The work of the Coast Survey is even more important than may appear on first thought. The law which instituted it required it to survey the sea for three leagues from the shore, the land for three miles inland, the navigable waters of the country, and when requested to do so by the States, to furnish them such information and such general surveys as they desired. The plan of this has been carried out, and nearly every State in the Union has been substantially aided by the excellent work of the Survey. It is continually surveying and resurveying our shores, the forms of which are subject to change; it is at work in our harbors—its charts, which closely follow any natural changes, being the mariner's safeguard; it is aiding in the development of new harbors, and it is giving its advice where such advice is deemed advantageous.

*   *   *   *   *   *   *

The movement against the Coast Survey does not seem in any way to be a partisan one, but it is rather brought forward through personal feeling against individuals. The attack is to be regretted, for it seems reasonable to assert that there is no department of our Government work in which experience is of more importance, and in which injury will more quickly follow hasty or ill-advised change than in this Survey. It is to be hoped, therefore, that scientific and commercial men may make their influence so strongly felt as to retain the present excellent system, which has been for so long a time an honor and a credit to our country.

Here is an article from the Commonwealth of Boston, Saturday, April 7, 1894.

*   *   *   *   *   *   *

The proposed transfer, therefore, should it be accomplished, means the end of good and reliable work for a long time to come, or until other assistants can have acquired the skill which the present men already have. The work is a specialized work of a high class, and its details can not be acquired in a moment. The transfer as suggested would not be unlike the action of a great newspaper, which issues an edict discharging the compositors and dividing their duties among the editors and reporters. The latter are bright men; they are intelligent and skillful; but, in the first place, they lack that experience and handiness at the case which is so necessary to the typesetter, and in the second place, they have other duties already which now occupy them and which, if followed out, would leave them but little time for their additional duties. The cases are very nearly parallel; it is proposed to abolish the present Survey, to discharge the experienced men, and to place the work in the hands of other men, intelligent to be sure, but lacking those most essential elements, technical skill and experience.

It is a little difficult to believe that such a proposition could be made in serious earnest; but it is indeed serious, and it behooves our scientific men and institutions to use their influence to prevent the destruction of this, one of the most creditable of our governmental institutions.

Here is an article from the Columbus Dispatch of Monday, April 16, 1894, which reads in this manner:

THE COAST AND GEODETIC SURVEY.

If strict attention to its legitimate business and unquestioned efficiency and success in doing its work could save any bureau of the General Government from the danger of unfriendly or experimental reconstruction, then, by all means, the U. S. Coast Survey should be exempt. It appears, however, that a bill is now before Congress, which, if passed, will result in the dismemberment of the bureau as at present constituted, and in greatly restricting the range of its work.   *   *   *

But what would this change involve? It would make the bureau a subordinate branch of one of the military arms of the Government, and consequently subject to the interruptions and suspensions which the primary and main business of this department would necessitate. It would put the survey under the control of officers whose ambitions and rewards would lie in an entirely different field. It would put an end to the civilian control under which all the credit of the Survey has thus far been won.

Then follows an article from the Guernsey Times, of Cambridge, Ohio, dated Thursday, April 19, 1894:

KEEP IT OUT OF POLITICS.

*   *   *   If there is any Bureau of the Government that has had an efficient, economical, and blameless administration it is the Coast Survey. It's work has been one of the honors of American science. If the rule "let well enough alone" is ever enforced, this is surely a proper case.

As now organized, the Survey makes up its staff from the best astronomers and mathematicians of the country, and to this free selection its great achievements are largely due. The change proposed would result in confining its selection to Navy officers, and even with these the Survey would hold second place. Their first duty and highest ambition would be found in the naval service proper, and if a war cloud should appear this outside work would be "whistled down the wind" forthwith.

The Times, of Minneapolis, of April 7, 1894, has the following:

THE GEODETIC SURVEY.

*   *   *   In time of war the Survey suffered because the Navy was busy with other matters. Yet the Survey was necessary to the successful prosecution of war. The Army and Navy during the late war depended at critical times upon the work done by the experts upon the Coast Survey. If they had waited for the Navy to have perfected the system they would have found the work done too late.

The Tribune, of Minneapolis, April 17, 1894, says:

* * * The State is in great need of the survey in order to draft for itself an accurate and reliable map. The maps which we now have may fairly be described as horrible. The distances as given on the maps are often miles out of the way. Important lakes are mislocated on the maps, or given out of shape, or left off the map entirely. The public does not know the exact area of Minnesota within a great many square miles. The surveys have been made by thousands of different surveyors, some of whom were competent and others of whom were not, and very few of whom had at hand the proper instruments for perfect work. As a consequence the exact length and width of the State are thought to be several miles different from the figures usually quoted. The shape of the State is a comparatively indifferent quantity. The latitude and longitude of places are indefinite, and no man knows perfectly where in the vast geographical system his farm, his road, his city, his county, or his State lie. In every European state the Government, by its scientific labors in geodetic work, gives each locality exact data and fixed landmarks by which to place itself. In this country our geography is known largely by guess. The Coast and Geodetic Survey is in the midst of the same work as that which Europe has carried to successful issue.

The Railroad Gazette, which as you know is a technical journal, says on April 6, 1894:

There is a movement on foot in Washington which engineers should watch. We say engineers especially, but all citizens who are concerned in preserving for future usefulness one of the old and honorable institutions of the country, should watch it. Its object is the destruction of the Coast Survey. This Bureau has existed for eighty-seven years, and its work is famous among scientific men all over the civilized world. We do not say that the Bureau has always been conducted in an ideal way. It has not been free from the evils of jealousy and sloth and expensiveness, which appear from time to time, and in greater or less degree, in all Government work if it endures long enough—in all human work, we might say—and which are inevitable in a country with such a shocking civil service as ours. * * *
Serious and patriotic engineers would do well to keep an eye on this movement, and if it shows signs of becoming important to write to their Representatives and Senators protesting against dragging the Coast Survey into the spoilsmen's net. It is in the interest of exact science and of professional work the world over that this wanton attack upon a great scientific bureau should not succeed.

I might multiply these notices very considerably, Mr. Chairman, but I wish to reduce my tax upon your time and patience as much as possible, so I will next refer to a few opinions of the Survey that have been expressed by very eminent authorities outside of the United States. I quote now from Sir Roderic I. Murchison, the celebrated English geodesist:

All unprejudiced persons must agree that the trigonometrical survey of the United States of America stands without a superior.
Capt. Smyth, R. N., president of the Royal Geographical Society and Admiral Beaufort, R. N., speak in high terms of appreciation of Coast Survey work and methods. They say that "the progress and character of the hydrography of Great Britain have severely suffered for the want of cooperation with the ordnance or land survey," a defect that is obviated by the organization of the Coast and Geodetic Survey.

That is an important point to which I ask your attention. In the opinion of these most competent witnesses, the present system of combining the hydrographic with the land work, which has always existed in our Survey, is far superior to that which exists in England.
The distinguished president of the Royal Geographical Society of London, Clements R. Markham, in his annual address, published in the Geographical Journal for December, 1893, says that "the U. S. Coast Survey is a monument of rigorous accuracy."

Gen. D. E. Sickles, of New York, said in the House of Representatives, March 17, 1894 (Cong. Rec., p. 3681), that the reports and maps of the Coast Survey excited the admiration of the chief admiral of the Russian navy at the International Geographic Congress at Paris, the admiral affirming that the work was an example to the world, etc.

Baron Humboldt, addressing Prof. Schumacher, says:

* * * In a region of the globe where the direction of oceanic currents, the differences of temperature produced by these currents and by the upheaval of the bottom and the direction of the magnetic curves, offer so important phenomena to the navigators, such a great work could not be placed in better hands than those of Dr. Bache. The Government of the United States has acquired a new right to our gratitude by protecting nobly that which has arrested the attention of the hydrographers and astronomers of Europe. I should be glad to think that in a country where I am honored with so much good feeling my feeble testimony might contribute to enliven the interest which is due to the excellent labors of Mr. Bache.

Mr. ENLOE. What is the date of that?

Prof. MENDENHALL. I can not tell you the date of it now, but it was when Humboldt was alive, so it was some years ago.

Mr. MONEY. Then it is no post mortem communication?

Mr. ENLOE. I did not know but what that might have been expressed at the time it was under the Navy.

Prof. MENDENHALL. I can assure you that that is not the case.

Admiral W. H. Smyth, R. N., president of the Geological Society of London in 1850, in speaking, in his address of that year, of the U. S. Coast Survey, says:

The Coast Survey of the United States is a truly national undertaking, and has been most creditably conducted through all its various departments of science. I have studied the question closely, and do not hesitate to pronounce the conviction, that though the Americans were last in the field, they have, *per saltum*, leaped into the very front of the rank.

Were I asked to give instances, I would say, look to their beautiful maps and charts; see their practice of establishing longitudes by electricity, and the probable extension of its wonderful chronographic applications; mark their novel method of taking and recording transits by galvanic circuit; and consider the excellence and refinement of their astronomical observations for geodetic purposes, as proved by their being able to detect the alteration of gravity, caused by a difference in the density of the earth's crust.

The president of the same society, in his address in 1852, while noticing with admiration the very efficient manner in which the Survey has been conducted, and the rapidity with which the work has been carried on along the western shores of the continent, classes it as "one of the most perfect examples of applied science of modern times."

The Survey has received medals or awards of distinction at several international expositions, etc.:

1858—The Victoria gold medal of the Royal Geographical Society of England.
1875—First premium at the Chilean Exposition, Santiago.
1880—Gold medal at the International Fishery Exposition at Berlin.
1881—Letter of distinction at the International Geographical Congress at Venice, Italy.
1892—Exposition at Madrid, medal.
1893—Six or seven medals at the World's Columbian Exposition at Chicago.

Finally, Mr. Chairman, I would like to summarize very briefly by saying:

(1) The relation of the two parts into which it is proposed to divide the work are such that it can not be done without certain loss of efficiency and an increase in cost.

(2) Twice in the history of the Survey it has been transferred to the Navy Department, and in each case the administration was found to

produce unsatisfactory results and it was soon returned to civilian control under the Treasury Department.

(3) The proposition to place a part of the work under the control of the Geological Survey has always met with opposition from the geologists of the country, besides being strongly and universally condemned by engineers, surveyors, engineering and scientific societies and journals, and others who are directly and especially interested in that part of the work of the Bureau.

(4) The assertions that the work as done under the present system is too elaborate and expensive; that money appropriated by Congress could be and was diverted from its legitimate channels; that no accounting of expenditures was made or could be gotten at; that the hydrographic work is now and has been exclusively executed by naval officers; that an attempt has been made to deprive these officers of proper credit for their services while detailed to the Survey; that the cost of the work has been steadily increasing by quiet additions to the annual appropriations; and many others of a like character have been completely disproved by the evidence of official records and the most competent witnesses.

(5) The all but universal testimony of those whose knowledge of the work of the Bureau is such as to entitle them to an opinion, including naval officers of distinction and experience in the operations of the Survey, is that the dismemberment proposed by this bill is extremely unwise and undesirable.

(6) The highest authorities in Europe have bestowed unstinted praise upon the work of the Survey, and have especially commended the combination of topographic, hydrographic, and geodetic surveying under one administrative head as certain to produce better results than their separate execution.

(7) The present organization offers a training and experience to the naval officers detailed to the service, the great value of which is testified to by these officers themselves, and it is greatly enhanced by the relations which exist between them and civilian officers by long experience in work of a high degree of precision. Under the scheme proposed in the bill such relations and associations will be impossible.

(8) After a thorough investigation of this subject, extending through two years, the Joint Commission of the House and Senate reported, in 1886, adversely to a division of the work of the Survey, such as is now proposed, and recommended that it be continued under existing regulations. And this occurred at a time when the Bureau was under the cloud of an investigation by Department officials of irregularities in administration.

(9) It is therefore submitted that no good reason has been given and no good reason can be given for the passage of the bill. The existing system is the result of a careful examination of the whole subject by a board of Army and Navy officers and civilians, the latter being in the minority, appointed by the President of the United States fifty years ago. It has been in successful operation for many years. It provides against a total suspension of the work in time of war and is advantageous to all parties concerned. It was imitated in many respects in the organization of the Light-House Establishment under the Treasury Department. There is not a single reason for the transfer of the work of the Coast Survey to the Navy which will not equally well apply to that of the Light-House Board. Both are in the interest of the vast commerce of the nation and not of the Navy. As such they flourish best under civilian administration, in a nation which is dis-

tinctly nonmilitary. The division proposed in the bill means the destruction of a Bureau which throughout its existence has had no superior in all the world. Its work has been such that it has everywhere been regarded as the most perfect illustration of the application of science to practical affairs. Intelligent Americans have felt a just pride in its reputation abroad, as well as its usefulness at home, and it is difficult to imagine that they will approve its destruction unless other reasons than any thus far presented shall be forthcoming.

Now, Mr. Chairman, I beg to thank the committee most heartily for the consideration which it has extended to me, and I wish to say, in conclusion, that I have strictly avoided any reference to personalities in the presentation of the claim of the Coast and Geodetic Survey in opposition to the passage of the bill. I have made no reference whatever to the origin of this movement or to any person connected with it. I have assumed the committee wished it argued upon its merits, and I have therefore attempted to present the question solely upon its merits and for no other reason. I would like to say I hope and believe personal considerations will not enter into the consideration of this question. Personal considerations should not enter into the action of any deliberative body upon a great question of this character, and I want to say whether the present administration of the Coast and Geodetic Survey is just what it should be or not is not a matter, in my judgment, which enters into this question at all. If the present Superintendent of the Coast and Geodetic Survey is not a proper man for the administration of the work of that Bureau, that is a disease which is very easily removed, and I hope the matter will have a consideration, as I have tried to present it, thoroughly free from personalities and simply and solely upon the merits of the question.

Gentlemen, I thank you very much.

The CHAIRMAN. We are very much indebted to you, professor.

Thereupon the committee adjourned to meet on Friday, June 8, 1894.

COMMITTEE ON NAVAL AFFAIRS,
Friday, June 8, 1894.

The Committee on Naval Affairs this day met, Hon. Amos J. Cummings in the chair.

STATEMENT OF HON. B. A. ENLOE, A REPRESENTATIVE FROM THE STATE OF TENNESSEE.

The CHAIRMAN. The committee will please come to order. The committee will hear Mr. Enloe on his bill proposing the transfer of the Coast and Geodetic Survey.

Hon. B. A. ENLOE then addressed the committee. He said:

Mr. Chairman and gentlemen of the committee, this is a discussion I did not expect when I introduced this bill. It has taken a very wide range and there might have been some doubt, it seems to me, in the minds of those who have listened to the discussion as to whether or not it is a discussion of the merits of this bill or a school in scientific instruction, somewhat primary in its character. Prof. Woodward, I think, was the first gentleman who appeared in opposition to the bill, voluntarily appeared, of course, to express his opinion to the committee. In making his remarks, aside from the general character of his argument, he took occasion to refer to me as the author of the bill, and to criticise or question my knowledge of matters that I had been discussing in the House. I find in his reported remarks—I was not present at the time he made them—he commented on this statement which I made in a former Congress in reference to the Coast and Geodetic Survey appropriation, which is as follows:

As it stands now it is expended under the direction of the Superintendent of the Coast Survey. He is in charge of the entire force and funds and directs where the work shall be done; but as the sum is appropriated in a lump and no particular direction given to it, he can take it and apply it anywhere in the country to any particular work he desires. He could spend every dollar of it in investigating the formation of ice bars.

Then this distinguished professor proceeds to explain to the committee that he at that time was engaged in the invention of an ice bar for the purpose of measurements, and that I had reference to that in making this statement on the floor of the House. I was not then aware of the fact that there was such a gentleman in the Coast and Geodetic Survey as Prof. Woodward and I did not know of the work in which he was engaged. I think as he has brought the matter up, however, it is well enough for me to state that I made his acquaintance about that time. He came here as a lobbyist and interceded with me to try to dissuade me from pressing certain amendments which I had offered to the annual appropriation bill in the House. He took me apart and interceded with me in regard to the amendments. That is the first knowledge I had of Prof. Woodward and his connection with the Coast Survey, and that is all the knowledge I had of him until he came before this committee. I, of course, declined to accede to his request and let up in my fight on the Coast and Geodetic Survey, and now he comes here and makes this imputation upon my knowledge of the subject I was talking about.

Here is a quotation from the annual report of the Coast and Geodetic Survey of 1887, showing that Assistant S. C. McCorkle was sent to the Delaware River and Bay for observing the formation and movement of ice. It is as follows:

Under instructions dated in October, 1888, Assistant S. C. McCorkle made the usual preparations for resuming observations of the formations, lodgment, and movement of ice in Delaware River and Bay, and also the temperature and density of the sea water at the Delaware breakwater. •

I found that was also referred to in the annual report of 1889. Well, I do not presume to question the value of this work; I do not know whether it was valuable or not to send a man down there to spend the entire winter to see exactly what time ice would begin to form, and what degree of thickness it attained, or what effect the tide had upon the formation, and all of those matters. I do not pretend to say that was a proper use of public money, or that it was of value to the Government to do this, but that was what I alluded to in stating the Superintendent might, if he saw proper, expend every dollar of the appropriation in stationing gentlemen over the country to investigate the formation of ice bars.

It is a sort of confession, it seems to me, of the weakness of a man's case when he comes before a committee like this and begins his argument by misrepresentations of the author of the bill in a foolish effort to make something out of nothing. He might have explained to the committee, if he wanted to deal in personalities, that my only knowledge of him was that of a lobbyist. He is not the only gentleman who did work of that kind since I began my effort to correct some of the abuses which I believe to exist in the Coast Survey. This same gentleman when he was before the committee made the statement that naval officers would not take off their coats and work. Prof. Mendenhall, the Superintendent of the Coast Survey, who has been before the committee, absolutely contradicts that statement. I have not brought anybody before this committee to testify as witnesses in this matter, and nobody has been here except voluntarily——

Mr. GEISSENHAINER. You will permit me to remark, Mr. Enloe, there have been no witnesses here.

Mr. ENLOE. Well, nobody has been here to make any statements. I expect it is well they were not under oath, because in that case some of the statements might not be so strong in some particulars and be a little less definite in others, but this gentleman voluntarily comes here and makes this statement in regard to naval officers, that they will not take off their coats and go to work. I met a naval officer at the door of this committee room one morning when you had a hearing here and asked the question whether that was true or not, he having been in the Coast Survey work. He said one of the things which made the Coast and Geodetic Survey unpopular in some sections of the country where it operated was that the officers sent out by the Coast Survey, the civilians who superintended this work, carried their tents, set up their household and lived in magnificent style on the shore, while the naval officers, the men in the Navy, took off their coats and went out and did the actual work while these other gentlemen managed their instruments and took observations, and he said that one he worked under had a magnificent umbrella about 6 or 8 feet in width and that he hoisted the umbrella and sat under it sheltered from the sun and made his observations, while he was sleeping in a tent or on a vessel and taking the common fare that the naval officers doing this work had to take, while this gentleman was living in luxury in a magnificent great big tent, where he had his family and furniture and everything fixed up in good style.

This same gentleman, Mr. Woodward, undertook to say to the committee very positively that if you undertook to transfer these men from the Coast and Geodetic Survey to the Navy Department they would resign their positions, and when he was pressed for the reason why this would be so he was greatly offended because some naval officer at sometime or other had referred to him as "a damn computer." Well, that was not a very elegant expression, perhaps, to apply to a gentleman who aspired to the title of a scientist, and I would rather be a damn computer than a damn lobbyist lobbying for my pay if I had to do one or the other. I reckon, Mr. Chairman, I had better leave that out as it is a little bit too personal.

Mr. MONEY. I would leave it out.

Mr. ENLOE. I would rather say that to him than the committee. Just instruct the reporter to leave that out.

Now, as to whether these men would be transferred, I do not think this gentleman is a competent witness or he is authorized to speak for anybody else but himself, and he certainly would not have stated that when he was in the Coast and Geodetic Survey.

The CHAIRMAN. I would state, Mr. Enloe, I understood Prof. Woodward came here on behalf of Columbia College.

Mr. GEISSENHAINER. I would like to say, Mr. Enloe, in speaking of witnesses, that no witnesses have been summoned, no side or action has been taken by this committee, or anything of that description. We have not summoned anybody, but they have all appeared voluntarily who have appeared, and we have heard them as they appeared.

Mr. ENLOE. I am not criticising the action of the committee in hearing those gentlemen. I have no objection to their having a hearing. I do not think there is anything in the argument which has been advanced against the transfer, and if there is no other reason assigned than has been assigned, it seems hardly worth while going on with the discussion. Now, they have assumed from the beginning and have attempted to inculcate the idea over the country—they know better themselves, the gentlemen in the Coast Survey, but they have attempted to inculcate the idea in the public mind that this is a movement to destroy the work of the Coast Survey—that it is a movement to destroy the Bureau of this character doing this work. Well, it is an effort to abolish the Bureau but not to destroy the work, and I insist if we pass this bill that the Navy Department will be better equipped to carry forward this work, all that ought to be carried forward, all that is essential, than under its present organization.

It is a very remarkable spectacle to me when a bill is introduced into Congress looking to the betterment of the public service, backed by the recommendation of the President of the United States, the head of the administration, backed by the Secretary of the Treasury, who has jurisdiction over the Coast Survey, backed by the Secretary of the Navy, a large part of whose force is employed in doing this work, and a man who has been chairman of the Committee on Naval Affairs, and who has thoroughly investigated this subject, I say it is a strange spectacle to see a subordinate under this administration coming before this committee and spending seven days in arguing against the policy of the administration under which he is serving. Sending out letters to the country, sending letters to the colleges of the country, and protesting against this measure. What do the college professors know about the purpose of this measure? They are not here on the ground. They are made to believe that we intend to destroy the scientific work of the Government and destroy the work of the Bureau now known as the Coast and Geodetic Survey, and under that impression, created by this Coast Survey, through its manipulation, they send letters here to be read to this committee to make an impression on the committee that a great wrong is about to be perpetrated against science and the scientific work of the Government.

Not only that, but the newspaper press of the country has been enlisted so as to flood this committee with clippings from newspapers, and a large part of the force employed in that Bureau, including its head, has been at work since the introduction of this bill, up to the conclusion of this hearing, in the preparation of matter and in the creation of matter to be brought before this committee to defeat the object of the administration under which that Superintendent holds his position. This is not the proper place to refer to that perhaps, but it seems to me to furnish a very strong argument in support of what I have always believed to be the correct position, that is, every man holding an important position under an administration ought to be in sympathy, politically and otherwise, with that administration.

We have had a discussion on this subject by the Superintendent of the Coast Survey covering seven days. The committee has heard it with a good deal of patience, and I have listened to it with patience and to portions of it with interest, because Prof. Mendenhall is a gentleman who comes nearer representing in words, if not in thought, the endless chain of perpetual motion, for it seemed to me there was never any conclusion to any part of his argument so long as you propounded a question to him, but a great deal of his information was very interesting to the committee and I was glad to have it; but I got so toward the last I had not the heart to ask him a question, because I was afraid it would continue the discussion until the end of this session of Congress, and I wanted a chance to have action on the bill, and therefore I avoided asking questions of which I had made notes during his discussion, with the intention of propounding the questions, as the gentleman stated he would answer them when he concluded his argument.

Now, we have heard some very interesting lectures before this committee on the subject of magnetics. We have heard a good deal about electricity and what the Coast and Geodetic Survey proposes to do if it is permitted to do it in the direction of producing 2,000 candle-power light, I think it was; but Mr. Woodward says they are not doing any electric work over there. I do not know who is right about it or in what time this remarkable achievement is to be accomplished if we do not interfere with the present organization. We have heard a good deal about triangulation in its various stages, which is all very interesting information. I have studied these charts of triangulation of the Coast Survey. I have marked with a good deal of interest what progress it is making in completing this transcontinental arc which they have started out to complete in the interest of science, and 1 have listened to the explanation of Prof. Mendenhall that the intention was to extend this along the line of States and the object was to furnish points for State surveys.

That was all very interesting to me because I had not been able to learn all of this until I heard him talking about it, but I have not been able yet and this committee does not now know what the cost of this' wonderful triangulation over the United States is going to be. I have tried in every way to find out something about it, what ultimately is to be the cost of furnishing points to State surveys, for that is all there is in this triangulation scheme that is of a practical character. I tried to find out how many of these States have asked in the last year, or even in the last two or three years, for points for State surveys. I got the general answer of probably ten or a dozen, but I understand if you bring it down to accuracy there are not that many, probably not more than two or three, that have asked for points for State surveys. Then I listened to the argument in regard to the variations of the magnetic needle and the work that was being done to show the variations of the needle at different points from time to time so as to regulate surveyor's instruments over the country, and I thought probably we had struck something there which could not be done anywhere else except in the Coast and Geodetic Survey, that we could not find anybody outside of the Coast Survey who could do it, and I followed the argument of the professor with a great deal of interest as long as he was on land, because it seemed to be pretty well backed up, but when he struck the edge of the water where he could not follow this line, that is, the land surveyors, the question arose then how could he tell anything about what this line was at any point on the water beyond sight or even beyond the shore?

Well, his argument was when they reached the shore the line would make a curve, and it was like coming to a curve of a railroad going around a mountain or some obstruction so you could not see where it ended, and the presumption would be that it continued to curve. Well, that seemed to me a very remarkable statement, that we had men smart enough in the Coast and Geodetic Survey to project a line, turning first to one point and then to another, as it did on shore, and when it struck the water it made a continuous curve, and I asked him if he could project a variable line in that way. Then it developed that it was necessary for somebody on the water to go and make observations beyond and establish points, and these observations were made and points were established, and all of this was done by the naval officers, and can be done by the naval officers just as well as it can be done by the men in the Coast and Geodetic Survey. So far as that is concerned, I will venture to say you can pick out surveyors in the Geological Survey who can go on the shore and follow every one of these magnetic lines and determine its variations just as well as any man in the Coast and Geodetic Survey can do it.

Next, I call attention to his argument on the subject of hydrography. He has asserted that on account of the peculiar organization of the Navy Department that hydrographic work could not be accurately done, that you must have a civilian organization, you must have long-continued service, you must have the continuous thought and attention of men to make correct hydrography. Well, as a matter of fact, when you come to ascertain who has been doing the hydrographic work ever since the foundation of the Coast and Geodetic Survey there has been a much larger percentage done by the Navy Department than by civilians in the Coast and Geodetic Survey proper. These naval officers are employed to make correct hydrographic observations everywhere else except when they approach our own shores. That is sacred territory that belongs to the Coast and Geodetic Survey, and I suppose their instruments become inaccurate, and useless, in fact, as soon as they invade this sacred territory of the Coast and Geodetic Survey. You will remember the professor in discussing that talked about these civilians who go on the land and made observations of points on the land, and they had signals by which at the proper moment the lead could be dropped and observations taken and the point established.

Now, he never did say to this committee why a naval officer who is competent to handle the instrument could not have taken the position on the shore and done that just as well as the Coast and Geodetic Survey officer did, and as a matter of fact, I presume there is not a member of this committee who for a moment will doubt the proposition that there are plenty of officers in the Navy who are capable of doing that work just as accurately as any in the Coast and 'Geodetic Survey, and wherever it has been necessary to demonstrate that fact they have demonstrated it.

We had a learned disquisition from the gentleman on the operation of the Coast and Geodetic Survey in connection with topography and the wonderful discoveries we are going to get soon from the topographical convention held here two years ago. We have heard of the wonderful work that has been done in geodesy. At some future time we will hear of the great geodetic convention which assembled here last winter. Then we had a learned disquisition in regard to the necessary knowledge of astronomy which is associated with this work, and how the telegraph has been brought into the operations of the Coast and Geodetic Survey. We have heard of the various wonderful achievements of these gentlemen. The point I want to make is that the argument is not sound that these gentlemen are alone able to put these agencies in operation, and that nobody outside of the Coast and Geodetic Survey would be able to do any such wonderful things.

As a lecturer on hydrography, physical hydrography, astronomy, magnetics, electricity, and everything pertaining to the applied sciences, I think Prof. Mendenhall is one of the most endless as well as interesting lecturers I have ever heard. There seems to be something of this kind going on. This Coast Survey organization has been in existence for many years, and I am under the impression that during all this discussion Prof. Mendenhall came here each day to the sessions of this committee just as an organ-grinder comes with his instrument set to new tunes. I think those officers of the Coast and Geodetic Survey who have been at work at it for years and have knowledge of every detail of its operations have been engaged ever since this hearing has been going on in getting up this information and cramming Prof. Mendenhall with it, and he comes in here and turns the crank and the committee gets the benefit of the prepared information. I am satisfied that if I had that scientific force at my command and I could have each one of them load me up each day for seven days, I could talk seven days about the operations of the Coast and Geodetic Survey just as intelligibly as Prof. Mendenhall talks about it, and any other man with a reasonably good memory and a fair knowledge of what the Coast Survey is and of the nature of its work could do the same thing.

I thought the point the committee wanted to hear discussed, and the point I think there is in this case, is, why should not the Coast Survey be transferred as proposed by this bill to the Navy Department and the Geological Survey? Prof. Mendenhall addressed himself very briefly to that part of it. He falsely assumed in the beginning that this work, if the transfer was made, would have to be done exclusively by the present force of naval officers or other naval officers. He ignored the fact that this bill proposes the transfer of the force now in the Coast Survey or such part as may be necessary, and under the provisions of this bill, if the transfer is made, the scientific force will be transferred. If the scientific force in the Coast Survey are not willing to serve under the Navy Department and prefer to resign, their places can be readily filled with others who are equally competent and would perform all of their duties equally well.

Mr. HULICK. Excuse me there, then you do not propose by your measure to confine it solely to the naval officers now in the service?

Mr. ENLOE. Not at all, sir; the bill does not propose anything of the kind, but that has been the lone argument, the false assumption upon which this committee has been addressed for seven days. The criticism has been pronounced upon the Geological Survey that it is not competent to do the geodetic work that is being done by the Coast Survey. Well, this bill proposes to transfer those gentlemen, as many as may be necessary, to continue all of this work that ought to be done, so that the Geological Survey will be equipped, if this provision is made, with exactly the same talent that the Coast Survey now employs. Then why should it remain as it is, under the Treasury Department, instead of under the Navy Department? What necessary connection is there between the Coast and Geodetic Survey and the Navy Department? There is no more connection between the Treasury Department and the Coast and Geodetic Survey than there is with the Interior Department or with the Agricultural Department, except the Bureau of Weights and Measures. If there is any other connection that is logical and convincing to the mind of any reasonable man, it must be a salary connection. That is the only part of it that is any more intimately connected with the Treasury Department than any other Department.

This bill does not propose to transfer the Bureau of Weights and Measures, about which we have heard so much. It is not really an important Bureau of the Coast Survey. That properly belongs to the Treasury Department, and this bill proposes to leave it there, and it can be as efficiently administered there as anywhere. In my opinion it would be better administered under the Treasury Department than under the Coast and Geodetic Survey as at present organized. Then we come down to the motive of this fight against the transfer. Why is it that Prof. Mendenhall and Prof. Woodward are making this fight against the transfer to the Navy Department and to the Geological Survey in the Interior Department? Why is it? When you come to narrow it all down, it turns on a matter of discipline. Prof. Mendenhall says the discipline of the Navy Department is too strict for scientific work like this. What is the meaning of that? The meaning of the discipline of the Navy Department is that men who are employed in the Navy Department are subject to rules, and required to account for their conduct, and for the expenditure of every dollar of money which passes through their hands in the very strictest manner.

Prof. Mendenhall held up before this committee the difficulty of buying a paper of tacks under the regulations governing the expenditure of money in the Navy Department. I am astonished that the gentleman should have entered upon that field, that he should have made that argument against it, for if there is any one argument stronger than another why this transfer should be made it is the fact that the Coast Survey, in its organization, has been loose, that its discipline has been bad, and the result has been scandals growing out of its management.

It has been investigated twice, once under the present administration. The Treasury officers have gone there and investigated the manner of disbursing the funds and found a defalcation.

Mr. MONEY. Was not that the Dockery Commission?

Mr. ENLOE. No, sir. The first instance in which anything wrong grew up in connection with the financial administration of the Coast and Geodetic Survey that we have any knowledge of was under Prof. Hillgard, whose administration was investigated in 1885. I have referred to that several times in the House, and most of the committee are somewhat familiar with that. A great scandal grew up in connection with it, from the fact that the men were not held accountable for their official conduct in the Coast and Geodetic Survey. There was a man appointed to the position, I believe, of observer of tides, at Mobile, from my State, under that administration, and he drew his salary and lived in the town where his home was, and he never once showed up at the station to which he had been assigned. This investigation developed that fact, and that gentleman went out of office.

Mr. WADSWORTH. Did he live in Tennessee?

Mr. ENLOE. Yes, sir. That not only occurred in one instance, but I do not know but what it occurred frequently about that time. Men were stationed here to observe tides or sent there to make surveys, or sent yonder on some particular work, but they paid no attention to the work, they did no work, they were accountable to nobody, and they simply drew their salaries and held sinecures.

Mr. MONEY. I can tell you another case which happened under the Navy rules. A man was appointed to go down to Florida and watch the Live Oak reservation, and he never left his home in Pennsylvania but drew his pay for four or five years.

Mr. ENLOE. That was possibly the fault of the Secretary of the Navy.

Mr. MONEY. Well, they had a pretty loose administration here then; that is what is the matter, I suppose.

Mr. ENLOE. To go on with this matter, Mr. Thorne investigated the management of the Coast Survey in 1885, or rather Mr. Chenoweth had it done, but Mr. Thorne was instrumental in having it done, and did more perhaps towards developing the inside of it than anybody else, and the result of it was Mr. Hillgard was removed and Mr. Thorne was appointed Superintendent of the Coast Survey. There were many things which occurred about that time which it is hardly necessary for me to mention in detail. I have heard much about how matters were managed after that occurred. I will not go further into that now, but will say that this Bureau, as at present organized, is not responsible, as it should be, for the use of the funds placed under its control. It does not have to render such an account to the Government for its expenditures as it ought to be required to render. I did find out something, but very little, from Prof. Mendenhall, while he was before this committee, in regard to that.

The Committee on Appropriations has long wanted to know something about it. The members of the Committee on Appropriations for the last two Congresses who have been talking to me wanted to know how the money was expended, to whom it was paid, and how much work is done in exchange for the payment. They give us a statement which shows so many men paid so much money, but where have these men been and what have they been doing? Nobody outside of the Bureau knows where they have been at work, or whether or not they have done any work which is a fair equivalent for the money, and it is very necessary, in my opinion, that this Bureau should be put under some administration where it will be held to a strict accountability for every dollar it expends. There was a gentleman in the Coast Survey, and he is there now, I referred to it in the House, who, though he may not have had any corrupt intentions, but indicating the loose system of doing business, who was found with a Government chronometer in his pocket. He was wearing a $300 watch belonging to the Government, and when he came before the Chenoweth investigating committee and they asked him about the chronometer he said he had it in his pocket. He pulled it out, and showed that he was using it as private property. The question arose whether he was charged with it. And he might have been. I do not know whether he was charged with it or not, but he had it. I understand they were in the habit of permitting men in that Bureau to dispose of property belonging to the Government without any sort of restriction which would protect the Government against loss in the disposition of the property. I heard of one instance where a horse costing over $100 was sold for $50. The officer had authority to sell the horse, and the Government, of course, had nobody to protect it except the officer, who had to account to nobody for the discretion he exercised. There was no check on him.

Mr. TALBOTT. How long had the horse been in use?

Mr. ENLOE. For a short time, I understand. I understand it was a very good horse.

Mr. TALBOTT. Maybe the Government got $50 out of him.

Mr. ENLOE. Here is a case in point outside of that. The Treasury officers under the former administration and under the present Superintendent investigated a young man in the disbursing office of the Coast Survey and they found he was a defaulter to the Government, and when that fact became known the Superintendent of the Coast and Geodetic Survay permitted him to go without any punishment whatever on his refunding the money. The matter was simply hushed up and that was the end of it. I went over there and asked him about that. When a man handles public funds and is a defaulter he is generally punished.

Why not punish this man? He told me that he was a young man and said he would not do it any more.

Mr. MONEY. When was that done?

Mr. ENLOE. Under the present superintendent. I have the statement here which I made in the House soon after I investigated the subject. Here is what I said about it on the floor of the House two years ago——

Mr. TALBOTT. Well, that would not have much weight with me, because the Government got the money, and I should rather the fellow should have a chance than go to the penitentiary.

Mr. MONEY. Mr. Spofford did the same thing.

Mr. TALBOTT. As attorney for my county I let a fellow out against whom there was a clear case because——

Mr. ENLOE. I do not know what your belief is in regard to public funds. That depends upon——

Mr. TALBOTT. But I say if the Government suffers no loss.

Mr. ENLOE. Where a man steals and returns the money it is a question whether it is a reason why he should not be put in the penitentiary. I know a man now who got $150,000 as a member of the whisky ring, and he was sentenced to five years in the penitentiary, and he thought he could make more money by keeping the money than by going free and giving up the money, so he went to the penitentiary and stayed there for three years and came out with his $150,000.

Mr. MONEY. He served at a high salary?

Mr. ENLOE. Yes, it paid him better to go to the penitentiary.

Mr. HULICK. Three years of that would be equivalent to the pay of the President of the United States.

Mr. TALBOTT. Without the wear and tear.

Mr. HULICK. Without the wear.

Mr. ENLOE. I think the proper rule is to punish defaulters. Prof. Mendenhall stated that if you attempted this division the records could not be divided. There is nothing in that suggestion, for there is no trouble in the world to separate the work. The work can be kept separate and distinct. You understand there is one branch of this work that has no relation whatever to the coast. The establishment of a transcontinental arc. That has no necessary connection with the Coast Survey.

The CHAIRMAN. That is geodetic?

Mr. ENLOE. Yes, sir; that could go to the Geological Survey, and whatever is necessary could be done just as well there as here. The Navy Department would receive the part of the records necessary to carry on the coast survey. The Interior Department would receive the records relating to the geodetic work. I understand, although I was not here at the time, that there was quite a considerable demonstration made in regard to the polariscope, as if that had something to do with it.

Mr. GEISSENHAINER. That has to do with weights and measures.

The CHAIRMAN. I want to suggest to my friend right here the propriety of ascertaining whether the Coast Survey had that rock down which the Columbia ran on in the Delaware River?

Mr. ENLOE. I was going to say in reference to the polariscope that it has more connection with the Internal-Revenue Bureau of the Treasury Department than it has with the Coast Survey, and I am not proposing to interfere with that at all, so it is not necessary to answer that argument. In regard to the charts, you will remember when Prof.

4561——12

Mendenhall was discussing the accuracy of the charts I asked him if the charts are accurate that are now used, and he said they were not absolutely accurate, and that was the object of extending the arc along the Atlantic coast so they might make them absolutely accurate. He went on to show what had been done in the matter of measurements of the base line. I showed in my argument before the House that we arr paying very extravagantly for every inch of accuracy we get in the measurement of the base line. That was shown, and the professoe stated here that they have devoted considerable time to correcting measurement of the base line, adding something to the accuracy. I have no doubt that is true. There has no doubt been some little addition to the accuracy, but for all practical purposes these charts which are now being used are as accurate as they will be when that are is completed. The whole purpose of the argument against this bill is to keep up the appropriations under present conditions, and to continue this expenditure of money to an indefinite period in the future.

I want to call the attention of the committee very briefly to some things which I said on the floor of the House. I will quote here from my speech delivered in the House of Representatives March 15 and 16, 1894:

This Bureau was organized in 1807, and the scope of its duties was clearly defined. The purpose of the organization of the Bureau was that it should make surveys of our coast line; that it should make charts or maps for the use of the Navy, and for the use of merchantmen engaged in commerce. From 1807 to 1871 this work went forward; and appropriations were regularly made by Congress for the purpose of carrying it on, and it seems to have been satisfactory in its character. But about 1871 it had nearly completed the survey of our coast, and it became necessary, in order to perpetuate this Bureau that it should connect something else with the Coast Survey. At that time an appropriation of $15,000 was asked for the purpose of forming a geodetic connection between the Atlantic and Pacific oceans. This was the nest egg for millions of dollars of appropriations to follow. This was an expansion of the work to an unlimited extent. If the geodetic work outlined at this time to be carried forward by the Coast and Geodetic Survey were completed, there is no means of arriving at an accurate estimate of what it would ultimately cost the country.

We have never been able to get the least ray of light on that subject, not an intimation even. Prof. Woodward announced to the committee that the work would never be completed, and that is exactly the point I make. Prof. Mendenhall is fighting, and Prof. Woodward is fighting for the extension of this work indefinitely in the future, regard less of its utility, in order that they may give employment to scientific men who are out of a job, and run it to suit themselves.

I have here a statement from the ex-Secretary of the Navy, Mr. Chandler, who is an earnest advocate of this measure. He said that this work then, in 1884, had been seven-eighths completed. I will quote his language before the joint commission reported in volume 4, Senate Miscellaneous Documents, first session Forty-ninth Congress, p. 63, to show that the Navy then, as now, did most of the Coast Survey work. He said:

The topographical survey of the coast proper having nearly arrived at completion there is very little left to be done except the continuation and revision of the hydrography. The latter has, for several years past, been intrusted exclusively to officers of the Navy, who also perform a considerable part of the topographic work on the coast. In these operations 57 officers and 275 seamen, drawing their pay from naval appropriations, are now employed under the Treasury Department.

I also call attention to the fact that Supt. Bache in 1857 said that the work would be finished in fifteen years from that date with the appropriations at the same rate. Congress has been going forward making appropriations from year to year at the annual rate of $463,000 up to 1885. From 1857 to 1886, a period of twenty-nine years, there was expended $549,190 per annum, an increase over the annual appropriation at the time Supt. Bache said this work would be completed in fifteen years at the same rate of appropriation. About $16,000,000 had been expended up to 1885–'86, and still the first survey of our coast line had not been completed. It seems to be no nearer completion to-day than it was at that time. If there has been any progress, it is so infinitesimal in its character that you can not discover it.

I find that Prof. Hilgard, in the investigation which was had in 1885 by the joint commission, testified that the survey of the Atlantic coast would be completed in five years, and the survey of the Pacific coast in nine years. We have advanced to the present time without showing any material progress toward the completion of this survey either on the Atlantic or on the Pacific coast. The appropriations since 1886, at the time this testimony was given, amount to $4,526,030.21. So that the Coast and Geodetic Survey has been engaged on this work for a period of eighty-seven years, and has spent nearly $30,000,000, yet nothing has been completed. It has not completed the survey of the coast, and it has not materially extended the line which it started in 1871, when it got that $15,000 to make the geodetic connection between the two oceans.

I cite here those authorities showing that there was from the foundation of this work a contemplation of its ultimate completion, except the mere revision of hydrography and the correction of maps. This whole argument on the other side contemplates no such thing as the completion of the work of the Coast Survey, but its indefinite extension.

Mr. TALBOTT. I would suggest we have some matters coming up in the House, and I think Mr. Enloe has also, and we had better adjourn at this point.

Mr. ENLOE. Very well, but I would like to be heard a little further at some future time, if the committee has no objection.

The CHAIRMAN. We will continue our hearing next Tuesday.

Thereupon the committee adjourned to meet on Tuesday, June 12, 1894.

COMMITTEE ON NAVAL AFFAIRS,
Friday, June 22, 1894.

The Committee on Naval Affairs this day met, Hon. Amos. J. Cummings in the chair.

The CHAIRMAN. The committee will come to order and we will go on with the hearing in regard to the Coast and Geodetic Survey. Mr. Enloe will please continue his remarks.

STATEMENT OF HON. B. A. ENLOE, A REPRESENTATIVE FROM THE STATE OF TENNESSEE.

Mr. ENLOE then addressed the committee. He said:

Mr. Chairman and gentlemen of the committee, at a former meeting of the committee I was proceeding to discuss the question as to the present condition of the work of surveying the coast, and the purpose of the Superintendent in his argument, and those who have aided him in that argument, to indefinitely continue the work of the Coast and Geodetic Survey. I had quoted some authorities showing

that originally the completion of the work at some time in the future
was contemplated. Various estimates have been made as to the time
within which the original survey would be completed, and that time
has been extended, and at every session of Congress the Coast and
Geodetic Survey comes up asking for its annual appropriation with
perfect regularity, and I have not been able to see that it shows any
material progress in the completion of the work which was originally
designed. I have here a map of the United States, a small printed
map, which comes from the Navy Department, showing the progress
which had been made in the work of surveying the coast. It will be
observed that the original survey of the entire coast on the Atlantic
and Gulf coast has been completed and that the survey of the Pacific
coast has been completed up to Cape Blanco, that is, the hydrography,
topography, and triangulation. Of course the committee understands,
and all who have investigated this subject——

The CHAIRMAN. Where is Cape Blanco? Hold the map up so we can
see.

Mr. ENLOE. Cape Blanco is on the map at this point here [illustrat-
ing] you see. The Pacific coast is surveyed from the southern boundary, beginning here near San Diego [illustrating] and running up here
to Cape Blanco. The blue lines show where the hydrography remains
to be completed, so you will see there is a very small section there which
is not completed.

The CHAIRMAN. On the California coast?

Mr. ENLOE. Oregon. And the red lines show where no triangulation
has been done nor topography begun. There has been a small section
of the coast which has never been completed and has been kept all the
time in an incomplete state, and the Coast and Geodetic Survey is not
willing, under its present management, that this original work shall be
completed, because that will leave nothing for the Coast and Geodetic
Survey—no coast survey work proper to be done whatever except the
revision of the hydrography. The changes that will occur on shore are
not of such a material character that there will be much necessity for
topography in the future where this survey has been made; but it will
always be necessary to revise the hydrography from time to time for the
purpose of making such corrections in it as may be rendered necessary
by the action of the tides or obstructions which arise to navigation
growing out of the action of the tides.

I want to call attention to that at this point, so that the committee
will see the force of the point I want to make against the whole argument on the other side, and that is, that the argument made here is for
the indefinite perpetuation of the Coast and Geodetic Survey in the
future. The intention is to perpetuate it as a scientific bureau. It is a
question for Congress to determine whether or not it is a proper use to
make of public money, to appropriate it strictly for the promotion of
scientific investigation that bears no relation whatever to the proper
operations of the Government, or at least only incidental relations.
The idea in establishing the Coast and Geodetic Survey in the beginning was that it was necessary to commerce and navigation. The geo-.
detic branch was afterwards added to it, but it had a very small
beginning. Now, it has very nearly absorbed the entire appropriation.

Mr. DOLLIVER. Does the pending bill provide for the abolition of the
Bureau?

Mr. ENLOE. For the abolition of this Bureau and the transfer of that
portion of work which is now practically done in the Navy Department
to the Navy Department, leaving the work in the Interior to be transferred to the Geological Survey.

I have talked with the present Director of the Geological Survey and I have talked with men who are employed in that work, and I am clearly satisfied, and I think this committee can satisfy itself, that there is no truth in the statement that the men employed in this work in the Geological Survey are not fully as competent to carry forward the work in the Interior as the officers who are employed in the Coast and Geodetic Survey; but, as I stated the other day, that question is obviated by the proposition in the bill to transfer this force, or so much of it as may be necessary, to the Geological Survey, so that the work would be practically in the hands of the very same men who are doing the work now. The Coast Survey work, now practically done by the naval officers, would be then done under the direction of the Navy Department, and it would be done with the assistance of the very same civilians who are doing the work under the present organization, so there is nothing in the argument against the abolition of the Bureau so far as it affects the character of the work. But there is this argument in favor of abolishing the Bureau at the present time, that it will enable Congress to intelligently appropriate money to continue the Survey. I have been trying for years to get some definite information as to whether the Government was receiving a fair equivalent in work for the money expended through that Bureau.

Mr. DOLLIVER. What amount is expended?

Mr. ENLOE. The amount that is appropriated—I have the appropriations here [examining papers].

Mr. GLASSCOCK. Half a million dollars.

Mr. ENLOE. The amount appropriated directly to it is not so much as half a million. The amount that was expended last year under the appropriation was $251,895; that was the amount of it. But then the Navy Department also expended a part of its appropriation in carrying on this work, and I have that statement here, and I think it is a very good place to refer to it showing what part is expended by the Navy and what part is expended under the Coast and Geodetic Survey appropriation proper. The total amount expended by the Navy Department during the last fiscal year for the Coast Survey was $209,048.63. The total amount expended by the Navy Department for the Coast Survey work during the fiscal year ending June 30, 1892, was $217,191.85. The total amount expended by the Navy Department during the fiscal year ending June 30, 1891, for the Coast Survey was $257,953.60. That was expended by the Navy Department in the actual surveys of the waters adjacent to the Coast of the United States. The amount expended by the coast and Geodetic Survey in an actual survey of the coast during the same fiscal year was $226,233.99.

Now you will see we make under the present system two definite appropriations, one for the Navy Department and the other for the Coast and Geodetic Survey, and a part of the naval appropriation is taken and expended on this work and it is done under the direction of the Coast Survey officers. The result is, when the Committee on Appropriations attempts to get any detailed information as to the use made of this money, as to the amount of work accomplished by the expenditure, it is not able to get anything which will enable the Committee on Appropriations to act intelligently. I went to Judge Holman when he was chairman of the Committee on Appropriations and asked him to call upon the Coast and Geodetic Survey for a specific and detailed statement of the expenditure of this money, showing where it was expended, so I could see what the practical results were from this appropriation, but Judge Holman did not get any such information about it, and when

I attempted to cut down the appropriation in the House, Judge Holman finally side tracked me with an amendment, general in its character, directing the Superintendent of the Coast Survey to make a recommendation to Congress for the reduction of this force. I asked him if he thought that would be done. I said, "If we appropriate this money, do you not think they will expend every dollar of it, and do you believe there will be any reduction in the amount of the appropriation or in the force employed." Well, he said, "If Prof. Mendenhall is the gentleman I take him to be and that he has been represented to me, he will make a considerable reduction."

I stated at the time that I had never known of an appropriation made to carry on public work yet placed in the hands of a public officer where any part of it was returned into the Treasury under any such general clause as that, and I was right about it because there was not a dollar of reduction in the expenditure, and there was not a reduction of a single man in the force as far as I have been able to learn. Mr. Sayers, chairman of the Committee on Appropriations at this session, attempted to get some detailed information about this matter and addressed a letter to the Superintendent looking to that, but when he received the reply it was so general and so vague and indefinite in its character that he did not know any more about the matter after he got the answers to the questions than he did before he asked them, and he and the committee determined to blindly cut down the appropriations, and proceeded to do it in the bill which passed the House.

In a speech which I delivered in the House the 15th or 16th day of March last, I referred to the use of this appropriation for the last year, and I said then:

Two hundred and fifty-one thousand eight hundred and ninety-five dollars was the amount of the appropriation actually used last year. Now, let us see what was done with it. I find, on examination of this communication of the Superintendent to the chairman of the Committee on Appropriations, that $139,075.40 was paid for the maintenance of the office force proper. I find that, in addition to that, the salaries of the assistants, belonging to the field force and carried in that part of the appropriation bill, but who are permanently employed in the office, amount to $19,400 a year. Then I find that the field force in the office during the three months, the 38 men specifically mentioned by the Superintendent in his communication sent to the chairman, received during that time $19,910.62 exclusive of the salaries of those permanently assigned to office work.

Now, this "period of comparative idleness" mentioned by Mr. Thorne extends from November until April, and in some portions of the country until as late as May. These men during that time are engaged, it is said, in working up their field notes; so they are paid for the six months of winter $39,821.24. By adding these sums together you get the amount expended in this office, across the street, for the maintenance of the office force, and for doing the work in the office $198,096.64, and you get for the work actually done in the field $53,598.36.

In other words, there is $4 in salaries paid in that office for every $1 of work that is done in the field.

Now, there was a question raised here as to what these men were doing the six months that they can not work in the field, and I raised that question in the House and the Superintendent of the Survey attempted to answer it here in his argument, and he explained that two years ago he held a topographical convention here, which had accomplished some results of great value, but we know nothing so far of what those results are, but we may sometime later learn. This winter it was claimed that these men were here in Washington, to all appearances doing nothing, and that was the general impression of those who observed that they apparently had nothing to do except to frequent the Capitol when it suited their convenience, or the hotels, and occupy themselves as gentlemen of elegant leisure. They were not about the office much, they were on the streets and other places more than the office according to the best information I have got, but we are told by the Superintendent they were constituted a geodetic convention, which was a convention not authorized by law, but authorized by the Superintendent of the Coast and Geodetic Survey. Those were of the force for whom we appropriate money to pay salaries to do a specific work, and here they were pursuing scientific investigations in a convention according to the statement of the Superintendent, and at some future time we are to be furnished with a report of the proceedings of that convention, and learn of the developments they have made in the interest of science during that six months.

There is another question to which I wish to call the attention of the committee, and that is the statement made by the Superintendent in reference to the revision of the salary list in the Fifty-first Congress. When the present Superintendent came into the office he stated to the committee that he was unfamiliar with the work there, and did not have time to prepare the estimates or did not prepare them, and they were prepared by his assistants in that office and sent to the Committee on Appropriations with his approval, and they asked for an increase in the appropriation. Mr. Cannon, of Illinois, chairman of the committee, informed the Superintendent that he must make a reduction in his estimates, and the Superintendent, when it was sent back to him for revision, revised his estimates for the appropriation, and he stated here to the committee the other day that he was assisted in that matter by the principal officers in the Coast and Geodetic Survey. He, however, said he assumed the entire responsibility for what was done. Nobody has ever doubted his willingness to assume it, because as the head of the Bureau he could not escape the responsibility if he wanted to do so.

I criticise that action, the action of the Superintendent and his assistants in revising the salary list in the Fifty-second Congress, and stated that it was a strange proceeding for an executive officer, called upon to revise his estimates, to intrust the revision to a set of gentlemen who were themselves interested in the results to be produced, and to follow their recommendation, when the revision itself showed that the men who were concerned in it increased their own pay, while they cut down the pay of the laboring men in the office. That was the way in which the revision was effected. They increased the pay of the men who were already receiving large salaries, and they decreased the pay of the laboring force in the office in order to come within the limitations placed upon them by the Committee on Appropriations.

Mr. DOLLIVER. Strictly in accordance with the Scriptures?

Mr. ENLOE. Gave it to those who had large salaries and took away from those who had small ones. Is that the portion of the Scriptures to which you refer?

Mr. DOLLIVER. Yes.

Mr. ENLOE. The effort to explain that transaction, which was heard by the committee, did not seem to me to be entirely satisfactory. One result which followed it was that the plate printers resigned their positions in the Coast and Geodetic Survey and went to the Bureau of Engraving and Printing, where they could get better compensation from the Government for their labor. The professor says that that was true, that they did resign, but that they attempted to return and get employment in the Coast and Geodetic Survey. Now, I am authorized by the Plate Printers' Union of this city to state that those gentlemen who resigned from that Bureau who belonged to the plate printers' organization never did attempt to go back to the Coast Survey; not one of them. There was one man employed as a plate printer there who did not belong to any organization. I do not know whether he was a very efficient man or not. Perhaps that might have something to do with his inability to make it more profitable to him to remain in the Bureau of Engraving and Printing, and therefore he would have been the one to make an effort to get back there, but competent men who left there, the men who were capable of doing this work in the highest style of the art, who went to the Bureau of Engraving and Printing and got employment, have not asked permission to return to the Coast Survey. There was only one man who left who tried to get back, and, as I stated before, he did not even belong to the plate printers' organization. I do not say whether he was an efficient or inefficient employé. That might have been his reason for wanting to return.

Now, the professor, in discussing this matter before the committee, called attention to another thing, and that was the rate of compensation. He submitted a statement here showing that these high-salaried men were not paid enough, and it was necessary to increase their salaries. That was his argument, that this increase was necessary in order to compensate them sufficiently for the work they were performing, and I have prepared here, on the same line his mind was running on, except I am on the other side of the question, a comparative statement showing the salaries those men received in 1887 and the salaries received in 1893, and I want to call the attention of the committee to the difference in salaries as shown on this comparative statement taken from the official record. Mr. Charles A. Schott, in 1887, received $3,200, and in 1893 he received $4,000. Mr. George Davidson——

Mr. DOLLIVER. What kind of work is he doing; do you know?

Mr. ENLOE. He is one of the assistants in the office. Mr. George Davidson received in 1887 $4,000, and was receiving the same in 1893; there is no change. Mr. B. A. Colonna, who was receiving $1,800 in 1887, is now receiving $3,600; Mr. Colonna is a pretty smart man.

Mr. McALEER. He must be a smart man to get that increase.

Mr. ENLOE. He is a very smart man, and I will tell you why he is smart. When they attempted to make the transfer in 1885, when it was investigated with the view of making a transfer, which was agitated about that time, Mr. Colonna was then a very efficient witness from the inside of the Coast Survey for those who wanted this transfer made, and wanted to change the Coast Survey methods, and his testimony, which is recorded in the investigation which took place at that time, is very valuable testimony now against present organization of the Coast and Geodetic Survey, but Mr. Colonna was too able a man and knew too much to be kept in any subordinate position in that office. He has been, not silenced exactly, but converted to the other side by a very simple process.

Mr. TYLER. Is not he a very efficient officer?

Mr. ENLOE. There is no doubt about the fact he is a smart man, and I have no doubt he is an efficient officer, but Mr. Colonna was then receiving $1,800 and he is now receiving $3,600, and now he is a very strenuous advocate of the present management of the Coast and Geodetic Survey, and naturally he would be. I have not seen many men who would throw away bread which is already buttered in order to take the chances of picking up crumbs elsewhere. Augustus F. Rogers in 1887 was getting $2,800 and he is now receiving $3,200. George A.

Fairfield was in 1887 receiving $2,400 and he is now receiving $3,000 and so on through the list it is the same. I will not take up the time of the committee to go through the entire list as it is of considerable length, and I will put it in the record.

	1887.	1893.		1887.	1893.
Chas. A. Schott	$3,200	$4,000	Ed. Smith	$1,800	$2,000
Geo. Davidson	4,000	4,000	J. F. Pratt	1,500	2,000
B. A. Colonna	1,800	3,600	C. H. Sinclair	1,500	2,000
Aug. F. Rodgers	2,800	3,200	E. F. Dicklus	1,500	1,800
Geo. A. Fairfield	2,400	3,000	D. B. Wainwright	1,500	1,800
A. T. Mosman	2,400	3,000	W. C. Hodgkins	1,400	1,800
Wm. H. Dennis	2,300	3,000	E. D. Preston	1,100	1,800
Jno. W. Donn	2,200	2,800	J. D. Bailer	1,400	1,600
Wm. Eimbeck	2,200	2,600	J. E. McGrath	900	1,800
Ed. Goodfellow	2,200	2,400	C. T. Iardella	1,400	1,600
Cleveland Rockwell	2,300	2,600	W. I. Vinal	1,400	1,600
Henry S. Whiting	2,100	2,400	C. H. Van Orden	1,400	1,600
Herbert G. Ogden	2,000	2,400	Isaac Winston	1,100	1,600
Otto H. Tipman	2,000	2,400	P. A. Welker	900	1,400
J. J. Gilbert	1,800	2,400	Fremont Moss	900	1,400
H. L. Marindin	1,800	2,200	J. A. Flemer	825	1,400
Andrew Braid	1,800	2,200	Jno. Nelon	825	1,200
F. W. Perkins	1,800	2,000	R. M. Bache	2,153	2,200
F. D. Granger	1,800	2,000			
				68,103	82,800

Before I get away from this subject, which is all incidental to the revision of salaries and resignation of these plate printers, I do not want to fail to call attention again to the plate printers of this city in their organized capacity. Without having any idea in my mind at the time that it would attract the attention of that body, I took up this matter as one of simple justice, and I espoused the cause of those men in the Geodetic Survey who had been treated, as I thought, in a shameful manner, and I tried to have it corrected in the House when the appropriation came up. I proposed to cut down the salaries of those gentlemen who had received the increase and put them back where they were, and to put up the salaries of the laboring men to the point from which they were reduced. In making that fight, I did not know that the plate-printers would take any interest in it, but they did, and at a meeting here in this city they adopted resolutions which I do not introduce here for any other purpose than to contradict the statement of Prof. Mendenhall here that he had never met with any protest from the laboring men on account of the manner in which the laboring force was treated in that office. I understood him to make that sort of a statement here. Here is a communication from the Plate Printers' Union, which was handed me some time ago.

WASHINGTON, D. C., *April 28, 1894.*

Hon. B. A. ENLOE:

DEAR SIR: At a regular stated meeting of the Plate Printers' Protective Union, 5041, American Federation of Labor, working under the auspices of the National Printers' Union of America, held on the above date, the following resolutions were unanimously adopted:

Resolved, That the thanks of this union are hereby extended to the Hon. B. A. Enloe, of Tennessee, for the able manner in which he defended the workingman's cause in a speech delivered in the House of Representatives in May, 1892, and again on the 16th day of March, 1894, when he exposed the outrages perpetrated by the Coast Survey officials on the workingmen employed in that Bureau by having their salaries reduced in 1890 so that the officials might have theirs increased: Therefore,

Be it further resolved, That we, the Plate Printers' Protective Union recommend the Hon. B. A. Enloe, of Tennessee, to the workingmen of the country and the State of Tennessee for their kind consideration and support.

Given under our hand and seal of this union this 28th day of April, 1894.

[L. s.]
EUGENE BETTES, *President.*
JOHN WOOD, *Secretary.*
ISAAC GIRRODETTE,
WM. JOHNSON,
JOHN T. CONNORS,
ARTHUR SMALL,
E. W. McRAE,
Committee.

Mr. DOLLIVER. That is a very persuasive document.

Mr. ENLOE. I should think so, but I read that not for campaign purposes, but simply for the purpose of showing to this committee how the laboring men feel in regard to this matter and how these men on the working force in the office felt about the reduction which was made in their pay in order that the salaries of the high officials, the better-paid officials, might be increased.

Now, I do not care to continue this argument at great length here, because I deem it entirely useless. The committee has had a very elaborate hearing on the other side of the question, and has heard Mr. Glasscock, who made a very strong presentation of the side of the question which I represent, and I do not think it is necessary to continue this at great length.

Mr. DOLLIVER. Before you leave the question of expenses, have you made an estimate of the actual saving which will be effected by the transfer of the Coast Survey to the Navy Department and by the transfer of the geodetic features of this enterprise to the Interior Department?

Mr. ENLOE. I have not been able to get any data which would enable me to get anything like an accurate estimate. The abolition of this Bureau here as a separate and distinct bureau in the Treasury Department would result in a considerable saving of expenses, because it would be merged into bureaus already organized. In the Navy Department it would go to the Hydrographic Office. In the Geological Survey it would go under the Director of the Geological Survey.

Mr. DOLLIVER. The executive expenses would be decreased?

Mr. ENLOE. The expense of administration would be decreased to that extent, which is one saving which is perfectly manifest on the face of it. Then, I take it, there would be less circumlocution and more direct methods, which would result in a saving. I think, too, there would be a saving in this respect, that the regulations of the Navy Department in regard to the use of money, its expenditure, use, and methods of keeping account, and the strictness with which it is done would result in a considerable saving also, and if it should not save in the appropriation I think it would result in an increase of the work done for the money.

Mr. DOLLIVER. You do not dispute the value of the work in surveying the coast or adjacent land?

Mr. ENLOE. No, but I do dispute the value of a portion of the work. I think that the present organization is doing work that ought not to be done by the Government.

Mr. DOLLIVER. For instance?

Mr. ENLOE. I have got a lot of maps which were furnished me by the Secretary of the Treasury in my committee room, the Committee on Education, which I had before the House at the time I addressed the House when the sundry civil bill was under consideration, and from an examination of those maps it is perfectly evident, and it must be to any unprejudiced mind, that there is a great deal of work done that is not of any practical value to the Government for commercial purposes and never could be of any value except in case of a war. If we became involved in a war and it became necessary to know everything of detail about the section of the country along the Atlantic coast where the principal part of this work has been done, then these maps would become valuable for military maps.

Mr. DOLLIVER. Which is quite an important matter?

Mr. ENLOE. That is quite an important matter, if we expect to become involved in a war and furnish definite and detailed information to any enemy which might invade the country. In other words, to lay the whole face of the country before them. Now, in making the cadastral maps, the work they are doing, it is done with such nicety of detail that it furnishes a complete view of the country covered. It is termed a cadastral map or detailed map, and it is used for military purposes in Europe. Now, these people in Europe are frequently engaged in wars with each other, and I suppose that they find it valuable for military purposes to have those accurate maps.

Mr. DOLLIVER. Are their maps published?

Mr. ENLOE. Well, I should hardly think it would be wise for France to have a cadastral map of Germany or Germany to have a cadastral map of France, and I believe they could not get such a map unless they got it surreptitiously.

Mr. MONEY. Every German soldier who was killed in France had a complete map of the country in his possession, that was one of the instances of the Franco-Prussian war.

Mr. ENLOE. I have no doubt that that is one of the results of making ● these military maps for any government.

Mr. DOLLIVER. Of course it is disastrous for us to have the enemy know in regard to the coast, but it is still more disastrous for us not to know it ourselves.

Mr. ENLOE. Yes, but I should think we would be likely to know more than the enemy about our own country.

Mr. DOLLIVER. Now, do we understand you to dispute the ability and general scientific efficiency of these people who are in charge of this business now?

Mr. ENLOE. No, sir; I am not disputing that, but they do not do all the coast work. Now, I was going on to say in reference to the other branch of the work, the geodetic work, as far as this transcontinental arc is concerned, which is a basis for surveys in the interior, that work can be completed by the Geological Survey just as well as under the present organization, but I do not believe that it ought to extended, as projected, to cover the entire United States. I think if that was done it would involve an expenditure of hundreds of millions of dollars without any corresponding benefit. The only argument that is made, and the only one made by Supt. Mendenhall in favor of it, was that it would furnish points for State surveys, and when I asked him how many States had applied for these .points he gave a very indefinite statement, and I have not yet been able to learn how many States have actually applied for these points for State surveys.

I have here letters from the Secretary of the Navy and the Secretary of the Treasury, bearing upon this subject, showing what their views are as to the desirability of this transfer.

Mr. DOLLIVER. Do they both concur with you?

Mr. ENLOE. They both concur with me, and as I understand from the expressions of the President in his letter to Congress in 1885, in discussing this question, he also believes in the wisdom of this transfer. Unquestionably these two secretaries do. I have letters here which I used in my speech in the House, but there is a still more elaborate letter here from Assistant Secretary McAdoo, of the Navy Department, which I will also insert.

NAVY DEPARTMENT, *Washington, March 14, 1894.*

SIR: In reply to your letter of the 12th, inclosing an amendment which you propose to offer to abolish the Coast and Geodetic Survey and to provide for the transfer of the Coast Survey to the Navy Department, I have had a conference with the honorable the Secretary of the Treasury, and the amendment as he will send it to you, which is substantially that proposed, is approved by Secretary Carlisle and myself.

In my opinion the work of the Coast Survey now remaining to be done, so far as it appertains to the Coast Survey proper, can be accomplished by the Navy Department quite as thoroughly and very much more economically than it is now being done by the Coast and Geodetic Survey.

The Hydrographic Office of the Navy Department is now making and engraving maps similar to those being made by the Coast and Geodetic Survey, the difference being that the Hydrographic Office is not permitted by law to make maps of the coast of the United States; its charts are of other portions of the seas, of which it publishes about 900, while the Coast Survey publishes only about 300 charts of the coasts of the United States.

This Hydrographic Office is well organized and does the work thoroughly and efficiently. About ten years since a joint commission, composed of three members of the House of Representatives and three Senators, made a very thorough investigation of the Coast and Geodetic Survey, the Hydrographic Office, the Geological Survey, and the Signal Service, and while there was a difference of opinion as to the manner in which each of these bureaus was performing the work allotted to it, the commission unanimously commended the method of the Hydrographic Office of the Navy Department.

An addition of one or more naval officers, already in the pay of the Government, by detail to the Hydrographic Office, would enable it to effectively supervise all the Coast Survey work now being done by the Coast and Geodetic Survey. Naval officers have heretofore done practically all the hydrographic work, the soundings, etc., for the Coast and Geodetic Survey. The topography and triangulation of the shore, so far as it is necessary for the charts made by the Coast and Geodetic Survey, have most of it been completed.

This organization has been in existence for more than seventy years past, and it has triangulated and mapped all the coasts of the United States except small portions of Florida, on the Gulf, and in Lower California. Naval officers are fully competent to do such triangulation as is needed to complete this work, just as the Army officers have done the triangulation along the shores of our lakes. The charts made by the Coast and Geodetic Survey are primarily for the benefit of the mariner, and it would seem that naval officers ought to know quite as well as civilians the requisites of a good chart for the guidance of mariners. The work to be done in the future is, therefore, to be largely hydrographic, and this must be done by the Navy Department.

If this work were all intrusted to the Navy Department, which is now forbidden by law to do hydrographic work along our own shores, men-of-war, when not needed elsewhere, could make the needed soundings, and thus our sailing charts could be rapidly improved. This would greatly benefit our commerce. Naval officers now make sailing directions not only of foreign waters, but they make all the sailing directions on charts published by the Coast and Geodetic Survey.

But few changes take place in the contour of the shores. Such changes there as time effects can be noted readily and at little expense. If the small amount of triangulation necessary to complete the mapping of the shores of the United States, heretofore alluded to, were completed, there would be, excluding from consideration Alaska and its coast, practically no field work along our coasts remaining to be done.

It will always be necessary to take soundings over and over again by reason of the changes in the bottoms of the ocean and of the streams caused by tides and currents. As this work is now being done by the Navy, though often credited to the Coast and Geodetic Survey, it would seem that the mapping and the charting our own coasts might very well be left to the Hydrographic Office.

The passage of your amendment, and the transfer you propose would, in my opinion, result in a large saving of money to the Government.

I also suggest that, as the work and responsibility of the Hydrographic Office will be largely increased if the transfer be made, the amendment to be forwarded by the honorable Secretary of the Treasury have added to it the following: "The Chief of the Hydrographic Office shall be an officer not below the grade of commander, and he shall be entitled to the highest pay of his grade."

Very respectfully,

H. A. HERBERT,
Secretary of the Navy.

Hon. B. A. ENLOE,
House of Representatives, City.

<hr>

TREASURY DEPARTMENT,
OFFICE OF THE SECRETARY,
Washington, D. C., March 13, 1894.

SIR: I have examined, as carefully as the limited time would permit, the amendment transmitted by you abolishing the Bureau of the Coast and Geodetic Survey, and transferring its work to the Department of the Navy and the Department of the Interior, and herewith inclose you a revised form of amendment, which I think will accomplish the purpose you have in view and obviate certain objections which might properly be made to some of the provisions contained in the original.

In my opinion, the measure proposed will result in a very considerable reduction in the expenditures, prevent duplications of work, and secure a service fully as efficient in all respects as that now existing.

Very respectfully,

J. G. CARLISLE,
Secretary.

Hon. B. A. ENLOE,
House of Representatives.

I wish now to read the views of the President of the United States on this subject:

The work of the Coast and Geodetic Survey was, during the last fiscal year, carried on within the boundaries and off the coasts of thirty-two States, two Territories, and the District of Columbia. In July last certain irregularities were found to exist in the management of this Bureau, which led to a prompt investigation of its methods. The abuses which were brought to light by this examination and the reckless disregard of duty and the interests of the Government, developed on the part of some of those connected with the service, made a change of superintendency and a few of its other officers necessary. Since the Bureau has been in new hands an introduction of economies and the application of business methods have produced an important saving to the Government and a promise of more useful results.

This service has never been regulated by anything but the most indefinite legal enactments and the most unsatisfactory rules. It was many years ago sanctioned apparently for a purpose regarded as temporary and related to a survey of our coast. Having gained a place in the appropriations made by Congress, it has gradually taken to itself powers and objects not contemplated in its creation, and extended its operations until it sadly needs legislative attention.

So far as a further survey of our coast is concerned, there seems to be a propriety in transferring that work to the Navy Department. The other duties now in charge of this establishment, if they can not be profitably attached to some existing department or other bureau, should be prosecuted under a law exactly defining their scope and purpose, and with a careful discrimination between the scientific inquiries which may properly be assumed by the Government and those which should be undertaken by State authority or by individual enterprise.—President's message, first session Forty-ninth Congress.

TREASURY DEPARTMENT,
OFFICE OF THE SECRETARY,
Washington, D. C., May 8, 1894.

SIR: In response to a communication received from the clerk of your committee, transmitting a copy of a bill "To abolish the Bureau in the Treasury Department known as the Coast and Geodetic Survey, and transfer the work of said Bureau to the Hydrographic Office in the Navy Department and the Geological Survey in the Department of the Interior," I have the honor to say that in a communication addressed by me to the Hon. B. A. Enloe on March 13, 1894, a copy of which is herewith transmitted, the opinion was expressed that the Bureau referred to could be advantageously abolished and the services now performed by it could be as well done in the Department of the Navy and the Department of the Interior, and I adhere to that opinion.

That the work performed by the Survey, or at least the greater part of it, is of great value to the Government, is not questioned, but I am unable to see the necessity for the maintenance of a separate and distinct bureau to carry it on, when it can be done as efficiently and more economically by the Hydrographic Office in the Department of the Navy, and the Geological Survey in the Department of the Interior.

Very respectfully,

J. G. CARLISLE,
Secretary.

Hon. AMOS J. CUMMINGS,
House of Representatives.

———

TREASURY DEPARTMENT,
OFFICE OF THE SECRETARY,
Washington, D. C., March 13, 1894.

SIR: I have examined, as carefully as the limited time would permit, the amendment transmitted by you abolishing the Bureau of the Coast and Geodetic Survey, and transferring its work to the Department of the Navy and the Department of the Interior, and herewith inclose you a revised form of amendment which, I think, will accomplish the purpose you have in view, and obviate certain objections which might properly be made to some of the provisions contained in the original.

In my opinion the measure proposed will result in a very considerable reduction in the expenditure, prevent duplications of work, and secure a service fully as efficient in all respects as that now existing.

Very respectfully,

J. G. CARLISLE,
Secretary.

Hon. B. A. ENLOE.
House of Representatives.

———

NAVY DEPARTMENT,
Washington, May 14, 1894.

SIR: In reply to the communication from your committee, dated April 25, requesting an opinion from this Department as to the merits of H. R. bill No. 6338, "To abolish the Bureau in the Treasury Department known as the Coast and Geodetic Survey, and to transfer the work of said Bureau to the Hydrographic Office, Bureau of Navigation, in the Navy Department, and to the Geological Survey, in the Department of the Interior," I have the honor to make the following statement as to such of the proposed changes as relate to this Department:

Prior to the request of your committee this Department had carried on some correspondence in regard to this subject with the Secretary of the Treasury and the chairman of the Committee on Appropriations of the House of Representatives, copies of such communications from this Department being annexed hereto and made a part of this reply. The Department believes now, as it did then, that the work of the Coast Survey Office, the larger portion of which is now done by naval officers and at the expense of the naval establishment, would be much better and more economically carried out did the Department have administrative control over it, and respectfully submits that it is most illogical to have this work continued under the present auspices, an opinion which is concurred in by the present Secretary of the Treasury, under whom the Coast Survey Bureau is placed.

The first positive advantage which would be gained by a transfer of this office to the Navy Department would be that Congress and the people would then know exactly the amount of money annually expended for Coast Survey work. As it is now the Coast Survey work is paid for out of two appropriations, made for two entirely distinct Departments of the Government. As will be seen by the annexed letters, a very large sum of money is annually taken from the amount appropriated by Congress for carrying on the naval establishment and expended upon this work; while, in addition, another sum is taken from the appropriation for the Coast Survey Office as a branch of the Treasury Department and charged to this work. There can be, therefore, no unity in the keeping of accounts, in the rendering of estimates, or in preparing statements of expenditures, in consequence of which nothing short of a painstaking and elaborate investigation will, at any time, show the actual cost of Coast Survey work to the Government. As will be seen, although the amount expended from naval appropriations for this work is larger than that expended by the Coast Survey Bureau itself, the impression might readily be produced that the entire expenditure was charged to the Coast Survey establishment. Were the whole work to be done by this Department, Congress would have an itemized estimate for the entire work before it each year, and a complete and accurate statement of expenditures could be easily prepared at any time, so that Congress and the people could always know just what the work of the Coast Survey was costing.

The Department can quite readily understand the difficulties in the way of a correct knowledge of this subject on the part of Congress and the public. By carefully concealing or entirely ignoring the work of naval officers on the Coast Survey, and with no published records to show the fact that over $250,000 of the money appropriated for the naval establishment is expended in this very work, it is not to be wondered at that the relations of the Navy Department to the work in question are very little understood. Many scientific gentlemen throughout the country, who are deeply interested in the investigations of the Coast and Geodetic Survey, have come forward in opposition to this transfer without apparently having any real knowledge of the facts in the case. Right here it is well to state that the Navy Department has no desire whatever to interfere with the pursuits, investigations, and speculations of the Coast and Geodetic Survey in any works pursued by it, other than the Coast Survey proper.

As a demonstration of the complete ignorance of many of those who have come forward to give their views of this question, I deem it but right that I should call attention to the fact that several of them have absolutely denied or ignored the services rendered by the Navy Department in Coast Survey work. It is unnecessary to do more than call the attention of the committee to the ignorance of the subject thus evinced. The expenditure of a quarter of a million of dollars by this Department every year, the detailing of a large number of its officers and men to Coast Survey vessels, and the hydrographic and scientific work done by these representatives of the Navy are completely ignored. The Department, seeking no controversy whatever on this subject, and having no desire to exploit itself, has made, and will make, no preconcerted movement for the control of this work, and will only make statements regarding the same when officially called upon by the Congress or by its committees.

As an evidence of the deliberate attempt to cover up the connection of the naval establishment with the present work, your attention is called to the statements in the annexed letters, wherein it is shown that the names of naval officers participating in the work of the Survey, and which, by long custom, were usually affixed to the charts, have been recently taken therefrom. On the other hand, the Coast Survey Office has constantly on dress parade long lists of its employés, in the full dress of all their official distinctions and learned titles.

The main object for which the Coast Survey was originally established has been greatly confused with the functions adroitly acquired by the present establishment. Gentlemen interested in various scientific pursuits, and wishing to advance their own interests, have found it convenient, from time to time, to add to the powers of the establishment through legislation.

The primary object of the Coast Survey was to survey and chart the coasts of the United States. This work should have been finished years ago, but as it approached its completion the Coast Survey began to extend in other directions, chiefly geodetic. The organization was finishing the task for which it was created by Congress, but the natural desire to perpetuate its existence was too great, and hence the consequent addition to the scope of its work and to the enlargement of its powers.

The statement made by certain of its friends as to the lack of qualifications of · naval officers for the work of the Coast Survey needs no other answer than to point to what they have already done in that direction. Indeed, to any one having a knowledge of the education and training of the officers of the Navy, it would not only be a waste of time but an absurdity to go into an argument on this subject.

The Navy Department has no desire to acquire work belonging to other departments of the Government, but it seems only just that it should control the work which is not only performed by its own officers but principally paid for from its own appropriations; a work which deals with navigation, a matter which naturally comes under the cognizance of the naval establishment. As to the geodetic work, that is a matter with which this Department has no concern. The only question before you, so far as the naval establishment is concerned, is as to the hydrographic work of the Coast Survey, a work which is intended to be primarily for the benefit of navigation and commerce.

The chart hereto annexed, and which was prepared by the Hydrographic Office of the Bureau of Navigation, will show that the unfinished work of the Coast Survey is exceedingly small. The chart in question rather over than under estimates the amount of work yet to be done. The work indicated in red would naturally be done by those not connected with this establishment; that in blue is Coast Survey work

pure and simple, and has been, is now, and will in the future be done by naval officers. The future work of the Coast Survey, which primarily relates to the safe-
guards of navigation, will largely consist in resurveys of the waters of the coast, in
order to determine and chart the natural changes which take place from time to
time. This work will, on account of the action of physical laws, always be necessary, and is one which can only be successfully performed by men who combine
scientific training with an actual and theoretical knowledge of navigation and
nautical surveying. The chief object of this work is to produce good navigating
charts for the use of mariners. It is a work only successfully done by sailors for
sailors. Changes of the land features near the coast will be of a very minor character, as may be readily perceived by the committee, unless we include cadastral
operations; that is to say, the mapping of farms and of the estates which suffer sub-
division and rearrangement, a work, the wisdom of which, as being done at Government cost, is a question for the Congress alone.

This Department has no opinion whatever to express as to the wisdom of Congressional action in advancing scientific investigation and speculative science
through the means of any Bureau or Department. It only recommends, as a matter of
wise administration and in the interest of economy, that it be given control of the
work now performed by those who are paid for the same out of the funds appropriated for the Navy.

When it is stated here that the naval officers and men do the hydrographic work
of the Coast Survey, it is meant to emphasize that they do the actual work, and all
statements to the contrary arise either from ignorance or from a deliberate attempt
to mislead Congress and the people. The services of a large number of officers, not
to mention the crews of the vessels of the Coast Survey, are every year provided
from the Navy. An inspection of the files of the Naval Register discloses the fact
that a great number of officers have served in the Coast Survey since 1832. Indeed,
so thoroughly dependent is the present Coast Survey upon the work of the naval
officers attached to it for its hydrography, that when this Department finds
itself unable, by reason of the exigencies of the service proper, to detail officers and
men to the Coast Survey vessels, the work has to stop. An examination of the notes
on the charts issued by the Coast and Geodetic Survey, and which, of course, is
evidence from that office, will attest the work done by naval officers and men. And,
in addition to the hydrographic work in the survey of our coast, all the great work
of deep-sea exploration is not only done by naval officers, but has been made successful through their inventions. At the present time, and for several years past, all
the work in connection with the survey of the Mexican coast has been done by naval
vessels, officered and maned, and supported by this Department.

The Hydrographic Office, attached to the Bureau of Navigation of this Department,
is well equipped to take entire charge of the Coast Survey work. This office has
made a reputation for itself throughout the world, and its charts and publications
receive the sanction of standard authority everywhere. The demands upon the
Department for hydrographic and other nautical information were so imperative
that it became necessary to equip and establish the Hydrographic Office in such a
manner that it now disseminates a great amount of invaluable information as safe-
guards for commerce on the waters, both at home and abroad. Yet, strange to say,
notwithstanding the reputation of our naval Hydrographic Office throughout the
world, and the fact that the actual work of the Coast Survey is performed by those
under the Navy Department, the office in question has no authority under existing
law to issue a chart of our own coast.

I therefore respectfully submit that the proposed transfer is in the interest of
economy and good administrative methods.

Very respectfully,

W. McADOO,
Acting Secretary.

Hon. AMOS J. CUMMINGS,
    Chairman Committee on Naval Affairs,
        House of Representatives.

NAVY DEPARTMENT,
Washington, February 7, 1894.

SIR: The total amount expended by the Navy Department during the last fiscal
year for the Coast and Geodetic Survey was $209,048.63.

The total amount expended during the fiscal year ending June 30, 1892, was
$217,191.85.

The total amount expended by the Navy Department during the fiscal year ending
June 30, 1891, for the Coast and Geodetic Survey was $257,953.60. This was expended

by the Navy Department in the actual surveys of the waters adjacent to the coast. of the United States. The amount expended by the Coast and Geodetic Survey in the actual survey of the coast during the same fiscal year was $226,233.99.

The work done by the Navy for which compensation was made by the Navy for the benefit of the Coast and Geodetic Survey during the last fiscal year and prior years, has been mainly hydrographic work, taking, locating, and plotting soundings; with incidentally some physical hydrography, current work, a small amount of topography, and minor triangulation. In other words, for a number of years naval officers have secured nearly all the data used by the Coast Survey in making the water portion of their charts, the officers of the Coast Survey furnishing the data used in making the land portion.

Except in unusual circumstances no officials or other employés of the Coast and Geodetic Survey act in conjunction with the naval officer in taking soundings, etc. But the Coast Survey officials furnish to the naval parties the data necessary for locating and plotting the soundings taken, except such soundings as are so far from the coast as to require astronomical observations before locating and plotting.

During the fiscal year ending June 30, 1891, 2,496 square miles of hydrography were executed by naval officers, and 190 square miles by Coast Survey assistants.

I am unable to make comparisons for the years 1892 and 1893, as the Coast Survey reports for those years have not been published.

Very respectfully,

H. A. HERBERT,
Secretary of the Navy.

Hon. JOSEPH D. SAYERS,
Chairman Committee on Appropriations,
House of Representatives, Washington, D. C.

NAVY DEPARTMENT,
Washington, February 2, 1894.

SIR: I have the honor to acknowledge the receipt of the letter of the Superintendent of the Coast Survey to the Secretary of the Treasury, dated December 28, 1893, which was referred to this Department. This letter of the Superintendent of the Coast Survey is a reply to a letter written by the Secretary of the Navy to the Secretary of the Treasury, dated December 19, 1893, relative to the omission from a recent Coast Survey chart of the names of naval officers who had made the survey from which the chart was constructed.

The Superintendent of the Coast Survey says in his reply:

"The omission of what has generally been called the 'authority note' from this chart was not an oversight, but was in accord with the policy adopted by this office more than a year ago after a careful and lengthy examination of all questions involved."

From this statement it appears that the omission is due to a recently adopted policy of the Coast Survey, which involves the exclusion from every Coast Survey chart of all recognition of naval participation in the surveys.

The new policy, so far as it relates to public acknowledgment due the naval establishment, certainly can not be satisfactory to the Navy Department, upon which falls the burden, each year, of diverting a large part of its appropriation and personnel for the work of the Coast Survey exclusively.

The latest annual report of the Coast Survey in print is for the fiscal year ending June, 1891. Its financial statement is not presented in a way to admit of comparing accurately the expenditure by the Coast Survey and the expenditure by the Navy for prosecuting the work done by naval officers on the Survey. But the report shows that the total expenditure of the Coast Survey for fieldwork of every kind, naval and civilian, was $180,760.73. For the items of hydrography and the coast pilot, the exclusive work practically of naval officers, it was only $63,778.45. Yet during the same fiscal year the naval establishment expended for this work of the Coast Survey the additional amount of $257,953.60.

In the following year the Superintendent of the Coast Survey decided to expunge from the hydrographic charts of the Coast Survey, for the production of which the naval establishment had expended more than the Coast Survey, all acknowledgment of naval participation in the Survey. During the year in question 81 naval officers served on the Coast Survey.

Although the great amount and specific purpose of this annual expenditure from the naval appropriation should be conspicuously set forth for the information of Congress and the people, the new policy of the Superintendent of the Coast Survey will operate in the direction of concealment.

4561——13

Nearly all the completed hydrography of the Coast Survey—practically all—has been done by naval officers, and that now under execution is in charge of naval officers exclusively. Sometimes the field work done by naval officers has been extended beyond the hydrography so as to include the whole survey; this is true in the case of the chart cited in the Department's letter of December 29, 1893, from which the names of naval officers, already engraved, were expunged, in execution of the policy of the Superintendent of the Coast Survey.

The Coast Survey Bureau was established to survey and chart the coasts of the United States. The charts that have resulted from the work of that organization are mainly for the use of mariners. In respect to those details of the charts which are most essential to navigation, it is submitted that the Navy is entitled to the chief credit. In fact the hydrography of the Coast Survey charts is a monument to naval officers; it is so regarded in the naval service and should be so regarded in the Coast Survey establishment.

In cases where the "authority note" is overburdened by names, it is believed that the names of technical employés may well be left off. The real authors of a chart are the surveyors. Handsome engraving can never make the nautical value of a chart greater than the value of the survey. It would hardly be thought a sufficient argument for withholding the names of the author of a technical book for the reason that it had been found inexpedient to mention upon the title page the names of the compositors, pressmen, proof-readers, engravers, foreman, and assistants of the printing establishment.

Contrary to the opinion of the Superintendent of the Coast Survey, this Department is assured that the "authority note" has great value to mariners, so far as it shows the names of the surveyors, but no value as setting forth the names of the assistants in charge of the branches of the Coast Survey office, or of the skilled workmen of that office.

To give credit to naval officers by tabulation in the annual reports of the Coast Survey, as suggested by the Superintendent of the Coast Survey, is not deemed sufficient. These reports are rarely referred to by mariners, and have only an occasional interest after the year of publication, while the charts constitute a continuous edition, and have a widespread circulation. The Coast Survey Report for 1892 has not yet been published.

It is nearly universal practice to give credit upon hydrographic charts to officers who executed the survey, and it is submitted that no sufficient reason has been given by the Superintendent of the Coast Survey for abandoning the usual practice. In other directions no great difficulty has been found in giving proper credit. On special charts special credit is commonly given by name, while on more general charts, involving the work of many surveys, more general credit is customarily given. It is believed that the Coast Survey, even on its general charts, should mention that the hydrography has been done by U. S. naval officers, and in cases where a chart results from the survey of a single party of U. S. naval officers, that the names of the contributing officers should be given. In certain cases the names of officers commanding parties might suffice.

Sixteen countries carry on surveys of their own coasts. In all but two of these, namely, the United States and Portugal, the surveys are made and the charts published by the naval establishments. Portugal alone offers an analogous example to that which prevails in the United States in respect to the division of the work. In Portugal, officers of the navy are placed temporarily under the minister of public works for the execution of the hydrographic work on the coast survey. In the titles of the resulting charts every one of the naval officers engaged in the work is mentioned by name.

Leaving the case of Portugal out of consideration, it is seen that the work of the U. S. Coast Survey is peculiar. Practically it is carried on by the labor and appropriations of two great departments, only one of which exercises administrative powers over the work. The Superintendent of the Coast Survey has put into execution a policy the practical effect of which is to exclude from public observation the participation of the other Government department.

It is requested that this policy of the Superintendent of the Coast Survey be set aside.

I have the honor to be, very respectfully,

H. A. HERBERT,
Secretary of the Navy.

The SECRETARY OF THE TREASURY,
Washington, D. C.

Mr. ENLOE. I desire now to submit to the committee a report of the Chenoweth investigation, which was an investigation of the management of the Coast and Geodetic Survey made in 1885. I made efforts heretofore to get possession of this report, so that I might have an opportunity to see what it disclosed in regard to the abuses of the administration which then controlled this Bureau. I was denied access to this report by the present Superintendent of the Coast and Geodetic Survey, when I applied to him during the sessions of the Fifty-second Congress, on the ground that the copy in his possession was the private property of Mr. Thorn. It seems that the Treasury Department has obtained a copy of the original report and papers and turned them over to the Committee on Naval Affairs. I desire the report to appear without the interlineations which I understand were made in red ink by Mr. Thorn after the report had been submitted and acted upon and made a part of the records. I do not think Mr. Thorn had any authority as an individual to revise the work of the committee or to attempt in any respect to alter the effect of the committee's report, whatever his individual opinion might have been at a subsequent period. This is a public document which should have been made public long ago, but was for some reason temporarily suppressed.

REPORT OF THE COMMISSION TO INVESTIGATE THE UNITED STATES AND GEODETIC SURVEY.

The SECRETARY OF THE TREASURY:

SIR: The undersigned, members of the commission appointed by you to investigate charges against the management of the office of the U. S. Coast and Geodetic Survey, respectfully submit to you, through the First Auditor of the Treasury, the following report:

In conformity with your instructions of July 23 last, we proceeded, on the morning of the 24th ultimo, to the office of said Survey in this city, took possession of the books, accounts, and such other papers as seemed necessary to the investigation, and from day to day examined the same; called, and under their oaths, examined a large number of witnesses, in nearly all instances reducing their testimony to writing in the form of depositions, and generally took such measures as seemed to us practicable and proper to enable us to report the actual condition and workings of said office. Our investigation, thus continued on each working-day until the date of this report, leaves no ground for doubt that the actual condition of the office of the Survey was one of demoralization, and its working, to a serious extent, inefficient, unjust, and, to some extent, disreputable.

That many of the defects in its condition and management are the result of gradual growth, under a system of regulations which afford excellent opportunities—if not even invitations—for the perpetration of abuses, is doubtless true; but it seems unquestionable that the responsibility for the lamentable condition, which was quite generally conceded by the employés, is due to a willingness on the part of the late Superintendent to avail himself of those opportunities for a continuance of abuses—to his weakness or procrastination in administering his office—to his toleration and apparent encouragement of vicious practices—to his exhibitions of favoritism and arrogance—to his continued and flagrant disregard, apparently, of regulations devised in the interest of honest, efficient, and economical administration—to his protection of exposed rascality, and to his own unfortunate, confessed, and locally notorious addiction to the use of intoxicants.

Either of these causes would seriously militate against efficient administration. In combination they seem to have been fatally effective, inasmuch as they afforded the demoralizing influence of a vicious example to such of his subordinates as chose to imitate it, while depriving him of the respect and confidence of nearly, if not quite, all.

A good deal of the testimony referred to, and some of that taken by us, was hearsay or inferential; but evidence afforded by books and papers, or by the testimony of witnesses, either undisputed or who carried conviction by their intelligence or integrity, or by both, establishes conclusively, to the minds of the commission, the following facts:

That moneys received from the Navy Department, from Office Engineers U. S. Army, for electrotyping, etc., and from the District of Columbia, for surveys, were not deposited in the Treasury, but after certain deductions for cost of material, etc., were divided among employés receiving regular salaries, as extra pay for extra work, in violation of law. (See sections 170, 1764, 1765, Revised Statutes.)

That the books kept in the Instrument Division, although exceedingly imperfect and incomplete, still show that many valuable instruments charged to persons no longer in the employment of the Survey have no been returned or accounted for; and that a number of valuable instruments have been loaned to institutions of learning and to individuals, without any apparent authority therefor, and that such instruments are still out. The books, however, are so defective that—as was demonstrated to your committee—little or no reliance can be placed in their statements or record.

That G. N. Saegmuller, late chief of the Instrument Division, was, while such chief, a partner in the firm of Fauth & Co., instrument-makers of this city, who have furnished a very large amount of the instruments purchased by the Survey since said firm was organized. Their trade with the Bureau in 1882, 1883, and 1884 was $24,369.46, and prior to June 30, 1884, their name seldom appeared upon the abstracts rendered to the Treasury, but their accounts were treated as subvouchers in the personal vouchers of the disbursing agent, who receipted direct to Government for the amount.

That property and material belonging to the Survey have been taken from the office to the house of Fauth & Co., and have not been returned, and some testimony was taken justifying a presumption that some property and materials have been wrongfully converted to the use of that firm.

That visiting cards for private parties, including Supt. Hilgard and family and other employés of Bureau, have been frequently printed in the copperplate-printing room of the Engraving Division of the Survey during office hours, at quite an expense and loss of time, by direction of Mr. H. G. Ogden, chief of the division.

That the chief of the drawing division, Mr. W. T. Bright, has been paid commissions on work done by employés of the division for outside private parties; also that moneys have been paid to employés of that division by Lieut. Col. Craighill and Lieut. Col. Warren, U. S. Army, for work done, out of appropriations made by the Government; that Mr. C. Junken received $400 from Maj. Lydecker, U. S. Army, for surveying done by him (Junken) for the fishways at the Great Falls of the Potomac, which amount was disallowed in the settlement of Lydecker's accounts at the Treasury; and that Mr. W. T. Bright, the chief of the drawing division, is much addicted to strong drink, and is frequently under the influence of liquor in office hours.

That traveling expenses have been incurred unnecessarily, and apparently with the view of favoring certain employés, rather than for advancing the real good of the Survey, as in the case of Morgan and Parsons making separate trips to New York to get a paper or evidence of authority from the Screw Dock Company in relation to a voucher for $120 suspended in his (Morgan's) accounts; in the case of clerk M. W. Wines, who has made several trips ostensibly to "inspect chart agencies," without apparent necessity, all the matter alleged to have been inspected, having been susceptible of easy ascertainment by mail; and in the case of employés sent out to make observations at points where it was altogether useless and unnecessary (as shown by testimony of Mr. Schott and Mr. Christie).

That in the case of Assistant J. S. Bradford, who presented false vouchers with his accounts, and, when discovered, refunded the amount thereof through his wife, and by an advance on his salary.

No action was taken, except to let him "lie by," as Prof. Hilgard phrased it, but he was continued in the employment of the Survey; which seems to have been a deliberate condonation of embezzlement, forgery, and drunkenness, to the inevitable demoralization of the service, and all respect for, or confidence in, its management.

That Prof. Hilgard, the Superintendent of the Survey, has been frequently seen at the office by various employés under the influence of liquor; that his drinking habits generally unfitted him for business every afternoon, and that of late years he has manifested a general unfitness and incapacity for the duties of his office.

That old and incapacitated persons have been and are still carried on the pay rolls of the Survey without rendering any service, in violation of the provisions of Section 87 of the regulations (as in the case of Mr. Samuel Hein, paid $150 per month as librarian, who renders no service, having been entirely disabled); that a number of ladies on the rolls never come to the office except to receive their pay, their work being sent to them, and being in some instances so light that the employés seem generally to classify them as "pensioners."

That valuable works belonging to the library of the Survey having been taken out by employés, and never returned (as in the case of about 200 volumes taken out by Prof. Pierce, as shown in the testimony of Mr. Christie and the present librarian, Reed, to whom Pierce excused his neglect to return books by the remark that he had had two fires and could not therefore be responsible for the books.

That Dr. Thomas Craig, while in the employment of the Survey, was also receiving pay from Johns Hopkins University, to wit, from 1880 to 1882.

That chronometer watches, belonging to the Survey, were found to be in the possession of certain employés, viz, J. E. Hilgard, M. W. Wines, and C. S. Peirce, and worn by them, some of whom are not connected with any scientific work. Hilgard had one stolen and was given another, and never accounted for the stolen one.

That a black mare, belonging to the Survey, was sold to a Mr. Shaw for $50. That the amount was received by Mr. M. W. Wines and by him turned over to Prof. Hilgard, the Superintendent, and that he retained the money and failed to account for it—as he now explains—by reason of "lapse of memory."

That an irregular voucher for $18.27 to cover various amounts for cab hire, paid at different times to different parties by Capt. C. O. Boutelle, the late assistant in charge of the office, was made out and signed by Mr. Shaw at Boutelle's request in December quarter, 1884; that Mr. Shaw never received a cent on account of the same, and said voucher was charged in the accounts of the disbursing agent, and check No. 240133, U. S. Treasurer, drawn to B. F. Shaw or bearer issued to Boutelle. This was in direct violation of the provisions of Section 5496, Revised Statutes. The allowance is also prohibited by section 67 of the Regulations of the Survey.

That Prof. Hilgard, during the time he was assistant in charge of the office, sent for Mr. E. J. Sommer, of the drawing division, and exhibited to him a voucher which he stated was in Russian, and would not pass the Treasury, and at the same time handed to him duplicate vouchers and requested him (Sommer) to sign them in the name of "Georg Bauer," which Sommer did; that the amount of the voucher was $175.

That on the resignation or death of an employé or employés of the Survey, the undrawn portion of the salary of such employé for the balance of the fiscal year is divided up amongst certain employés, by means of a system of so-called promotion, which generally gives the greatest portion to persons who were already drawing higher salaries than the incumbent who happens to die or resign. This is, in fact, no promotion, but a device for using up and distributing the portion of the salary of the employés dying or resigning, which would otherwise revert to the Treasury. As for example, on the resignation of W. H. Dall, September 20, 1884, the sum of $1,326.97, the balance of his salary not drawn or paid, was distributed and divided up by this so-called promotion among certain employés, some of whom were receiving higher pay than Dall; and so, on the death of H. W.Blair, December 16, 1884, the undrawn balance of $874.26 was divided and distributed in like manner.

That requests have often been made from the computing division, the work of which is badly in arrears, that assistants who had completed their work in the field and were idle and unemployed might be assigned to the office for office work, but that such requests have always been disregarded, on the pretext that there would be no money for paying to such assistants their per diem subsistence if brought to Washington and assigned to the office for duty. Such subsistence actually rests in the discretion of the Superintendent, who might, therefore, have properly withheld it, and provided for work of such assistants for a time without it.

That bottles containing liquor have been at various times, and frequently, passed by the messengers to the rooms of certain employés of the Survey, also to the room of the Superintendent.

That a tide-gauger, who had neglected his duties for five months without making regular reports, and whose reports, when received, were so inaccurate and imperfect as to be practically useless, was paid his salary or compensation for the full time, although the facts were known. (See testimony of L. P. Shidy.)

That for several years, beginning in 1873, C. S. Peirce, assistant, and in charge, nominally, of division of weights and measures, has been making experimental reseaches with pendulums, without restriction or limitation as to times or places. That since 1879 the expenditures on account of those experiments—aside from salaries of chiefs of parties and office employés detailed to assist him—amount to about $31,000. That the meager value of those experiments to this Bureau is substantially destroyed by his utter disregard of the regulations requiring the filing of their records, duplicates, or computations. From 1879 to 1881 Mr. Pierce was lecturer at Johns Hopkins University at a salary of $1,500, and in 1882, 1883, and 1884, at a salary of $2,500 per annum, and at all times has apparently been independent of control or the semblance of discipline.

That one of the messengers has been twice detailed to act as nurse for sick "assistants": Once, at Providence Hospital, Washington, two months, by Capt. Boutelle; and once, four days, at the same time receiving his salary as messenger. (Testimony of Atwell Richardson.)

That "acting assistants" are paid $4 per day for every day instead of for "working days," as per paragraph 17 of Regulations (deposition of Fagin, accountant), and Marcus Baker was paid $1,650 per annum during fiscal years 1883 and 1884, as such.

That expenditures were made from wrong appropriations. Instance, analyzed by Schott & Courtenay, in New Jersey, where a few hours "magnetic observations" were made to cover a season's expenses "Triangulation."

That E. August Reubsam, an inexperienced boy, was paid $1,758.36 during the six months from January 1, 1885, ostensibly for engraving. That after examining H. G. Oyden, in charge of the engraving division, and Reubsam himself, it was only a severe catechism of the latter that elicited the fact that all but $90 of the above sum had been turned over by him to other engravers in the office, with whom, by permission and at the suggestion of Ogden, he had made subcontracts to do engraving for which he had made contracts in his own name with the Bureau. When this fact was extorted from Reubsam, Mr. Ogden's explanation was to the effect that "it was the understanding in the office that it might not appear well on the vouchers if the extra work on contract was given directly to employés of the office—that explanations would be needed," and so the contracts were let to a minor outside of the Bureau, who acted as broker or middleman between the office and the competent employés at a confessed commission of 3 per cent. Whether the queer arrangement imparted an appearance of respectability to anything besides vouchers, that "might not appear well" we were unable to ascertain.

That Mrs. Brainard has been carried on roll at $50 per month, five months, without rendering service; and Hilgard wants now to withdraw the account presented for her services; that the payments were made ostensibly and upon vouchers for "services as tide keeper."

That Superintendent Hilgard admits that he might have cut down the field force to advantage after reduction in appropriation last year and year before, but did not want to be invidious to employés as long as the money was appropriated.

That C. O. Boutelle caused to be constructed in the office an elevator for passengers, which, owing to the slowness of motion and the convenience and shortness of stair flights, is of doubtful utility.

That Disbursing Agent W. B. Morgan uses intoxicants to excess, and is habitually absent from the office, so that mail matter and matter requiring his signature has very frequently to be sent to him; that he knew the circumstances attending the spurious voucher in favor of Shaw for Boutelle's cab fares, and aided the transaction by making the check payable " to bearer," as well as by passing an invalid and deceptive voucher.

That on the occasion of the funeral of Assistant Blair at Lexington, Va., about December 19, 1884, Edwin Smith, assistant, and F. H. Parsons, subassistant, went from Washington, D. C., and C. H. Sinclair, assistant, went from Charlottesville, Va., and attended the obsequies. Upon their return, and apparently on December 21, in the cases of Smith and Sinclair, and on December 31 in the case of Parsons, traveling expenses incurred upon that trip to the amount of $29.10 for Smith, $7.20 for Sinclair, and $16.85 for Parsons were paid to them upon the usual form of voucher purporting to have been predicated upon the Superintendent's instructions. Examination of the letter press of instructions shows that the following letter of instructions was sent to each:

" WASHINGTON, *December 16, 1884.*

"DEAR SIR: You will please proceed to Lexington, Va., and *transact such business as I have designated to you*, upon the completion of which report to me in person at this office.

"Yours respectfully,

" J. E. HILGARD,
" *Superintendent.*"

The phrase " and transact such business as I have designated to you," shows how easy it is, by specious and deceptive "instructions" to give a scientific turn to the most melancholy "business." When it appears, as it does by an examination of the "instruction book," that those letters, apparently written prior to the excursion, were really written about January 10, 1885, and antedated to December 16, 1884, quite a vivid idea may be had of the complaisance with which "star-eyed science" sometimes winks at crooked practices and gives unlawful excursions by Coast Survey employés, a semblance of propriety.

That G. N. Saegmuller, an alien, entered the service of the Bureau in July, 1873, and became a naturalized citizen of the United States in 1883, notwithstanding the regulation, Section 84, prohibiting the employment of an alien more than six months.

That an arrangement was made with the superintendent by which R. M. Harvey swears he was carried on the rolls as tidal observer, at $50 per month, from April 15 to July 1 last, without performing any service. Superintendent Hilgard admits that he made a similar arrangement by which N. Y. Cavitt, for two months after resigning as janitor, was paid $100 per month for service as "special observer at Mobile," while rendering no service and being in Washington or Tennessee.

That the salaries of S. Hein, $1,800, superannuated librarian, and T. D. Reed, assistant librarian, $1,000, make the cost of caring for the Coast Survey library $233.33 per month, when $83.33 per month pays for all the services actually rendered.

That G. N. Saegmuller continues to be really a partner in Fauth & Co., notwithstanding his pretended withdrawal, which was merely a substitution of a liquidated sum instead of contingent profits.

The sworn statements of J. E. Hilgard and B. A. Colonna would appear to warrant the opinion that under the present rate of appropriations the force might be considerably reduced under a judicious system of natural selection, or, rather, rational rejection.

Of the moneys hereinbefore referred to as having been received from the Navy Department, from Office Engineers, U. S. Army, and from the District of Columbia, by employés of this Bureau, and not turned into the Treasury, there was, as nearly as can be ascertained, received for extra work:

For electrotyping:
By Anton Zumbrock—

April 25, 1882	$130. 32
July 24, 1882	123. 66
August 4, 1882	51. 71
January 12, 1883	206. 15
Total	511. 84

By Frank Over—

April 25, 1882	60. 16
July 24, 1882	61. 82
August 4, 1882	25. 85
January 12, 1883	103. 07
Total	250. 90

For office work, District of Columbia survey:

By A. E. Burton (not now an employé), July 21, 1882	83. 00
By E. J. Sommer, August 9, 1882	50. 00
By Chas. Junken	400. 00

For tracing of maps, charts, etc.:
By L. Karcher—

From Lieut. Col. G. K. Warren, February 10, 1882	21. 00
From Lieut. Col. W. P. Craighill, March 30, 1882	35. 00
From Lieut. Col. G. H. Elliott, January 19, 1884	10. 00
Total	66. 00

By E. Willenbucher—

From Lieut. Col. W. P. Craighill, January 25, 1882	45. 00
From Lieut. Col. W. P. Craighill, February 24, 1882	45. 00
Total	90. 00

By E. J. Sommer—

From Lieut. Col. W. P. Craighill, January 25, 1882	50. 00
From Lieut. Col. W. P. Craighill, February 24, 1882	47. 00
From Lieut. Col. W. P. Craighill, April 17, 1882	95. 00
From Lieut. Col. G. H. Elliott, February 27, 1883	25. 00
Total	217. 00

By W. T. Bright—from Lieut. Col. G. H. Elliott, February 17, 1884	5. 00

With the exception of the extra work on electrotyping, which from its nature had to be done concurrent with the regular electrotyping work of the Bureau, the foregoing extra work was performed out of office hours. Nevertheless, the retention of the money, which was paid to them out of funds appropriated by the U. S. Government and for work done for departments or officers of that Government, and therefore for the Government, appears to be in violation of sections 170, 1764, and 1765 of the Revised Statutes United States. It is but fair to say, however, that the work was done and pay received without any thought of illegality, with the full assent of the Bureau officers, and in pursuance of a custom which has long openly prevailed, though it has ceased as to electrotyping. Enforced restitution would involve serious hardship in nearly every case. In view of these facts and of the possible legality of the transaction, we venture to suggest the propriety of a reference of the question of its legality to the Hon. Attorney-General before proceedings are taken to compel restitution.

There is no system of bookkeeping in the office of the Coast and Geodetic Survey by which the receipts from sales of charts, maps, and Coast Survey publications, by sale agents, and at the chart room of the office can be verified. Duplicate certificates of deposit show that from April 6, 1877, to July 31, 1885, the sum of $26,568.77 has been deposited in the Treasury on account of receipts from such sales. Remittances from sale agents are made by drafts, checks, and post-office money orders, payable to different employés of the office, and, under existing practice, are turned into cash and placed in the safe of the assistant in charge, who from time to time makes deposits of the aggregate amounts on hand. Prior to January 1, 1881, no book account of the receipts seems to have been kept, and the book kept since that date is very imperfect, and is not a correct statement of all receipts from sales. It appears that the sum of $7.80 received at the chart room for sales for September, 1884, has never been entered on the book, and that there is a balance of $13.33 still to be paid on account of receipts to February 6, 1883, the deposit of that date being $13.33 short, making the total amount (as far as can be ascertained) to be accounted for and paid into the Treasury $21.13.

It is recommended that a book account of the charts, maps, and other publications now on hand, and such as may be hereafter published, be kept by valuations, and in such a manner that it may at any time be determined whether all receipts from sales have been accounted for and deposited in the Treasury.

It would also seem that systematic business methods would require that one officer only should be charged with the duty of receiving and accounting for these moneys as well as moneys received from all other sources.

An examination of the accounts of the disbursing agent was made which showed that at the close of business on the 23d ultimo there was an excess of assets over liabilities of $5.91, according to the vouchers exhibited to us. A detailed statement of the condition of his accounts will be made as soon as his balances in the hands of the Treasurer of the United States and the assistant treasurers at New York and San Francisco shall have been verified by the accounts current of those officers.

The sum of $96.87, corresponding with the balance shown by the memorandum book of the account of electrotyping for the Navy and Engineers' Office, U. S. Army, and office work for District of Columbia survey, was found in the safe of the assistant in charge, which is ready to be deposited in the Treasury of the United States.

While the instructions, in pursuance of which the investigation was undertaken, do not require the framing of an indictment of the individuals who appear to have been compromised by the evidence, it seems proper that—in the interest of the more or less extensive reorganization which a due regard for the prosperity of the Bureau imperatively demands—we should refer, by name, to the individuals who, to a greater or less extent, appear to be implicated by that evidence.

If the intemperate habit of Prof. Hilgard, late Superintendent, confessed by him and established by abundance of testimony, were not of itself a complete disqualification for the discharge of the responsible duties from which he was suspended, his own deposition affords abundant evidence of either such failure or faculty or perversion of moral sense as must be held to quite unfit him for a position of responsibility; while the evidence of his large share of responsibility for the unsatisfactory condition and recent dubious reputation of the Bureau, and the substantially unanimous concurrence of opinion among the principal employés of the office, quite emphatically suggest the impropriety of his restoration to any office duty.

There is some evidence—mainly his own testimony—to show that C. O. Boutelle has made efforts to correct some of the irregularities revealed by the investigation. Those efforts have not been very strenuous, and he has perhaps manifested an undue respect for the official dignity of his superior and been too diffident about complaining to their common superior, the Secretary of the Treasury. His personal integrity is indorsed with considerable vehemence by some of the prominent office employés. His procurement of liveryman Shaw to sign a voucher for promiscuous cab fares, of which Shaw had received no part, and simply to enable Boutelle to recover $18.27, to which he was not entitled under the regulations of the Bureau, seems to justify the opinion that if he is personally honest, he might with advantage be more scrupulously careful or keenly intelligent. He perhaps does not deserve dismissal from the service, but his restoration to the position of assistant in charge would seem to be a measure of quite dubious propriety.

While there was no conclusive evidence of the conversion of any property of the Bureau to the use of G. N. Saegmuller, or the firm of which he was a member, there was enough of testimony to raise a strong suspicion that there has not always been a scrupulous distinction between the articles and materials of the Bureau and those of the firm. The antagonism between the interest of Saegmuller, partner in an instrument manufactory, and his duty as foreman of the Instrument Division of the Bureau was so patent and the incongruity of his relations so glaring that he appears to have been the object of general suspicion and his partnership the inspiration of a long scandal in which the Bureau and its good name were seriously involved. That scandal appears to have been but slightly mitigated by his professed dissolution of partnership with Fauth & Co. His restoration would be detrimental to the *morale* of the Coast Survey, the dissolution of his partnership with which should be made permanent, especially so in view of the practical continuance of his objectionable partnership relations with Fauth & Co.

No evidence was brought to our attention indicating that Mr. W. B. Morgan, the late disbursing agent of the Bureau, had in any wise appropriated to his own use any of the funds coming to his hands. But he appears to have been entirely passive in the matter of objecting to, or calling the attention of, the Superintendent to "unusual items" or "unnecessary charges."

He was fully cognizant of the signing of a spurious voucher by Shaw to accommodate Boutelle, and so testified. He also, at Boutelle's request, deviated from the usual custom of making the check payable "to order" and caused it to be made payable to Shaw "or bearer," as if to aid in the foolishly irregular process by which payment was obtained of an illegal account, in a method specifically forbidden by section 5496, Revised Statutes. Besides some other evidence, the testimony of Mr. Morgan's office accountants afforded quite convincing proof to us that he has become addicted to the habitual, and occasionally excessive, use of intoxicants, and has been from once to four times a week, during the last year and a half, absent from the office, so that mail and matters for his signature had to be sent to him at his house or elsewhere. He appears, also, to have been cognizant of the fraudulent character of J. S. Bradford's transactions, and to have done nothing to prevent or make them public.

In the light of those facts, we do not feel warranted in recommending his restoration to his former duties.

The somewhat dilatory confession of Mr. H. G. Ogden, after its proof by another, that E. A. Reubsam—an inexperienced minor, who appeared on the rolls of the Bureau as a largely paid contract engraver—was selected to make subcontracts with other engravers in the office, because vouchers for contract work would look better in the name of an outsider than in the names of employés, and his equally dilatory confession—after proof by others—of the frequent gratuitous printing of visiting cards for the friends and acquaintances of himself and others in the office hardly indicate the possession of that keen sense of propriety which would secure to him the respect and confidence of the employés in the extensive printing and engraving division of which he is in charge—sentiments essential to proper discipline and honest work.

Conclusive evidence, notwithstanding his denial, of the almost invariable daily intoxication of W. T. Bright, clerk in charge of the drawing division, and equally conclusive evidence that he has demanded, from employés in his division, a share of the work done for "outside information," and has received a share ranging from 10 to 20 per centum, either from the employés or by adding the amount to their bills rendered to "outside" employers, suggest the propriety of an early change, in the interest alike of morals and discipline, in that division.

The evidence indicates that R. Zumbrock, late in charge of the electrotyping room, was unconscious of wrong or irregularity while engaged in extra work, hereinbefore referred to, for the Navy Department and Engineers' Office, U. S. Army; it was done with the sanction and at the request of his superiors, and after estimates prepared at their request, and with plant increased for the purpose by their order. When he was advised of its illegality, he was, at the same time, informed by the then assistant in charge that the matter had been properly arranged and required no further attention.

Another feature of the present organization and condition, which seems open to criticism, relates to the compensation of the office force, which would appear to require redistribution, and, in some respects, a better defined limitation. The Superintendent's salary of $6,000 is liable to an indefinite increase by special appropriation like that of $1,200 for his traveling expenses, as well as by a not over scrupulous exercise of his discretion in personal inspections of "the operations of parties and persons employed in the Survey," prescribed by regulation 3. The present compensation of the assistant in charge of the office and topography is $4,000 and $2.50 per diem, subsistence, for every day in the year. We believe that the salary of no assistant needs to exceed $3,000 per annum with the abolishment of subsistence, except for parties actually in the field. The salaries appear to be temporarily guarded against any reduction, by the naming of specific amounts in the last appropriation.

Part of the money now liberally dispensed in office—subsistence—might be justly employed to advance the compensation, to a just and decent rate, of underpaid office workers, like computers, who receive from $1,100 to $1,400 per annum, and clerks who receive $60 per month.

There is some evidence that assistants in the field have practiced a species of extortion by collecting the entire subsistence allowance of their subordinates, without allowing the difference between such subsistence and the actual expense, and then dividing it pro rata among the party to lighten the mess bills, the effect of which is make the mess bill of the highest-paid o o r lighter than that of his most poorly paid subordinate.

The regulations prohibit the allowance of traveling except on business of the Survey. There seems to be, very rarely, any difficulty in providing business for a favored employé who desires to travel. When there is such difficulty it is conveniently avoidable under that rule, section 66, which makes effective a "voucher indorsed 'approved' by the Superintendent." If the voucher or transportation account were required, in every instance, to show fully the practical necessity and purpose of the trip it might tend to discourage the making of excursions not fairly justified by the exigencies of the service.

It appears from the records of the Bureau that 63 parties, at present engaged in field work, are distributed as follows: Topography, 19; hydrography, 16; triangulation, 20; astronomical, 4; magnetic, 2; reconnaissance, 1: gravity, 1; total, 63. Of the assistants, subassistants, and aids in the field, and not attached to the office, an estimate, made after a laborious analysis of the general record of each, gives them the following classification: Very able and efficient, 12; efficient and reliable, 32; able, but not very efficient, 6; either inefficient or not well informed, 2; usefulness impaired by age or infirmity, but still capable of efficient work, 2; not capable of efficient work by reason of age or infirmity, 4; total, 58.

We transmit herewith a tabulated list of the assistants, subassistants, and aids, with their assignments. Also the deposition of witnesses examined by us and such other items or copies of evidence as seem necessary or proper in support of the statements or suggestions of our report.

Respectfully submitted,

F. M. THORN,
I. R. GARRISON,
A. T. HUNTINGTON,
Committee.

Mr. DOLLIVER. Will you permit me to ask, Mr. Enloe, whether there is any friction, personally or professionally, between the managers of these bureaus, the Coast and Geodetic Survey and the Geological Survey?

Mr. ENLOE. None that I have been able to discover. One thing I have heard stated. I think it was a gentleman connected with the Geological Survey who came to me the other day and stated he wanted to know if Prof. Mendenhall had been reflecting upon the ability of the men employed in that Bureau—that is, the Geological Survey. I stated that I did not so understand his remarks before the committee, except to this extent, that I thought he stated that the Coast and Geodetic Survey could do the work in a little higher style of the art than could be done by the Geological Survey. This gentleman said he would like to have an opportunity if the committee had any such impression to come before it to show the character of the work they do.

Mr. TALBOTT. As far as I understood, he did not reflect upon anybody's ability.

Mr. ENLOE. Did I say he reflected upon their ability?

Mr. TALBOTT. I did not understand him to call anybody's ability in question.

Mr. ENLOE. His statement here will show what he did say about it, and I understood him to say, and I think the committee understood him to say, and I think the record will bear me out in this statement, that the Geological Survey was not prepared to do work in the style and with the accuracy it is being done in the Coast and Geodetic Survey.

Mr. DOLLIVER. I have received from various scientific societies and various colleges throughout the country very high testimonials about the Geodetic Survey business and the way it is maintained. I do not know whether they know anything about it or not.

Mr. ENLOE. I suppose you have received them, as a great many others have, largely through the instrumentality of Prof. Mendenhall, who has been very industriously working to prevent this bill from passing. He admitted before the committee here that he had addressed communications in regard to this bill to presidents of colleges and other gentlemen of distinction throughout the country to get up this protest against the proposed transfer.

Mr. TALBOTT. He did not say that he sent communications for this purpose, but he said he had sent copies of the bill and asked their views on the subject without intimating to them what sort of answer he wanted.

Mr. ENLOE. He intimated very clearly what sort of an answer he wanted, when it was published throughout the press of the country that he was opposed to it, and that he proposed to stay here and fight it, and refused a position tendered him in order that he might stay here and fight his enemies.

Mr. MONEY. I think he stated he sent these men a copy of the bill and asked for their opinion.

Mr. ENLOE. Say that is true; admit that is what he said, and what I state is true, that it was at the instance and the solicitation of Prof. Mendenhall that these letters were written here. Grant that. Prof. Mendenhall's position was well known in the country, because he had spread broadcast throughout the country, through the press, that he was opposed to this transfer, that it was an effort to break up this scientific work, that his enemies were trying to do it because they were hostile to him, that he had been tendered a position as the head of an institution of learning and he would not accept it, and he was going to remain here and fight the battle out to the end.

Mr. MONEY. I have no doubt that he received none but favorable responses, but I am telling you what he said.

Mr. ENLOE. Well, I state the facts.

Mr. DOLLIVER. Well, I did not introduce that for the purpose of suggesting; the writing of these letters amounted to an argument on the subject.

Mr. ENLOE. But letters were produced in large numbers and placed in the record by Prof. Mendenhall when you were not present, and they were in the nature of an argument against the passage of this bill and were prepared for that purpose.

A number of newspaper extracts were read also. There is no doubt about the fact that it was an easy matter for an institution like the Coast Survey to build up a support throughout the country from people who do not really know what is being done by the Coast and Geodetic Survey. They have a general idea that it is doing valuable work for the Government, and that is true; it is doing some valuable work for the Government, and we do not propose to discontinue that work, but we propose to do it in a different way.

Mr. TYLER. Do you propose to limit it in any way?

Mr. ENLOE. I would place some limitations upon it. I am not proposing to limit it, because I have no power to put a limit on it. This bill proposes a change in the methods of administration, to give the jurisdiction of the work to the Secretary of the Navy so far as the coast is concerned, and give to the Secretary of the Interior the jurisdiction of the work in the interior, through the Geological Survey. Now, as to how the work shall be prosecuted in the future, whether on the scale mapped out by this Coast and Geodetic Survey or on some reduced scale, depends upon those secretaries' recommendation to Congress, and it depends upon the judgment of Congress in making the appropriations.

Mr. DOLLIVER. You say that the present scope of the enterprise seems to have no end?

Mr. ENLOE. Prof. Woodward stated in the beginning of his argument that it would indefinitely continue.

Mr. TALBOTT. Prof. Mendenhall says you can never stop this character of work.

Mr. MONEY. Here is what Prof. Woodward says, that as long as the tides, currents, and winds were shifting there would be a continuation of the work of the Coast and Geodetic Survey.

Mr. ENLOE. Nobody disputes that proposition, and that has never been disputed.

Mr. DOLLIVER. I understood you to say the general scope of the work was without an end?

Mr. ENLOE. The general scope of work of the Geodetic Survey is as broad as the territory of the United States, including Alaska, and there is no limitation to it, either in the amount of work that may be done or the extent to which it may be carried. They first go and make a primary triangulation of the country, and then they go and make a second triangulation of the country, and then a tertiary triangulation, and I suppose they might go and refine it and make a map of the entire surface of the United States, that would show every stream, that would show every hill, and every valley, and every mountain, and every tree, and everything on the face of nature. It may extend to that ultimately.

Mr. TALBOTT. What objection would there be to that?

Mr. ENLOE. I will tell you my objection to it very clearly. I believe that would be an unwise expenditure of public money, and I believe, furthermore, that it would be an unwarranted expenditure of public money.

Mr. DOLLIVER. I quite agree with you in that, but the substantial features of it present a different problem, of course.

Mr. ENLOE. I am not objecting to the substantial features, but I am objecting to the scope of it as planned by those men who have appeared before the committee and propose to continue the appropriations for this service until the end of time and spend enough to keep employed all the unemployed scientists who want jobs at the expense of the Government. Perhaps not all of them, but a great many of them. I think really that a part of the hostility to this transfer is because it is believed if we take it out from under the present control and put it under the two Secretaries, men will not be employed there unless the Government actually needs their services, and they will not be permitted to stay unless they render a fair equivalent for their pay.

Mr. MONEY. Why should the Secretary of the Treasury retain a man who is useless any more than the Secretary of the Interior?

Mr. ENLOE. The Secretary of the Treasury does not know any more about what is going on there than you.

Mr. MONEY. Would the Secretary of the Interior know any more if it was under the Geological Survey?

Mr. ENLOE. If the Secretary of the Treasury appoints a man under him he is responsible to him and he ought to know, but this gentleman is appointed by the President and he is not responsible to the Secretary of the Treasury, and the Secretary of the Treasury can not remove him.

Mr. MONEY. But is not the Chief of the Geological Survey appointed by the Secretary of the Interior?

Mr. ENLOE. I do not know whether he is or not.

Mr. MONEY. I think he is appointed by the President.

Mr. ENLOE. I believe he is appointed by the President.

Mr. MONEY. Then the Secretary of the Interior has no more to do with the Superintendent of the Geodetic Survey in that case than the Secretary of the Treasury would have to do with the Superintendent of the Coast Survey?

Mr. ENLOE. I know, but he does. I was down there and talked with the Director of the Geological Survey and he told me that the Secretary of the Interior proposed to pass upon every single appointment or promotion and everything of that character that was done in that office, and to see that it was administered——

Mr. MONEY. The Secretary of the Treasury has the same power?

Mr. ENLOE. The Secretary of the Treasury can not even control the Superintendent to the extent of having him restore practices there which, ever since the foundation, there——

Mr. DOLLIVER. Then that is the fault of the Department then?

Mr. ENLOE. There is the Superintendent having the charts, Coast Survey charts, printed, omitting the names of the officers who did the work.   •

Mr. TALBOTT. If the——

Mr. ENLOE. He was ordered or requested to put the names back on the charts and I asked him the question whether he obeyed the order, and he did not say; he stated it was not an order but a request. This committee did not find out and you do not know now whether or not he paid any attention to the requirement of the Secretary. Prof. Mendenhall explained why he took them off; explained how it was done. I have not time to go into it, but I can give a good deal of history in regard to that, but nobody's name was to appear upon that chart but the Superintendent's name. There was complaint made about his not giving credit to the naval officers. The Secretary of the Treasury called the attention of the Superintendent to the omission and requested that the names be restored to the maps as heretofore, but whether that request has been complied with or not I do not know, and this committee does not know, from the statement made by Prof. Mendenhall here.

Mr. MONEY. I was very well satisfied from the explanation why the names ought not to be on the chart.

Mr. DOLLIVER. It would appear that the utility depends largely upon the superiority of the Secretary of the Navy over the other secretaries; I mean in regard to executive ability.

Mr. ENLOE. No; you are mistaken about that, because the Secretary of the Navy has complete jurisdiction of the Hydrographic Office of the Navy Department, and unquestionably, so far as a valuable part of the Survey is concerned, the Coast Survey will be under a better administration than it is at present organized under the Coast and Geodetic Survey. As to the geological part of it, the same conditions may exist, and that might interfere with the efficiency of the administration in the Department of the Interior.

I have no personal feeling about this matter, and I am pursuing it with no personal object in view. In answer to a number newspaper publications bearing upon the propriety of this change which was quoted by Prof. Mendenhall and incorporated in his extended remarks, I want to quote an expression from the Marine Journal published in New York, and I will just quote a brief expression from it:

This work is all of the highest importance, and that it be performed by the most skilled men is essential. No more question of dollars should stand in the way. But when it is shown that the work is done by the naval hydrographers, whether they receive credit for it or not, and that it would be an actual saving to transfer the service bodily to the Navy Department, the transfer should be made without delay.

Now, I have attempted to show here reasons for the transfer. Prof. Mendenhall made an extended argument before this committee in hearings on seven different days, and during that time Prof. Mendenhall never advanced a single reason that I thought ought to have been conclusive to the minds of the committee why the transfer should not be made. The Secretary of the Treasury thinks he can not manage it under him as it should be managed, and he advises its transfer to the Navy Department, and the Secretary of the Navy, who has been chairman of the Committee on Naval Affairs in the House, and who is perfectly familiar with these matters, believes that it would be an advantage to navigation and to naval interests to have transferred to the Navy Department that part of it relating to the Coast Survey proper.

Secretary Chandler, who was formerly Secretary of the Navy, now a Senator of the United States, also advocated it. The naval officers generally, as I understand it, favor it, and the only question raised was as to the competency of men in the Geological Survey to do this work and the competency of the naval officers to do Coast Survey work. This, I think, has been sufficiently answered. I think it is sufficiently answered in the fact that everywhere else, except on the coast of the United States, the naval officers have this work to do, and they do it in a way that seems to be satisfactory and seems to be working well. I notice, with all the knowledge that has been claimed as belonging peculiarly to the officers of the Coast and Geodetic Survey, they can not locate all obstructions to navigation. The chairman of the committee suggested to me the other day that it was the time to find out why the Coast and Geodetic Survey did not locate the rock on which the *Columbia* ran in the Delaware River.

Mr. DOLLIVER. That was a shoal, well understood, I believe.

Mr. ENLOE. Certainly it was a shoal, but this was a place where there was nothing to indicate that it was a shoal dangerous to navigation. It should have been marked.

Mr. MONEY. Judging from the letter of the Secretary of the Navy it was a matter of universal knowledge.

Mr. ENLOE. It was a matter of universal knowledge that it was a shoal, but there was no knowledge of the obstruction on this particular point on the shoal, and there was nothing to indicate that the vessel could not pass over it.

Mr. MONEY. The Secretary reprimanded the officers for running over it.

Mr. TYLER. And they took the risk——

Mr. ENLOE. They took the risk of running over the shoal that they were in the habit of passing over. The censure was for not reducing speed. It was not until after the attempted passage of the ship that they found that rock. I will tell you all the talk about the work being done by these civilians over there in the Coast Survey in locating obstructions is to be discontinued. Obstructions are often first found by vessels coming in contact with them, and then these gentlemen go out and locate and mark them. A great many obstructions are first found in this way.

Mr. MONEY. The Assistant Secretary told me that log came down in the late freshet.

Mr. ENLOE. Well, I did not discover that from the official investigation, and the letter of the Secretary of the Navy to the commanding officer of the ship did not indicate it was a log.

Mr. TALBOTT. That seemed to indicate that it was the bottom of the river.

Mr. ENLOE. I think that Prof. Mendenhall has not shown in his argument that the greater part of the Coast Survey work is not now done by naval officers, and that they are not as capable of doing it as the civilians in the Coast and Geodetic Survey.

Mr. TYLER. Just one question. Is it the intention of this bill that the present scope of the work should be continued?

Mr. ENLOE. This bill does not place any limitation upon the work at all.

Mr. TYLER. You say the present scope of work could be continued under this bill?

Mr. ENLOE. It could be, but I do not know whether it would be or not.

Mr. TYLER. That depends upon——

Mr. ENLOE. That is a matter of administration, and I could not tell you in regard to that. It would depend upon the judgment of the Secretary of the Navy, the Secretary of the Interior, and the President of the United States as to the extent to which this work in the interior should be carried, and ultimately it would depend upon the judgment of Congress whether it was wise to appropriate the money.

Mr. TYLER. It does now depend upon the judgment of Congress?

Mr. ENLOE. Entirely.

Mr. TYLER. If the present scope was continued after the transfer was made, can you state to the committee in what respect would there be a cheapening of the work?

Mr. ENLOE. I made the statement just a few minutes ago which I thought answered that in one particular. I just stated in answer to Mr. Dolliver awhile ago that the abolition of this Bureau would be a considerable saving in the administration, because the work would go to other bureaus already organized in other Departments, and already prepared to go on with the work, so it would save the expense of the organization of this Bureau. That is one thing. As to the saving in other respects I stated that I believed that it would result in a saving of expenditures, either in the amount of the appropriation, or it would result in an increased amount of work done for the money appropriated, and that would be brought about, I think, by strict discipline and stricter supervision of the expenditure of money and work performed. That was my argument on that. If my judgment were followed in the matter, I am sure that unless I thought there was more necessity for military maps in this country than I now think, I would not follow the policy of continuing this detailed survey, extending it from the coast back into the country, nor would I favor an extension of the lines from the transcontinental arc on State lines to give points to the States. I do not believe it is a necessity, and I do not think it is wise to use the public money in that way. It would be time enough to deal with that if we shall ever have need of it for military operations.

Mr. DOLLIVER. It would be too late then if we should get into a war?

Mr. ENLOE. We are not going to get into any war at the present time, unless it is with our own people. We are not in much danger at this time of getting into a foreign war unless we do that in order to build a larger Navy, to make more ships, to build larger guns and furnish employment to the Committee on Naval Affairs.

Now, Mr. Chairman, Prof. Mendenhall has not shown any use for the geodetic work except to furnish points for State surveys, although he admits that is its only use. He gives no definite answer to the number of States which have asked for them, notwithstanding the fact he was questioned particularly on that point.

The evidence which has been produced before this committee as to the utility of this work, its cost, its duplication, as to who does the hydrographic work and its duration, and the maladministration of the affairs of the office has been furnished by this side of the question. Such witnesses as Prof. Hilgard, Commander Bartlett, Prof. ———, Secretary Chandler, Mr. Colonna, now of the Coast and Geodetic Survey, and Mr. Ogden, now of the Coast and Geodetic Survey, have testified upon this point, and the evidence is in this record, placed there by Mr. Glasscock in his opening argument before the committee.   Prof. Mendenhall has not attempted to impeach that testimony nor has he offered any of his own to sustain any assertions unfriendly to this transfer, except clippings from newspapers, to which I referred a moment ago, and some personal letters written, as I stated, at his instance, if not at his solication.

Mr. TYLER. I have memorials from several colleges protesting against this transfer.

Mr. ENLOE. I had one myself.   I received one from the Cumberland University of Tennessee, an institution which I attended.   I know the professors there well, and it appears that they believe I am a regular iconoclast.   I presume they think I am attempting to break down and destroy everything scientific.   They appear to be of the impression that this whole work is to be destroyed.   I judge from the communication that that was the impression on their minds.

Mr. DOLLIVER. That is, that you were making war on science in general?

Mr. ENLOE. Yes; I did not suppose that the fact that one of the professors there has been in the employ of the Coast and Geodetic Survey had anything to do with it.   But that fact occurred to my mind when I received the communication, as it naturally would.

The Secretary of the Navy, as I have stated to you, the Secretary of the Treasury, and all the authorities that I regard as most competent to speak on this question are in favor of this transfer, and I want to call the committee's attention just in a single sentence to a curious anomaly which is here presented, and I believe I called attention to it in my opening remarks, and that is, that this Superintendent, holding an office under this administration, owing his position to the President, did for sometime practically suspend the practical workings of the Bureau in which he was engaged, to load this committee with information and arguments protesting against the very policy which the administration was attempting to carry out.   There were the two Secretaries of the Navy asking for it, and there was the subordinate voluntarily coming here for seven days talking against the policy of the administration under which he holds his office.

Mr. DOLLIVER. Would it indicate that the usual law of subordination does not apply to the domain of science?

Mr. ENLOE. That is what I have said all the time about this Coast and Geodetic Survey, that if there ever was a bureau organized under the Government that was independent of and superior to everything in the nature of a governing power it was this Bureau.

Mr. TYLER. But ought not science to be independent and not subordinate?

Mr. ENLOE. Science is superior, and is not subordinate, but I deny that this Bureau is, or ought to be, the embodiment of science.   I hope the committee will consider the matter.   It is a matter in which I feel no personal interest whatever, except when I attempt a thing I like to succeed in it, as I always believe I am right before I begin.   I thank the committee for the patience with which they have heard me.

Thereupon the committee adjourned.

○